Also by Christopher Caldwell

Reflections on the Revolution in Europe: Immigration, Islam, and the West

Left Hooks, Right Crosses: A Decade of Political Writing
(edited with Christopher Hitchens)

THE AGE OF
ENTITLEMENT

America Since the Sixties

Christopher Caldwell

Simon & Schuster

NEW YORK · LONDON · TORONTO · SYDNEY · NEW DELHI

Simon & Schuster
1230 Avenue of the Americas
New York, NY 10020

First Simon & Schuster hardcover edition January 2020

SIMON & SCHUSTER and colophon are registered trademarks of Simon & Schuster, Inc.

For information about special discounts for bulk purchases, please contact Simon & Schuster Special Sales at 1-866-506-1949 or business@simonandschuster.com.

The Simon & Schuster Speakers Bureau can bring authors to your live event. For more information or to book an event, contact the Simon & Schuster Speakers Bureau at 1-866-248-3049 or visit our website at www.simonspeakers.com.

Interior design by Paul Dippolito

Manufactured in the United States of America

1   3   5   7   9   10   8   6   4   2

Library of Congress Cataloging-in-Publication Data is available.

ISBN 978-1-5011-0689-7
ISBN 978-1-5011-0693-4 (ebook)

to Neal Kozodoy,
Wladyslaw Pleszczynski,
and Richard Starr
in friendship and gratitude

Contents

Part I

THE REVOLUTIONS OF THE 1960s

1
―――

1963

The assassination of Kennedy

I
n the mid-1960s, at a moment of deceptively permanent-looking prosperity, the country's most energetic and ideological leaders made a bid to reform the United States along lines more just and humane. They rallied to various loosely linked moral crusades, of which the civil rights movement, culminating in the 1964 Civil Rights Act, provided the model. Women entered jobs and roles that had been male preserves. Sex came untethered from both tradition and prudery. Immigrants previously unwanted in the United States were welcomed and even recruited. On both sides of the clash over the Vietnam War, thinkers and politicians formulated ambitious plans for the use of American power.

Most people who came of age after the 1960s, if asked what that decade was "about," will respond with an account of these crusades, structured in such a way as to highlight the moral heroism of the time. That is only natural. For two generations, "the sixties" has given order to every aspect of the national life of the United States—its partisan politics, its public etiquette, its official morality.

This is a book about the crises out of which the 1960s order arose, the means by which it was maintained, and the contradictions at its heart that, by the time of the presidential election of 2016, had led a working majority of Americans to view it not as a gift but as an oppression.

The assassination of Kennedy

The era we think of as the sixties began with relative suddenness around the time of the assassination of President John F. Kennedy in 1963. Americans are right to say that nothing was ever the same after Kennedy was shot. You can hear the change in popular music over a matter of months. A year-and-a-half before Kennedy was killed, "Stranger on the Shore," a drowsy instrumental by the British clarinetist Acker Bilk, had hit number one. A year-and-a-half after the assassination, the musicians who would form Jefferson Airplane, the Grateful Dead, Big Brother and the Holding Company, and various other druggie blues and folk-rock bands were playing their first gigs together in San Francisco.

This does not mean that the assassination "caused" the decade's cultural upheaval. The months before Kennedy's death had already seen the publication of Thomas Kuhn's book *The Structure of Scientific Revolutions* (August 1962), which upended notions about science's solidity and a lot of social and political assumptions built on it; Rachel Carson's exposé of pesticides, *Silent Spring* (September 1962); and *The Feminine Mystique* (February 1963), Betty Friedan's attack on what she saw as the vapidity of well-to-do housewives' existence. Something was going to happen.

The two conflicts that did most to define the American 1960s— those over racial integration and the war in Vietnam—were already visible. In October 1962, rioting greeted attempts to enforce a Supreme Court decision requiring the segregated University of Mississippi to enroll its first black student, James Meredith. The last summer of Kennedy's life ended with an unprecedented March on Washington by 200,000 civil rights activists. Three weeks before Kennedy was killed in Dallas, Vietnamese president Ngo Dinh Diem was ousted and then murdered in a coup that Kennedy had authorized.

Kennedy's death, though, gave a tremendous impetus to changes already under way. Often peoples react to a political assassination, as if by collective instinct, with a massive posthumous retaliation. They memorialize a martyred leader by insisting on (or assenting to) a radicalized version, a sympathetic caricature, of the views they attribute to him. The example most familiar to Americans came in the wake of Abraham Lincoln's assassination in 1865, when the country passed constitutional reforms far broader than those Lincoln himself had sought: not only a Thirteenth Amendment to abolish slavery but also a broad Fourteenth Amendment, with its more general and highly malleable guarantees of equal protection and due process.

Something similar happened in the 1960s. A welfare state expanded by Medicare and Medicaid, the vast mobilization of young men to fight the Vietnam War, but, above all, the Civil Rights and Voting Rights acts—these were all memorials to a slain ruler, resolved in haste over a few months in 1964 and 1965 by a people undergoing a delirium of national grief. Kennedy's successor, Lyndon B. Johnson, was able to take ideas for civil rights legislation, languishing in the months before Kennedy's death, and cast them in a form more uncompromising than Kennedy could have imagined.

Civil rights ideology, especially when it hardened into a body of legislation, became, most unexpectedly, the model for an entire new system of constantly churning political reform. Definitions of what was required in the name of justice and humanity broadened. Racial integration turned into the all-embracing ideology of diversity. Women's liberation moved on to a reconsideration of what it meant to be a woman (and, eventually, a man). Immigration became grounds for reconsidering whether an American owed his primary allegiance to his country or whether other forms of belonging were more important. Anti-communist military adventures gave way, once communism began to collapse in 1989, to a role for the United States as the keeper of the whole world's peace, the guarantor of the whole world's prosperity, and the promulgator and enforcer of ethical codes for a new international order, which was sometimes called the "global economy."

There was something irresistible about this movement. The moral prestige and practical resources available to the American governing elite as it went about reordering society were almost limitless. Leaders could draw not just on the rage and resolve that followed Kennedy's death but also on the military and economic empire the United States had built up after World War II; on the organizational know-how accumulated in its corporations and foundations; on the Baby Boom, which, as the end of the twentieth century approached, released into American society a surge of manpower unprecedented in peacetime; and, finally, on the self-assurance that arose from all of these things.

The reforms of the sixties, however, even the ones Americans loved best and came to draw part of their national identity from, came with costs that proved staggeringly high—in money, freedom, rights, and social stability. Those costs were spread most unevenly among social classes and generations. Many Americans were left worse off by the changes. Economic inequality reached levels not seen since the age of the nineteenth-century monopolists. The scope for action conferred on society's leaders allowed elite power to multiply steadily and, we now see, dangerously, sweeping aside not just obstacles but also dissent.

At some point in the course of the decades, what had seemed in 1964 to be merely an ambitious reform revealed itself to have been something more. The changes of the 1960s, with civil rights at their core, were not just a major new element in the Constitution. They were a *rival* constitution, with which the original one was frequently incompatible—and the incompatibility would worsen as the civil rights regime was built out. Much of what we have called "polarization" or "incivility" in recent years is something more grave—it is the disagreement over which of the two constitutions shall prevail: the de jure constitution of 1788, with all the traditional forms of jurisprudential legitimacy and centuries of American culture behind it; or the de facto constitution of 1964, which lacks this traditional kind of legitimacy but commands the near-unanimous endorsement of judicial elites and civic educators and the passionate allegiance of those who received it as a liberation. The increasing necessity that citizens *choose* between these two orders, and the poisonous conflict into which it ultimately drove the country, is what this book describes.

2

Race

*The Civil Rights Act—Freedom of association—What did
whites think they were getting?—What did blacks think they
were getting?—Not civil rights but human rights—Origins of
affirmative action and political correctness*

The very first days of the 1960s saw the publication of a scholarly landmark. In January 1960, Harvard University's Belknap Press brought out a new edition of the *Narrative of the Life of Frederick Douglass* (1845), edited by the historian Benjamin Quarles, a professor at Morgan State University in Maryland.

Today, with the figure of Douglass towering over American culture, in high school curricula and museum exhibits, on postage stamps and television specials, we might assume that what made the publication important was Quarles's new interpretation of a classic American autobiography. We would be wrong. Far from being thought a classic in 1960, Douglass's earliest memoir, covering his years as a slave, had been out of print for more than a century and almost unmentioned in print since the Civil War. Douglass's career as an abolitionist orator, newspaper publisher, and diplomat was important to historians of the nineteenth century. But his struggles as a slave were not of obvious relevance to mid–twentieth century Americans.

Today slavery is at the center of Americans' official history, with race the central concept in the country's official self-understanding. Never before the 1960s was this the case. For almost all of American history, racial conflict was understood as a set of episodes—some shameful, some glorious—set against a larger story about building a constitutional republic. After the 1960s, the constitutional republic was sometimes discussed as if it were a mere set of tools for resolving larger conflicts about race and human rights.

The Civil Rights Act

If the 1960s were a revolutionary time, the core of the revolution was race. Black people in Southern states, with a few reform-minded white allies across the country, were challenging, and demonstrating and marching against, various local systems built up in the century since the Civil War to keep black people apart from white people. The whites who had erected and enforced these systems used them to claim the best fruits of the local economy.

World War II had knit the country together, exposing Southerners to the variety of European-descended ethnicities now present in the Northeast and Midwest, and introducing Americans to the problems of other regions. (But not directly to the problems of other races, for the armed forces would not be integrated until 1948.) In the 1950s, highways, televisions, and corporate expansion made it hard to hide any part of the country from any other part. Systems of racial separation, known collectively as Jim Crow, lost much of their logic and, with it, their power to enforce, intimidate, and control.

The Civil Rights Act of 1964, passed by Lyndon Johnson in the immediate aftermath of John F. Kennedy's death, was meant to deliver the coup de grâce to Jim Crow, and to end the black marches and police crackdowns in Mississippi and Alabama that television viewers were seeing almost weekly. The act banned racial discrimination in voting booths (Title I); hotels, restaurants, and theaters (Title II); public facilities, from libraries to swimming pools to bathrooms (Title III); and public schools (Title IV).

But that was not all it did. It also empowered the federal government to reform and abolish certain institutions that stood in the way of racial equality and to establish new ones. By expanding the federal Civil Rights Commission (Title V); by subjecting to bureaucratic scrutiny any company or institution that received government money (Title VI); by laying out hiring practices for all companies with more than 15 employees; by creating a new presidential agency, the Equal Employment Opportunity Commission (EEOC), with the power to file lawsuits, conduct investigations, and order redress—by doing all these things, the act emboldened and incentivized bureaucrats, lawyers, intellectuals, and political agitators to become the "eyes and ears," and even the foot soldiers, of civil rights enforcement.

Over time, more of the country's institutions were brought under the act's scrutiny. Eventually all of them were. The grounds for finding someone or something guilty of discrimination expanded. New civil rights acts—notably the Voting Rights Act of 1965 and the Fair Housing Act of 1968—brought new rights for black citizens and new bureaucracies to enforce them.

Civil rights transformed the country not just constitutionally but also culturally and demographically. In ways few people anticipated, it proved to be the mightiest instrument of domestic enforcement the country had ever seen. It can fairly be described as the largest undertaking *of any kind* in American history. Costing trillions upon trillions of dollars and spanning half a century, it rivals, in terms of energy invested, the peopling of the West, the building of transcontinental railways and highways, the maintenance of a Pax Americana for half a century after World War II, or, for that matter, any of the wars the country has fought, foreign or civil.

On top of those conflicts, the United States has had two massive domestic policy programs that mobilized public resources and sentiments so thoroughly that they were presented to the public as what the philosopher and psychologist William James called a "moral equivalent of war": the War on Poverty in the 1960s and the War on Drugs in the 1980s and '90s. Both were mere battlefronts in a larger struggle over race relations. The reinterpretation of America's entire history and purpose in light of its race problem is the main ideological legacy of the last fifty years.

The scholar Derrick Bell described the quarter-century after the Supreme Court's school desegregation decision *Brown v. Board of Education of Topeka* (1954) as "the greatest racial consciousness-raising the country has ever known." This consciousness-raising has only intensified since. Race is the part of the human experience in which American schoolchildren are most painstakingly instructed. Their studies of literature, of war, of civics, are all subordinated to it.

Race was invested with a religious significance. It became an ethical absolute. One could even say that the civil rights movement, inside and outside the government, became a doctrinal institution, analogous to established churches in pre-democratic Europe. And yet there was something new, something mid–twentieth century, about the way the U.S. government sought to mold the whole of society—down to the most intimate private acts—around the ideology of anti-racism. You could see this ideology emerging in the way Quarles reimagined the young Frederick Douglass:

> Naturally the *Narrative* does not bother to take up the difficulties inherent in abolishing slavery. These Douglass would have dismissed with a wave of the hand. Similarly the *Narrative* recognizes no claim other than that of the slave. To Douglass the problems of social adjustment if the slaves were freed were nothing, the property rights of the masters were nothing, states' rights were nothing. He simply refused to discuss these matters. As he viewed it, his function was to shake people out of their lethargy and goad them into action, not to discover reasons for sitting on the fence.

It is true that, in the years before the Civil War, not only the young Douglass but also the New England abolitionists in whose orbit he moved sometimes spoke in such an absolutist way. But when Quarles wrote in 1960, such a stance was still out of favor. As most historians till then had understood it, the absolutism of Douglass and others had hurried the country into a bloody civil war and unnecessarily complicated the reconstruction that followed. In fact, the constitutional and social obstacles to abolishing slavery had been formidable, making attempts to "shake people out of their lethargy and goad them into action" correspondingly dangerous. When Rutherford B. Hayes, on taking the presidency in 1877, ended the military occupation of the South and, with it, efforts to reform race relations there, it was not because he was a coward or a reactionary. Barely a decade after a civil war that had cost 600,000 lives, the entire country, even the North, had turned against Reconstruction. The costs of solving the American race problem had risen beyond what voters were willing to pay.

So when the historian C. Vann Woodward described the twentieth-century civil rights movement as a "Second Reconstruction," he meant it partly as a warning, a warning that later historians and polemicists have been deaf to. Like the young Douglass, they "dismissed with a wave of the hand" the notion that there might be costs to keeping intolerance at bay. Until the election of 2016, the Second Reconstruction appeared to have fared better than the first. A half-century on, its institutions were still standing.

What was innovative about the reformers of the 1960s was neither their morality nor their perspicacity. Few Americans could contemplate segregation without feelings of hypocrisy, scandal, and shame. It had always been understood, surely even by many of its Southern defenders, that government-sponsored racial inequality was a contradiction of America's constitutional principles and an affront to its Christian ones. Those who stood up to segregation in the middle of the twentieth century did not have any special insight into this. Nor were they braver or more humane than, say, Homer Plessy had been when he boarded a "whites only" train car in Louisiana in 1895 to challenge the state's recently enacted segregation laws.

What made the modern framers of civil rights different from the nineteenth-century ones was their conception of power and their genius for wielding it. They succeeded where their forebears had failed because they were confident in resorting to coercion, indifferent to imposing financial burdens on future generations, and willing to put existing constitutional freedoms at risk in order to secure new ones.

Why wouldn't they have been? They were the heirs to a civilization that had just vanquished totalitarianism on two continents and come to produce a quarter of the world's GDP, and was now sending rockets out to explore space. The folkways of the South clashed intolerably with mid-century Americans' self-image. Americans were civilized, modern, gentlemanly. Segregation was sleazy, medieval, underhanded. Fulton County, Georgia, kept black people from voting by requiring them to complete a 30-item questionnaire demanding that they lay out the legal bureaucratic procedure for changing the seat of a county, name the state comptroller and all of the state's federal district court judges, and state how many votes Georgia had in the federal electoral college. The smugness and cruelty of the system, the way it appeared to taunt, demean, and demoralize its victims even as it threatened and bullied them—it was infuriating, and not only to blacks.

The reaction, when it came, was pitiless. The Civil Rights and Voting Rights acts provided permanent emergency powers to smash the sham democracy of the segregated South. They mixed surveillance by volunteers, litigation by lawyers, and enforcement by bureaucrats. This was a new model of federal government, with a transformative power that was immediately apparent. Thoroughgoing and versatile, often able to bypass the separation of powers, civil rights law became the template for much of American policy making after the 1960s, including on matters far removed from race. This was mostly on the grounds of its efficiency, but that efficiency rested on certain assertions about values. To set oneself against civil rights was to set oneself against the whole moral thrust of American government.

Freedom of association

The United States is today a free country in a very different sense than it was between the administrations of George Washington and John F. Kennedy.

Brown v. Board of Education of Topeka (1954), the unanimous Supreme Court decision that ordered the desegregation of all the country's schools, was not just a landmark decision but an unusual one. It was brief to the point of curtness: Shorn of footnotes and case references, each of its two parts ran about the length of a newspaper column. It was less a judicial argument than a judicial order.

The justices ignored the subject to which they had devoted most of their deliberations: whether the Fourteenth Amendment—drafted in the wake of the Civil War to guarantee "equal protection of the laws"— had intended to permit segregated schools. Instead they asked whether the doctrine of "separate but equal," used to justify school segregation, was possible in practice.

It may surprise readers of a later generation to discover that the justices believed it *was* possible, not just in cherry-picked cases taken from model schools but in the actual schools that the National Association for the Advancement of Colored People (NAACP) had chosen to argue over. The justices noted findings "that the Negro and white schools involved have been equalized, or are being equalized, with respect to buildings, curricula, qualifications and salaries of teachers, and other 'tangible' factors." They nonetheless repudiated the separate-but-equal doctrine for primary schools on the grounds that, because of "intangible considerations" and "qualities which are incapable of objective measurement," segregation "is usually interpreted as denoting the inferiority of the Negro group."

Even many ardent opponents of segregation were troubled by *Brown*'s project to rewrite the Constitution on the authority of vague pronouncements about the way things are "usually interpreted." In an article published at the end of 1959, Harvard Law School professor

Herbert Wechsler described *Brown* as "an opinion which is often read with less fidelity by those who praise it than by those by whom it is condemned"—the most circumlocutory way imaginable of saying that it was wrongly decided. Wechsler showed in devastating detail that *Brown* would have been impossible under any faithful reading of what the drafters of the Fourteenth Amendment had meant by equality. He also argued that the *Brown* justices had blundered when they focused on equality in the first place.

The "heart of the matter" with segregation was not equality but the conflicts it created with the implicit First Amendment right of freedom of association. These conflicts were not easily solved, Wechsler showed:

> If the freedom of association is denied by segregation, integration forces an association upon those for whom it is unpleasant or repugnant. . . . Given a situation where the state must practically choose between denying the association to those individuals who wish it or imposing it on those who would avoid it, is there a basis in neutral principles for holding that the Constitution demands that the claims for association should prevail?

Wechsler hoped to find such a basis. But in constitutional terms, the decision was arbitrary and open-ended. *Brown* granted the government the authority to put certain public bodies under surveillance for racism. Since the damage it aimed to mend consisted of "intangible considerations," there was no obvious limit to this surveillance. And once the Civil Rights Act introduced into the *private* sector this assumption that all separation was prima facie evidence of inequality, desegregation implied a revocation of the old freedom of association altogether. Just as assuming that two parallel lines can meet overturns much of Euclidean geometry, eliminating freedom of association from the U.S. Constitution changed everything.

Within a decade of *Brown*, the philosopher Leo Strauss was warning that attempts to root out discrimination could backfire badly. In an off-the-cuff talk about Jewishness and identity that he gave to the Hillel Foundation at the University of Chicago, he spoke about the difficulties under which minorities, and specifically Jews, labored—but he warned about the dangers of doing too much to change them:

> A liberal society stands or falls by the distinction between the political (or the state) and society, or by the distinction between the public and the private. In the liberal society there is necessarily a private sphere with which the state's legislation must not interfere. . . . liberal society necessarily makes possible, permits, and even fosters what is called by many people "discrimination."

Tempting though it might be to attack this discrimination at its root, the cure could wind up worse than the disease, Strauss warned: "The prohibition against every 'discrimination' would mean the abolition of the private sphere, the denial of the difference between the state and society, in a word, the destruction of liberal society."

From the start it took courage to dissent from the intellectual consensus in favor of *Brown*. The University of Chicago First Amendment scholar Harry Kalven, Jr., tried to disguise his own misgivings as praise:

> One of the most distinctive features of the Negro revolution has been its almost military assault on the Constitution via the strategy of systematic litigation. . . . Here there has been no waiting for the random and mysterious process by which controversies are finally brought to the [Supreme] Court; there has been rather a marshaling of cases, a timing of litigation, a forced feeding of legal growth. This has been a brilliant use of democratic *legal* process, and its success has been deservedly spectacular. I am old-fashioned enough to read the development, not as political pressure on the Court which then as a political institution responded, but rather as a strategy to trap democracy in its own decencies.

In his own esoteric way, Kalven invites us to view the civil rights revolution as a potential constitutional catastrophe. In what healthy society is an "almost military assault on the Constitution" worthy of praise? What upstanding political actor takes advantage of another's "decencies" to entrap him? And when court cases do not arise "naturally" out of a country's ordinary social frictions but are confected by interested parties, doesn't the entire tradition of judicial review lose its legitimacy? Especially since, in a country where lawyers must go through an expensive training and a guild-like selection, those interested parties are likely to be the country's elites.

Kalven implicitly accepts, lock, stock, and barrel, an argument that back then was usually put forward by Southerners: that much civil rights litigation amounted to barratry, a gaming of the justice system through the creation of stylized cases. Such scruples were clearly on the way out. Today, the "staging" of court cases is such a standard strategy for activist litigators that even many lawyers are unaware that until the 1950s it was widely considered a straightforward species of judicial corruption, and not just in the South.

The *Yale Law Journal* had already leveled a similar accusation: that the National Association for the Advancement of Colored People had been allowed to take up a role in the various civil rights cases as a "private attorney general." The NAACP not only staged events, it scripted them. The plaintiffs it hand-picked to carry them out were chosen for their sympathy and skill.

One example is Rosa Parks. Over decades, Black History Month has taught millions of schoolchildren to think of her as a "tired seamstress," whose need to rest her weary legs in the white section of a Montgomery, Alabama, city bus unleashed a storm of spontaneous protest. But she was considerably more than that. Five months before the Montgomery bus boycott began, she had attended the Highlander Folk School in New Market, Tennessee, an academy that the Congress of Industrial Organizations had set up for training social agitators. She was an organizer of considerable sophistication, one of the intellectual leaders of the Montgomery NAACP chapter.

Americans have in recent years been fond of boasting that—unlike most nations, where it is heritage, history, and race that bind people together—the United States is a place that one can belong to regardless of background. That is true enough, but there is a reason most countries are not multi-ethnic countries and why most of those that have tried to become multi-ethnic countries have failed. Where a shared heritage is absent or unrecognized, as it is in the contemporary United States, all the eggs of national cohesion are placed in the basket of the constitution. Hence a paradox: With the dawn of the civil rights era, the U.S. Constitution—the very thing that made it possible for an ethnically varied nation to live together—came under stress.

The problem is that rights cannot simply be "added" to a social contract without changing it. To establish new liberties is to extinguish others. This difficulty would be at the root of the earliest debates over civil rights legislation. In the summer of 1963, well before Kennedy's assassination, one anecdote from the Senate's debates captured the imagination of the public. Senators skeptical of civil rights legislation hinted that "Mrs. Murphy"—a hypothetical old widow who rented out a room in her house in a northern city—might wind up bearing the brunt of federal surveillance and law enforcement if she got too picky about whom she accepted as a tenant. The legislation's backers treated the question as ridiculous—of course a boarding house, unlike the hotels that would be covered in any civil rights legislation, was Mrs. Murphy's "personal" property, with which she could do as she pleased.

But the distinction was not as obvious as pro–civil rights legislators claimed, and the certitudes that rested on it proved complacent. In his opening remarks at the 1963 March on Washington, A. Philip Randolph, organizer of the Brotherhood of Sleeping Car Porters (and of the march itself), warned that "real freedom will require many changes in the nation's political and social philosophies and institutions. For one thing we must destroy the notion that Mrs. Murphy's property rights include the right to humiliate me because of the color of my skin. The sanctity of private property takes second place to the sanctity of the human personality." And so it was after the Civil Rights Act of 1964. Property simply would not enjoy the same constitutional protection that it had before.

Neither would the traditional understanding of freedom of association. Florida's segregationist governor, C. Farris Bryant, was able to describe this understanding as something all Americans shared:

> We would all agree that the traveler is and should be free not to buy. He can pass a motel because he doesn't like the town, he doesn't like the color, or he doesn't like the name. He can stop and go in and when he sees the owner he can decide he doesn't like him because he doesn't like his mustache, or his accent, or his prices, or his race, or his other customers. He can turn around and walk out for any reason, or for no reason at all. Why not? He's a free man. So is the owner of the property. And if the traveler is free not to buy because he doesn't like the owner's mustache, accent, prices, race, other customers, or for any or no reason, the owner of the property ought to have the same freedom. That's simple justice. The wonder is that it can be questioned.

It tended to be segregationists who philosophized in this vein. Progressive politicians were seldom comfortable conveying to white voters that, in exchange for civil rights, they were going to have to surrender certain basic freedoms they had until then taken for granted. Naturally it was a delicate moment, because the white public was sending mixed signals about whether it wanted to get rid of segregation in the first place.

What did whites think they were getting?

The mood of that public is hard to gauge. Certainly, many white people did wish for the civil rights revolution. In the last summer of John F. Kennedy's life, a plurality (49 to 42 percent) said they favored a law that "would give all persons—Negro as well as white—the right to be served in public places such as hotels, restaurants, theaters, and similar establishments." That right would be at the core of the Civil Rights Act of 1964, signed by Kennedy's successor, Lyndon Johnson. But the act, as we have seen, went further still, and five months after pushing it through Congress, Johnson won the presidency with 61 percent of the popular vote—the highest tally in American history.

It does not seem likely that Johnson's election victory constituted a voter endorsement, given the two decades of steady, nationwide conservative drift that began almost simultaneously. Democrats would lose 47 House seats at the next midterm election, making the 1964 landslide look less like a validation of Johnson than a tribute to Kennedy. Johnson had framed his civil rights legislation as such a tribute; for a while after Kennedy's death, he framed most issues that way. "No memorial oration or eulogy could more eloquently honor President Kennedy's memory than the earliest possible passage of the civil rights bill for which he fought so long," Johnson said in an address to Congress five days after the assassination. "And second, no act of ours could more fittingly continue the work of President Kennedy than the early passage of the tax bill for which he fought all this long year."

The Gallup polling organization routinely asked Americans in the early 1960s whether they believed the pace of integration was "too fast," "not fast enough," or "about right." In August 1963, the month of the March on Washington at which Martin Luther King gave his "I have a dream" speech, 50 percent said the country was moving "too fast" on integration, versus 10 percent who said "not fast enough"—a ratio of 5 to 1. That ratio fell to 2 to 1 (30 to 15 percent) in January, during the debate over the Civil Rights Act. But in October, on the eve of the election, it was back over 3 to 1 (57 to 18 percent) again. It never disappeared.

Whites were muddle-headed on the subject of race. It is clear that they did not understand that the Civil Rights Act was a big constitutional deal. Three weeks before the 1964 elections, Gallup asked the following question:

Some people say the Civil Rights law guaranteeing equal rights for Negroes should be strictly enforced right from the beginning. Others say a gradual persuasive approach should be used at first. Which approach would you rather see used?

What a question! The law had already passed. It was on the books. It had capped a months-long political campaign that aimed to resolve a centuries-long legacy of quarreling and bloodshed. And now Gallup was asking whether the country should *enforce* it? The pollsters, however, had a reason for asking. Fewer than a quarter of Americans actually did want the law to be enforced. Here is how they answered:

23%   strictly enforced
62%   gradual, persuasive approach
10%   depends on circumstances
6%   don't know

The answer was no fluke. *After* the election the Opinion Research Corporation asked a similar question ("In the area of civil rights, which government policy do you favor . . . vigorous enforcement of the new civil rights law or moderation in enforcement of the new civil rights law?") and got almost identical results:

19%   vigorous enforcement of the new civil rights law
68%   moderation in enforcement of the new civil rights law
13%   no choice

For all their pious sentiments about desegregating the South, whites opposed every single activist step that might have brought desegregation about, and every single activist who was working to do so. In 1961, they thought, by a margin of 57 to 28 percent, that the black students staging sit-ins at North Carolina lunch counters and the "Freedom Riders" occupying segregated buses between Washington, D.C., and New Orleans "hurt" rather than "helped" the cause of civil rights. In 1964, on the eve of the Civil Rights Act, only 16 percent of Americans said that mass demonstrations had helped the cause of racial equality—versus 74 percent who said they had hurt it. Sixty percent even disapproved of the March on Washington, at least in the days leading up to it, while only 23 percent approved.

Most Americans, liberal as well as conservative, saw the race problem as something distant. It had to do only, or mainly, with the exotic culture of the South, where segregation was legal. The problem was almost one of foreign policy. The sociologist of race Alan David Freeman wrote of how, sitting in an all-white fifth-grade classroom in New York City in 1954, he had found out about the *Brown* decision: "I can recall distinctly the response of my own naïvely liberal consciousness . . . The Law is now going to make those bad Southerners behave."

As white people in the northern and western states saw it, racial harmony had arrived long ago. In August 1962, with the school year about to begin, 83 percent of Americans told Gallup that the blacks in their community had "the same opportunities as white children to get a good education." Gallup kept asking this question as the 1960s wore on and white Americans' views changed little. At the end of the 1967–68 school year, 70 percent told pollsters that blacks in their community were treated "the same as whites" and only 20 percent that they were treated not very well or badly.

Outside the South, white people seemed to believe it would be a simple matter to get rid of segregation, as if a system of racial oppression so intricate and ingenious that it had taken three-and-a-half centuries to devise could be dismantled overnight—by sheer open-minded niceness, at no price in rights to anyone. The country could solve a problem of institutional racism without altering any of its institutions. "What we find most amazing about this ideological structure in retrospect," Kimberlé Crenshaw and a group of scholarly race theorists would write three decades later, "is how very little actual social change was imagined to be required by 'the civil rights revolution.'" Crenshaw and her colleagues were right—that is indeed the most amazing thing about the civil rights revolution. Americans' basically wrong assessment explains why problems emerged so soon after the passage of civil rights legislation. It may also explain why the legislation passed in the first place.

As a practical matter, whites did not suspect they would see the vast increase in federal government oversight that would become the sine qua non of civil rights. The congressional debate leading up to the Civil Rights Act of 1964 is filled with outright mockery of those who warned of some hitherto unimaginable federal government infringement: not just the regulation of Mrs. Murphy's rooming house, mentioned above, but also mandatory school busing, public and private hiring quotas, and immigration quotas. In the spring of 1964, when Florida Democratic senator George Smathers worried that attempts to equalize school enrollment might lead to busing, his Pennsylvania Republican colleague Hugh Scott scoffed, "Does the Senator not agree that there is nothing whatever in the bill which relates to the transportation of schoolchildren by bus from one district to another? I find nothing in the bill which pertains to any such provision." By the 1970s, there was race-based busing nationwide, and not just in Southern states. All sorts of constitutionalist and libertarian fears, chuckled at and pooh-poohed on the floor of the Senate, came to pass. Those who opposed the legislation proved wiser about its consequences than those who sponsored it.

White civil rights supporters, even the most street-smart among them, were inclined to view the civil rights movement not as an attack on America's Constitution and culture but as an opportunity for everyone in the South to "buy into" it. Southern whites, whether they realized it or not, would be getting a better deal: full membership in the country's constitutional culture. And it was hard to imagine that blacks, who would be getting a *much* better deal, would respond with anything other than gratitude. Looking back from the late 1970s at a vanished golden age of harmony between whites and blacks, the Harvard sociologist Nathan Glazer recalled that interracial fraternity "was certainly the objective of the American Negro civil rights movements until the late 1960s—black leaders wanted nothing more than to be Americans, full Americans, with the rights of all Americans." But by the time Glazer wrote, he could see what Wechsler had predicted: Giving blacks access to "the rights of all Americans" would mean redefining those rights, starting with freedom of association.

The proudest achievement of the American model of ethnic assimilation was its pluralism. Even if suburban parts of the country appeared to be growing blander and more homogeneous, they had issued out of, and still co-existed with, a thrilling and varied culture of mostly European inheritance: Jewish yeshivas, Chinese restaurants, Italian Catholic folk festivals, Slovak veterans' lodges, Irish musical groups, Polish trade unions, and even Anglo-Saxon yacht clubs. Civil rights legislation put not just Jim Crow but all of American culture up for re-examination and renegotiation. "For one of the major groups in American life," Glazer wrote of black people,

> the idea of pluralism, which has supported the various develop-
> ments of other groups, has become a mockery. Whatever concrete
> definition we give to pluralism, it means a limitation of govern-
> ment power, a relatively free hand for private and voluntary or-
> ganizations to develop their own patterns of worship, education,
> social life, residential concentration, and even distinctive eco-
> nomic activity. All of these enhance the life of some groups; from
> the perspective of the American Negro they are exclusive and dis-
> criminatory.

Subcommunities, as Glazer called them, were often suspicious, hostile to outsiders. They were also indispensable for giving people of humble prospects a dignified place in the social order, and keeping the ruthless machinery of market competition at bay. "The force of present-day Negro demands," Glazer wrote, "is that the subcommunity, because it either protects privileges or creates inequality, *has no right to exist*." Now government would set about destroying those subcommunities—eventually doing so in the name of "diversity," although that is a story for another chapter.

What did blacks think they were getting?

The mainstream (white) assessment of the race problem in the 1960s, and of the scope of the actions needed to remedy it, was mostly wrong. It erred wildly on the side of optimism. White people knew a lot less about black people than blacks did about white people. Whites had not thought much about what it would be like to live in close proximity to blacks—if indeed they thought that would be the result of civil rights legislation at all.

In part they were blinded by their privileged position, Alan David Freeman explained. Even when they concur in seeing a system of racial discrimination as evil, outsiders and insiders—or "victims" and "perpetrators," as Freeman called them—tend to look at different things. Victims see racial discrimination as a *system* of corruption that burdens them in a variety of practical, measurable ways—with "lack of jobs, lack of money, lack of housing." They are unlikely to view the system as repaired until those practical burdens are removed. Perpetrators, on the other hand, see an ethical failure on the part of society's leaders and feel society will have done its duty as soon as most people are behaving ethically—speaking out against prejudice and refraining from acts of overt discrimination. The mostly Northern whites who legislated against Jim Crow saw themselves as making a grand and magnanimous gesture, cutting a heroic figure. They would affirm the moral principles on which the Constitution rested by extending its legal principles to a region where they had never really been applied. Black people, and the most zealous among the civil rights activists of all races, saw whites as having entered a guilty plea in the court of history, and thus as repudiating the moral posturing on which the good name and the good conscience of their constitutional republic had rested.

These are matters of perspective. There is no point in describing one interpretation as morally "right" or "wrong." We can say, though, that where the black consensus differed from the white consensus, it was blacks' views that were more congruent with the reality of what would be required, and what would be effective, in bringing racial equality about.

The major polling companies did not do intensive work on black opinion until the late 1960s—itself an instructive datum concerning the kind of reform American elites thought they were launching. When the pollsters looked, they discovered that blacks' views were in most cases the opposite of whites'. Sixty percent of blacks believed that progress on civil rights was too slow—not, as most whites did, too fast. By 69 to 9 percent, blacks reckoned federal anti-poverty programs a boost rather than a hindrance. And when riots eventually came, in big cities and on college campuses, blacks leaned toward thinking they helped more than hurt integration (by 41 to 30 percent and 40 to 32 percent, respectively), versus the 74 percent of whites, mentioned earlier, who said just the opposite. Civil rights, as many blacks saw it, was not just a reform but also an uprising.

Not civil rights but human rights

So did whites confer those rights, or did blacks wring them out of a reluctant political system? It was a bit of both. The civil rights movement was not precisely a movement of civil rights, in the sense of giving American blacks access to the ordinary rights of *cives*, or citizens. If it had been, the laws would not have required changing, only enforcing.

Congress had thought in terms of citizenship when it passed the Civil Rights Act of 1866. So had the Supreme Court when it tried the Civil Rights cases of 1883. The term "civil rights" survived even as the approach failed. What was being fought over in the 1960s was something different from civil rights. It was a conception of *human* rights that had arisen in the twentieth century.

Gandhi had advanced it. So had the Universal Declaration of Human Rights, promulgated at the United Nations in 1948. American liberals were inclined to think it an improvement on the country's own constitutional traditions. "The time has arrived in America for the Democratic party to get out of the shadow of states' rights and walk forthrightly into the bright sunshine of human rights!" Minneapolis mayor and senatorial candidate Hubert Humphrey said in a speech at the 1948 party convention that launched his national career. "People—human beings—this is the issue of the twentieth century."

In the mid–twentieth century, human rights was not a milquetoast moralism but a fighting doctrine. The Black Muslim orator Malcolm X, who professed indifference as to whether the civil rights struggle succeeded by the ballot or the bullet, embraced something he described as human rights in the spring before the passage of the Civil Rights Act. His vision overlapped only partially with that of the United Nations.

Worldwide, as Malcolm X saw it, white people were panicked that rising incomes in the Third World were leading to rapid population growth, thence to power, thence to revolution. In a speech he gave before a mostly white audience at a forum sponsored by the socialist newspaper *The Militant*, he treated rights and revolution as part of a seamless whole. "Revolution is never based on begging somebody for an integrated cup of coffee," he said. "Revolutions are never fought by turning the other cheek. Revolutions are never based upon love-your-enemy and pray-for-those-who-spitefully-use-you. And revolutions are never waged singing 'We Shall Overcome.' Revolutions are based upon bloodshed." This was not necessarily meant to be a racist doctrine. Malcolm X urged sympathetic whites to turn the civil rights struggle into a struggle for human rights, which "opens the door for all of our brothers and sisters in Africa and Asia, who have their independence, to come to our rescue."

Malcolm X made that speech a week after his only meeting with Martin Luther King, Jr. The two bumped into each other in the U.S. Senate while attending the debate on the civil rights bill and spoke for, literally, one minute. It has become common to present the two as having taken opposite approaches to civil rights. The motto of the Southern Christian Leadership Conference, the civil rights umbrella group King founded in 1957, was "To save the soul of America." It summarizes well the role King plays in twenty-first-century civil rights pageantry, but King himself soon moved beyond it. By 1967, when he had come to see the Vietnam War as a strategic and humanitarian catastrophe, he was changing tack. In a rueful and sarcastic address at New York's Riverside Church, King used Vietnam to sharpen the focus on America's racial hypocrisy:

> We were taking the black young men who had been crippled by our society and sending them eight thousand miles away to guarantee liberties in Southeast Asia which they had not found in southwest Georgia and East Harlem. So we have been repeatedly faced with the cruel irony of watching Negro and white boys on TV screens as they kill and die together for a nation that has been unable to seat them together in the same schools. So we watch them in brutal solidarity burning the huts of a poor village, but we realize that they would hardly live on the same block in Chicago.

King felt compelled to explain "why I believe that the path from Dexter Avenue Baptist Church—the church in Montgomery, Alabama, where I began my pastorate—leads clearly to this sanctuary tonight." America had become "the greatest purveyor of violence in the world today," to the point where he would no longer speak only in its name. "I speak as a citizen of the world," he said, "for the world as it stands aghast at the path we have taken." Then he reframed his point in terms that would not have been out of place in a speech by Malcolm X: "If we are to get on the right side of the world revolution, we as a nation must undergo a radical revolution of values." Although many American whites did not realize it even many decades later, black civil rights leaders had turned down a different path. The problem was not just America's exclusion of blacks. It was something deeper about American values.

Two weeks after Johnson signed the Civil Rights Act, policeman Thomas Gilligan shot dead 15-year-old James Powell in Harlem. Powell had been either (as police said) attacking Gilligan with a knife or (as Powell's friends said) caught up in a mostly peaceful protest of a landlord's anti-loitering policies. The neighborhood exploded in riots, which lasted for six nights, one of which saw 200 police and civilians hospitalized. No sooner had they ended than Rochester, New York, blew up. Jersey City, Philadelphia, and Dixmoor, Illinois, followed. Observers were slow to tie the wave of violence to the movement for civil rights, describing it as a kind of coincidence. "The civil rights movement itself was winding down," the *New York Times* reporter David Halberstam would later write. "There was a new and growing Negro discontent. There was a new anger in the air, particularly in northern cities." But the word "new" reflects wishful thinking. The riots *were* the civil rights movement—not the whole of it, certainly, but an important element of it.

Many American race riots in the half-century that followed, from Watts in 1965 through Los Angeles in 1992 to Ferguson in 2014 and Baltimore in 2015, would take the form of Harlem's in 1964. All would have the half-political character best described by the historian Eric Hobsbawm in his work on medieval uprisings and Mediterranean "banditry." To part of the country the riots were a social movement: a protest against the legitimacy of law enforcement that favored whites over blacks. To the rest of the country, the riots were just crime: a protest against nothing more than the rule of law. In the mid- to late 1960s, that was true especially for whites outside the South. For many, the riots were their *introduction* to blacks, and brought a change of perspective. It seemed to white people that the country had somehow pressed the wrong button and was now getting the "bad" civil rights movement instead of the "good" one they'd been promised—the burn-down-the-business-district version instead of the shake-hands-on-the-White-House-lawn version.

Starting in the early 1960s, an astonishing spike in crime, in which blacks made up a disproportionate share of both perpetrators and victims, took on aspects of a national emergency. The emergency would pass through various stages: the looting episodes in Memphis that preceded the assassination of Martin Luther King on April 4, 1968, and a new wave of deadly riots that followed it, the Attica Prison Revolt of 1971, the New York blackout of 1977, the crack epidemic of 1986, the Los Angeles "Rodney King" riots of 1992, O. J. Simpson's acquittal in his 1995 murder trial. After that, crime rates fell in general, but the overrepresentation of blacks in the criminal statistics never went away. By 2011, toward the end of Barack Obama's first term in office, blacks, who make up 13 percent of the U.S. population, still accounted for 39 percent of the arrests for violent crime.

During the election season of 1964, B'nai B'rith commissioned a poll on anti-Semitism and other bigotries. It found 37 percent of whites less sympathetic to blacks than they had been a year before, with only 15 percent more sympathetic. A measure that had been intended to normalize American culture and cure the gothic paranoia of the Southern racial imagination had instead wound up nationalizing Southerners' obsession with race and violence.

Origins of affirmative action and political correctness

The legislation of the mid-1960s made legal equality a fact of American life. To the surprise of much of the country, though, legal equality was now deemed insufficient by both civil rights leaders and the government.

Once its ostensible demands had been met, the civil rights movement did not disband. It grew. It turned into a lobby or political bloc seeking to remedy the problem according to what Freeman would call the victims' view: "lack of jobs, lack of money, lack of housing." The federal government made it a central part of its mission to procure those things for blacks. The results were disappointing on almost every front—naturally, since the country had never signed up for such a wide-ranging project.

Americans were by no means opposed to black advancement—but they had accepted the government's assurance that de jure racism was the main obstacle to it. They were probably surprised when the advance in blacks' fortunes slowed after 1964, relative to its rate in the two decades after the Second World War. It was not the first such disappointment in American history. In 1914, half a century after the Emancipation Proclamation, the historian Charles Beard lamented, "Whatever the cause may be, there seems to be no doubt that the colored race has not made that substantial economic advance and achieved that standard of life which its friends hoped would follow from emancipation."

So it was now. Though no one had thought that those brought up under segregation would be able to make up for the opportunities they had been denied in their youth, it had been assumed that the first generation to benefit from standard American higher education would thrive, on the model of immigrants before them. That did not happen. Blacks, as Allan Bloom put it in his 1987 bestseller, *The Closing of the American Mind*, proved as "indigestible" in university systems as they had been in earlier generations.

Bloom had been a professor at Cornell University in upstate New York when black radicals bearing assault rifles rousted visiting parents out of bed on parents' weekend in 1969 and demanded concessions from the university administration—which were granted, over the objections of the faculty. He left for the University of Toronto the following year. The indigestibility and the radicalism were two sides of the same coin, as Bloom saw it. "Cornell," he wrote, "now had a large number of students who were manifestly unqualified and unprepared, and therefore it faced an inevitable choice: fail most of them or pass them without their having learned. . . . Black power, which hit the universities like a tidal wave at just that moment, provided a third way."

Whites were looking for excuses, too. The commencement speech Lyndon Johnson gave in front of the Howard University library in Washington on a June evening in 1965 has become a hallmark of civil rights oratory:

> You do not take a person who, for years, has been hobbled by chains and liberate him, bring him up to the starting line of a race and then say, "you are free to compete with all the others," and still justly believe that you have been completely fair.
>
> Thus it is not enough just to open the gates of opportunity. All our citizens must have the ability to walk through those gates.

Many who had gone to war against segregation had done so in the expectation that they would be greeted with flowers by those they had "liberated." Only now did the builders of civil rights realize that this was not something they could pronounce on with certitude. Two months later, Johnson would sign the Voting Rights Act and the black Los Angeles neighborhood of Watts would undergo race riots that left dozens dead, a thousand injured, and thousands more in prison.

There had always been a good deal of bluff about Johnson and other Southern white apostles of civil rights, a whiff of the nineteenth-century Southerner's claim to know the ways of "our" black folk better than you ever could. Now their reputation for expertise and fine-tuned sympathy was damaged. The country's political leadership was thrown into a consternation from which it would not emerge for at least half a century.

Every corner of American political culture would be affected by the effort to explain that failure away. Every corner would be racialized. No one would be permitted to sit back and just allow social change to happen. Every American had to be enlisted as a zealous soldier in the war on racism. "Authentic" voices of the black community were now desperately enlisted by the establishment, and Potemkin achievements for the civil rights movement just as desperately sought. Johnson called this "the next and the more profound stage" of civil rights.

Section 706(g) of the Civil Rights Act allowed the government to compel "affirmative action"—ordering the hiring of black people "or any other equitable relief as the court deems appropriate," provided an employer or institution "has intentionally engaged in or is intentionally engaging in an unlawful practice." But the act had opened almost all American businesses to lawsuits for discrimination, whether they had engaged in it intentionally or not.

One way to shelter one's business from the government's investigative zeal was to act in the spirit of voluntarism—to establish preemptively a government-approved affirmative action program, along lines laid out in Section 718 of the act. President Johnson's Executive Order 11246, promulgated in the same summer as the Voting Rights Act, had already required that any private company with at least 51 employees set up an affirmative action program if it was going to seek government contracts.

There was nothing race-neutral about the system. In fact, the judges who interpreted it wound up explicitly repudiating race-neutral solutions. The American anti-racist regime developed in such a way as to *exclude* the most obvious race-blind solution to prejudice: neutral civil service, college admission, and hiring exams. In *Griggs v. Duke Power Co.* (1971), the Supreme Court justices asked whether a power plant in North Carolina could give aptitude tests to its employees. Title VII (Section 703) of the Civil Rights Act had said they could. But Chief Justice Warren Burger and a unanimous Court decided they could not, if such tests disadvantaged blacks in any way: "Good intent or absence of discriminatory intent does not redeem employment procedures or testing mechanisms that operated as 'built-in headwinds' for minority groups," Burger wrote.

Government could now disrupt and steer interactions that had been considered the private affairs of private citizens—their roles as businessmen or landlords or members of college admissions boards. It could interfere in matters of personal discretion. Yes, this was for a special purpose—to fight racism—but the *Griggs* decision made clear that the government was now authorized to act against racism even if there was no evidence of any racist intent. This was an opening to arbitrary power. And once arbitrary power is conferred, it matters little what it was conferred for.

That seemed to worry people. Skepticism about the civil rights revolution spread quickly in the wider public, if slowly among opinion leaders. In 1966, former B-movie actor Ronald Reagan, an opponent of both the Civil Rights and Voting Rights acts, unseated California governor Edmund "Pat" Brown, a popular public servant and master campaigner. The episode was so bewildering to the educated classes that *Commentary* magazine commissioned the Harvard political scientist James Q. Wilson, himself a native Californian of humble origins, to write a "Guide to Reagan Country" for its readers. "I do not intend here to write an apology for Reagan," Wilson explained at the outset. "Even if I thought like that, which I don't, I would never write it down anywhere my colleagues at Harvard might read it." Intellectuals seldom wrote that way at the time. Wilson, known among his colleagues as original and indomitable, was acknowledging the power of peer pressure to constrain what was said. Half a decade later, his Harvard colleague Nathan Glazer wrote:

Members of white ethnic groups say, "We worked hard and suffered from discrimination, and we made it. Why don't they?" And blacks retort, "You came after us and were nevertheless favored above us and given all the breaks, both when we were in slavery and since." It is a question that cannot be asked without arousing emotions so strong that one wonders just how far scholarship will be allowed to go on this issue.

Truth was among the first casualties of the affirmative action regime. At the simplest level the term "affirmative action" meant discarding prevailing notions of neutrality in order to redistribute educational and employment chances on the basis of race. The idea that it could be a permanent solution to the problem of racial prejudice required doublethink. "Affirmative action requires the use of race as a socially significant category of perception and representation," as Kimberlé Crenshaw and her colleagues put it, "but the deepest elements of mainstream civil rights ideology had come to identify such race-consciousness as racism itself." Just half a decade into the civil rights revolution, America had something it had never had at the federal level, something the overwhelming majority of its citizens would never have approved: an explicit system of racial preference.

Plainly the civil rights acts had wrought a change in the country's constitutional culture. The innovations of the 1960s had given progressives control over the most important levers of government, control that would endure for as long as the public was afraid of being called racist. Not just excluded and exploited Southern blacks but all aggrieved minorities now sought to press their claims under this new model of progressive governance.

The civil rights model of executive orders, litigation, and court-ordered redress eventually became the basis for resolving every question pitting a newly emergent idea of fairness against old traditions: the persistence of different roles for men and women, the moral standing of homosexuality, the welcome that is due to immigrants, the consideration befitting wheelchair-bound people. Civil rights gradually turned into a license for government to do what the Constitution would not previously have permitted. It moved beyond the context of Jim Crow laws almost immediately, winning what its apostles saw as liberation after liberation.

The new political style was not suited to every goal. It was designed for breaking traditional institutions, not building new ones. But it drove some observers to transports of speculation. The Jamaica-born Harvard sociologist Orlando Patterson enthused in the early 1970s:

Bleak though the system is, it also presents an awesome opportunity. . . . Black Americans can be the first group in the history of mankind who transcend the confines and grip of a cultural heritage, and in so doing, they can become the most truly modern of all peoples—a people who feel no need for a nation, a past, or a particularistic culture, but whose style of life will be a rational and continually changing adaptation to the exigencies of survival, at the highest possible level of existence. . . . It is clear that the next great cultural advance of mankind will involve the rejection of tradition and of particularism.

That is not how civil rights had been sold to the American public. Its toolbox of reform measures had been advertised as a remedy to one heinous constitutional exception. Americans who felt that civil rights were justified by an especially shameful history also thought it was *limited* by that history. They would not have consented to it otherwise. Patterson was one of the few who understood that there were no logical grounds for limiting its work to desegregation. The Yale University law professor Robert Bork, in his own very different way, was another. Immigrant rights, children's rights, gay rights, and the rights of the aged were not in the civil rights legislation, but they could easily be induced from it. The civil rights movement was a template. The new system for overthrowing the traditions that hindered black people became the model for overthrowing every tradition in American life, starting with the roles of men and women.

3

Sex

The GI generation and its failures—The Feminine Mystique *and male sexism*—Playboy *and male sexuality*—Gloria Steinem, *capitalism, and class*—Roe v. Wade *and the Supreme Court*—Our Bodies, Ourselves—*The Equal Rights Amendment*

Second-wave feminism began in 1963. Betty Friedan published *The Feminine Mystique* a few months before President Kennedy was shot. Her preoccupations were not those of the "first wave" of nineteenth-century abolitionists, prohibitionists, and suffragists. She did not philosophize about the inequalities, incompatibilities, and quarrels that the feminist Robin Morgan called "a five-thousand-year-buried anger." Friedan was describing something more modest: the ground women had lost since she herself had gone to all-female Smith College in western Massachusetts in the late 1930s.

The GI generation and its failures

It was a hard argument to make, because most of that ground had been lost in World War II. The U.S. military enjoyed vast prestige. Its victories on two continents were vivid in most people's memories. At its urging, scientists had invented a weapon of unprecedented destructive power. So much devastation had the war wrought on the industrial bases of other advanced nations that in the war's immediate aftermath America not only set the rules for most of the world's economy but also produced 60 percent of its manufacturing output. Until the war, though, the Great Depression had put America's civilian institutions on a decade-long losing streak. It now seemed reasonable to reassign the country's only successful leadership class (and its only successful culture of leadership) from the battlefield to the boardroom, the shop floor, and the faculty club.

That is what happened. By the mid-1950s, half the seats in Congress were held by (mostly quite young) veterans. Their domination of Congress would keep rising through the decades, peaking in 1971, when vets held 75 percent of the seats. They dominated journalism, too. "The intimate interaction between press and president in the thousand days of John F. Kennedy's administration . . . ," recalled *Washington Post* journalist Robert G. Kaiser, "depended on the existence of a like-minded cohort of World War II veterans (soldiers and journalists who covered the war) who shared a view of America's destiny."

It was a manly world knit together socially out of wartime memories and guided in its decisions by wartime rules of thumb. Vets called society's tune. Their tastes and preoccupations were presented as normal for the whole country. Advertisements from the color magazines of the 1940s and 1950s followed the arc of a GI's fantasies across the years; they were a mix of technology and animal spirits. Everything was dressed up as rocket science. Oldsmobile had the "Rocket 202 Engine," while Pontiac had the "Strato-Streak V-8 + Strato-Flight Hydra-Matic." Post-war women's swimsuits were as animally sexual as those of the supposedly libertine 1970s would be, albeit in a different fashion idiom (reticulated singlets for the earlier decade, string two-pieces for the later). As the 1950s progressed—as the GIs entered middle age—bust lines rose, hemlines fell, and women loaded up with jewelry.

Naturally, men too young to have fought in the war carried themselves as if they had. To shuffle through a stack of Topps baseball cards from 1963 (or even, baseball being at the time a relatively conservative sport, from 1969) is to see an almost uninterrupted procession of military-looking crew cuts. Twenty-four teams, 600 young men, and not a single mustache or beard among them. When Richie Allen of the St. Louis Cardinals and Felipe Alou of the Oakland Athletics began growing mustaches in 1970, they were the first players to have worn them since the 1930s.

Socially, the country was conservative. The early 1960s, we can see now, had more in common with the turn of the last century, two generations back, than with the turn of the next, only one generation away. Smoking was cool, not semi-criminal. President Kennedy himself smoked Petit Upmann cigars, his wife menthol cigarettes, either Newports or Salems. You could take German in public high schools but not Chinese, and poetry made up a considerable part of a high school English curriculum. Mary, the most popular girl's name in the United States for generations, nosed out only briefly by Linda after World War II, had fallen again to number-two in 1962, behind Lisa. By early in the twenty-first century, it would fall completely out of the top hundred.

Weeknight television was made up almost wholly of Westerns and army serials. For the 1962–63 season, ABC showed in its prime-time slot (7:30 p.m. back then) *Cheyenne* on Monday (followed by *The Rifleman* at 8:30), *Combat!* on Tuesday, *Wagon Train* on Wednesday, *The Adventures of Ozzie and Harriet* on Thursday, and *Gallant Men*, a World War II drama, on Friday. (Odd that in later years *Ozzie and Harriet* would become a symbol of post-war American conformism—at ABC in 1963, it broke the macho mold.)

NBC's Tuesday-through-Thursday offerings in that time slot were *Laramie*, *The Virginian*, and *Wide Country*, with the high-ranking *Bonanza* as a 9:00 p.m. Sunday-night treat. CBS had less of a Western orientation during the week, confining its 7:30 p.m. shows to *Marshall Dillon* (Tuesday) and *Rawhide* (Friday), leaving its main Western programming for late Saturday, with *Have Gun-Will Travel* and *Gunsmoke*. You would think women didn't watch television at all: A *TV Guide* from early in the Johnson administration featured an article expressing mild astonishment that ladies' golf would be shown on television ("The Fair Sex Takes to the Fairways"), followed by a profile of a foreign correspondent, "the American Broadcasting Company's woman reporter, Lisa Howard."

All of the countries that fought World War II emerged from it with deep-grained habits of regimentation in both political and civilian life. Unlike the other countries, though, the victorious United States lacked any reason—such as humiliation, atonement, economic crisis, lost empire, or foreign occupation—to re-examine the habits of that martial era. Americans still believed with their whole hearts in science and progress, in a way that would have been hard for, say, Germans to do. Magazine ads presented various synthetic polymers—Nylon, Acrilan, Orlon—as fashionable to wear, largely because they were newly invented.

But there wasn't as much progress as Americans wanted to think. The smashed industrial infrastructure of Western Europe was being thoroughly rebuilt. America, the "New World," suddenly found itself the most ancient part of the industrialized West. From coast to coast, even in larger cities, there was a hokiness, a Victorian provinciality. Many women in the 1960s and 1970s still sewed their own clothes. Most mothers owned sewing machines. Most of the products of high technology—color TV sets, for instance, which would come, by 1972, to outsell black-and-white—were cabineted in wood, as if they had come out of a lumber mill.

Despite the promise of limited exploration in space, in the early 1960s the Industrial Revolution was no longer producing anything revolutionary. The theorist of management Peter Drucker noted that the world's markets were beginning to unify, the world's technology leader, IBM, was now producing an astonishing thousand computers a month, and plastics appeared to be a new industry of major importance. But otherwise the country remained stuck in the age of Edison, Bell, and Westinghouse. Drucker warned that the economy

has been carried largely by industries that were already "big business" before World War I. It has been based on technologies that were firmly established by 1913 to exploit inventions made in the half-century before. Technologically the last fifty years have been the fulfillment of promises bequeathed to us by our Victorian grandparents. . . . Almost all the steel mills built since World War II use processes that date back to the 1860's and were already considered obsolescent fifty years ago. . . . And there is not one major feature on any car anywhere today that could not have been found on some commercially available make in 1913. . . . Measured by the yardsticks of the economist, the last half-century has been an Age of Continuity—the period of least change in three hundred years or so.

When the countercultural historian Theodore Roszak introduced his study of "post-industrial" problems in *Where the Wasteland Ends* (1972), the problems were the same urban-industrial ones you'd have found in the mid–nineteenth century: the slums, the repetitiveness of factory work, the sameness of mass-produced merchandise, the joylessness of small-town life.

World War II vets would in their old age be lionized as their country's Greatest Generation for their achievements abroad and at home. But considered as a generation of domestic policy makers, they compiled a record that was modest in most things, dismal in many. We need to look not only at how they stormed Omaha Beach but also at the identically shoddy, low-slung, asphalt-moated, asbestos-lined brick junior high schools that they built from coast to coast and deemed good enough for their children; not only at how the managers of the Marshall Plan provided the resources to rebuild the bomb-wrecked city centers of Rotterdam and Frankfurt but also at how between 1962 and 1968 Boston's city planners, led by the architect I. M. Pei, destroyed eight acres of ancient streets, apartments, factories, and stores around Scollay Square in order to build . . . *nothing*, except Kallmann McKinnell & Knowles's windblown wasteland, City Hall Plaza, centered on a mildewy concrete monument to government high-handedness. "Go right to it—that's the way I feel about it," President Harry S Truman had said in 1952, urging Washington, D.C., authorities to proceed with a plan that would demolish the downtown row houses in which 25,000 residents lived (they had included Al Jolson and Marvin Gaye), and replace them with concrete towers.

There was a "male"-ness to these failures. The country worked, all right—but in a way that was transactional, aggressive, and indelicate. Uniformity marked the post-war built landscape, from billboards to housing projects to corporate headquarters. When the dyspeptic University of Michigan literature professor John Aldridge looked out on America's post-war suburban neighborhoods, then still under construction, he saw army attitudes brought home and a war zone along with them. "It resembled nothing so much as the military world we had just escaped," he recalled in the late 1960s. "From coast to coast we bulldozed the land into rubble, tore out the grass, uprooted the trees, and laid out thousands and thousands of miles of company streets all lined with family-sized barracks."

In President Dwight D. Eisenhower's view, the great boon of the Highway Act of 1956 was that it made the country easier for U.S. military vehicles to traverse and thus easier to defend against attack. It incidentally tied the country together in ways that promoted trucking and automotive vacationing and eviscerated, enervated, and devitalized many small towns and urban neighborhoods.

Still, the glow that surrounded Americans' reminiscences of the Second World War, and their understanding of their role in the world, was hard to dim. It suffuses memoirs of the 1950s and 1960s. Americans were prospering, according to the news anchorman Tom Brokaw, from "the same passions and disciplines that had served them so well in the war." The historian George Marsden recalled his 1950s childhood as a time when the United States "had been thrown into a position of world leadership." "Thrown into"! Americans, like many victorious peoples, mistook the fruits of conquest for the rewards of virtue. They repressed, for the most part, their memory of the Korean War, the deadly stalemate into which Truman had drawn them in 1950.

What marvels might America not accomplish if it could only sharpen its sense of purpose? Modern people, after all, were smarter than anybody else had ever been. When the Gallup polling group asked Americans in the first month of the 1960s whether "the human race is getting better or worse from the point of view of intelligence," 73 percent said better, 7 percent worse. This is the sort of confidence you would expect from a country about to put a man on the moon—or about to sacrifice the lives of tens of thousands of its young men in the jungles of Southeast Asia.

The Feminine Mystique and male sexism

As surely as World War II had advanced the integration of blacks into the mainstream of American academic and work life, it had reversed the integration of women. The war done, women were shunted from the jobs they had filled, to make way for the returning heroes. Between 1920 and 1958, women went from a third of college students to a quarter. The GI Bill put universities at the service of millions of demobilized veterans. However storied its contribution to the smooth reintegration of American fighting men, the bill was one of the greatest impediments to working women ever erected. The boom of the 1950s wound up affecting the sexes in different ways. Men became titans of, or at least soldiers in, the industrial economy. Their women were left stranded in empty houses full of high-powered cleaning machinery. This had never been their lot before.

Today The Feminine Mystique reads like a collection of magazine articles—exciting, insightful, gripey. It is hard to say exactly what it is about as a whole. Friedan blamed women's tendency to place their womanliness before their humanity. She spoke of a "problem that has no name," and called women's predicament a "sexual" one. But there are many meanings of "sexual." It could describe the civil disadvantages a woman labored under because of her gender, her role in the typical American family structure, or a whole range of erotic questions.

Friedan meant a bit of all three, but it would be a decade before the society began to grapple with such distinctions.

Americans groped their way only slowly toward an understanding of what a liberated woman was. Everyone, no matter what his viewpoint, understood the stakes of civil rights. But the public didn't *get* women's lib. In 1968, the Philip Morris tobacco company brought out Virginia Slims, a brand that would pitch cigarette smoking as a component of the emancipation under way. "You've come a long way, baby" was its motto. With a financial stake in figuring out what women yearned for and (just as important) claimed to yearn for, the brand sponsored frequent polls. In October 1971, it asked women how often they felt that "being a woman has prevented me from doing some of the things I had hoped to do in life." Only 7 percent said "frequently"; 12 percent said "occasionally"; 79 percent said "hardly ever." As for what women thought of feminists, the results were chastening. Twenty-two percent respected the journalist Gloria Steinem, versus 4 percent who did not. But 65 percent had never heard of her. Sixty-three percent had never heard of the author Germaine Greer, and 64 percent had never heard of the theorist Kate Millett. For most women, the "problem that has no name" was not a problem.

During the Kennedy administration, polls showed no attitudinal gap of any kind, on any important issue, between married and unmarried women. Ninety percent of married women and 87 percent of unmarried believed in the existence of a superior "women's intuition." Sixteen percent of married women thought it was excusable in some circumstances to have an extramarital affair, versus 15 percent of unmarried women. Fifty years later, married and unmarried women would disagree about almost everything. The conditions for women's lib, not yet ripe in the 1960s, would be more favorable a decade later. Bureaucratic and judicial procedures first worked out to punish civil rights violations would by then have been analogized into remedies for other grievances. In the 1970s, a generation of women would come of age who could take advantage of them, not having already wagered their happiness on a traditional mating and family-forming system. Universities grew, admitted more women, and insulated a critical mass of elite women from child-rearing expectations. It was they who would mobilize against "sexism."

The word did not exist when Friedan's book came out. It was coined in 1968 by the writer Caroline Bird, who had enrolled at Vassar in 1935, three years before Friedan (then Bettye Goldstein) went to Smith. "Sexism," Bird wrote, "is judging people by their sex where sex doesn't matter." It is an admirably simple definition, reminiscent of the definitions of racism that were current before the Civil Rights Act of 1964. But it reveals the perennial political difficulty of feminism, which is that sex often matters, and matters more than anything. It is fundamental in a way that race or class is not. Men don't carry babies. Feminism had to contend not just against bigotry but also against nature. Faced with the scale of their project, feminists showed an ambivalence that besets them even today. Was this a call to order or a movement of liberation? Was sex supposed to matter less or more? Did women want to fend off men or engage them in a freer, more "male" culture of sexuality?

Men took feminism as a straightforward indictment of their own attitudes. They were right to. Sexism as Bird defined it was everywhere. The succinct explanation that *New York Times* war correspondent David Halberstam gave in 1972 for the high-quality work he and his fellow journalists had done in Vietnam was that there had been no women in their lives to mess things up. "Because only one of them was married," he wrote of his colleagues, "there was no wifely pull to become part of the Saigon social whirl, to get along with the Noltings or the Harkinses, the kind of insidious pressure which works against journalistic excellence in Washington."

Women meant compromise and intellectual mediocrity. If you asked women to name the quality they most admired in women, "intelligence" ranked tops, at 57 percent. If you asked men, the best thing about women was "gentleness," at 38 percent; only 1 percent of them cited intelligence. It is obvious what the consequences of such attitudes would be in any man-run workplace. Look at the TV commercial and marketing campaign that Eastern Air Lines ran in the summer of 1967. Entitled "Presenting the Losers," it announced that the company had hiring standards so rigorous that only one in twenty applicants for a job as stewardess was hired. Rather than describe those standards, it paraded a dozen young women across the screen and invited the viewer to check them out, accompanied by a narrator's contemptuous assessments: "She's awkward. . . . Not very friendly. . . . She bites her nails. . . . She wears glasses. . . . *Oh!* . . . Aww, she's married." One is too tall, one too short, another chews gum. Eastern's standards were wholly physical. Sexual.

The feminine sexuality they reflected was preposterously, cruelly, pointlessly narrow. Yet a woman who did not want to find herself left alone in life would do well to conform to it. "Maybe the real you . . . is a blonde," ran a 1966 magazine ad for a Clairol product called Born Blonde. "Often a woman who looks merely pleasant with dark hair can be a beauty as a blonde. How about you?" Women's choices and options were of a demeaning and fetishistic kind. A 1968 ad for Heublein cocktails showed a man with seven women, each of them got up with erotic accoutrements: the socialite with the mink and the pearl choker, the sexy cleaning lady with the too-short black-and-white French maid's outfit, the island woman with a bare midriff, the mannish woman in gaucho hat and high heels. They would all roll on a bed with you if you could just pour enough Heublein cocktails into them: "Everything to make it happen comes inside the bottle. Uncap the new free spirit in liquor . . . 17 uninhibited drinks from Heublein—all very strong on flavor."

You could see how such ads might render contact with the opposite sex so stupid, humiliating, and exploitative as to turn certain people off it altogether. Throughout the early years of women's lib, men's "objectification" of women seemed to be its main underlying grievance. Male sexual desire demanded too much obedience and conformity from half the population, and that was leaving aside what it did to men. Both sexes needed to be liberated from it.

Playboy and male sexuality

If that had been the real grievance, it would have been a logical thing for second-wave feminism to ally itself—as first-wave feminism had done—with those forces of prudery that had always worked to trammel or civilize male sexuality, above all the churches. There were still such forces at work in the early days of feminism. Until the mid-1960s, college dormitories were all single-sex and parietal rules were enforced with suspensions and expulsions. They would not last long. By 1969, elite colleges were full of "Men and Women Copopulating," as a Williams College T-shirt of the time put it.

Feminists almost never allied with moral tradition. For all their outspoken misgivings about male sexuality, liberated women were on the side of more, freer, and "better" sex. Certainly a large part of feminists' aspiration was simply to live with the same freedom that men did. Barry Mann and Cynthia Weil's "It's Getting Better," which "Mama" Cass Elliot made a hit in the summer of 1969, was a renunciation of romantic feminine ideas about love:

> Once I believed that when love came to me
> It would come with rockets, bells, and poetry
> But with me and you
> It just started quietly and grew
> And believe it or not
> Now there's something groovy and good
> 'Bout whatever we got.

In this telling, love and sex were not mysterious or irrational—they were "natural and right." Trying to gird love round with conventions and roles had only cut people off from what was most true and noble about it. Now this demystified, straightforward way of looking at sex had its own transgressive thrill. As a whisper can gain more attention than a shout, objectivity was more erotic than objectification. Bliss, when one encountered it, would be something like common sense.

There were a lot of reasons why, in the 1960s, eroticism seemed to overflow the levees of tradition. They included the prestige attached to manliness (and even machismo) in the wake of the Second World War, the bringing to market of an almost perfectly effective birth control pill in 1960, and, with the Baby Boom, an unprecedented temporary concentration of people of sexually active age.

Sudden demographic spikes like the Baby Boom create shifts in power relations between the sexes. Men tend to marry (or, in our day, pair up with) women on average three years younger. Other things being equal, babies born at a time when the birth rate is rising will come of age, two decades or so later, in a society where eligible women outnumber eligible men. Men can therefore drive a harder mating bargain. This means not just that individual men born into a baby boom get better mates than they "deserve" but also that, collectively, the era's style of sexuality, of gender relations, will be more "male." When women outnumber men, they must compete for male favor by offering sex and companionship on male terms. This probably means more promiscuity and more out-of-wedlock births.

The reverse is true, too. When a society is in demographic decline, men outnumber the women they are most likely to marry or pair off with. As a consequence, mores will be more "female." James Q. Wilson offered the example of female suffrage in the turn-of-the-century United States. All the movement's prominent theorists and agitators were in the northeast, but all eleven of the states that had given women the vote before World War I were in the west, where the male-female ratio (and therefore male deference to women) was highest.

The 1960s were as wildly skewed toward an excess of women as any period since the aftermath of the Civil War. In 1970, the ratio of unmarried white men ages 23 to 27 to unmarried white women ages 20 to 24 was 2 to 3. For blacks it was close to 1 to 2.

However inevitable the sexual disruption of the 1960s and 1970s might have been, a variety of sexually enthusiastic and culturally influential men sought to promote it as a "sexual revolution," as if it had been somebody's brilliant idea, probably theirs. John Updike, Gore Vidal, Norman Mailer—for such novelists, the trend to more open sexual relations offered new opportunities in culture, art, and society. Hugh Hefner felt the same way. In 1953, he had founded the monthly *Playboy*, a magazine that included ample political and cultural coverage but was known best for its color photo centerfolds of pneumatic nudes.

Hefner envisioned the Playboy Clubs that he set up in several American cities as outposts of a new culture. His Playboy Mansion in Chicago resembled the airless, lightless, weatherless utopias of the spacecraft on *Star Trek* and *Lost in Space*. It had a basement pool with an underwater barroom where you could look up through windows at naked swimmers. It was, Hefner wrote,

> a place where one could work and have fun without the trouble and the conflicts of the outside world. Inside, a single man had absolute control over his environment. I could change night into day, screening a film at midnight and ordering a dinner at noon, having appointments in the middle of the night and romantic encounters in the afternoon.... Being brought up in a very repressive and conformist manner, I created a universe of my own where I was free to live and love in a way that most people can only dream about.

The bed, the most important item in the Hefner hedonist habitat, was circular. It rotated and vibrated next to a closed-circuit TV system and all kinds of other gadgetry. The London designer Christopher Turner later compared it to an air traffic control tower: "The headboard of his bed was crammed with the buttons and levers with which he controlled both his environment and his ever expanding empire." When the journalist Tom Wolfe came for an interview, Hefner told him he hadn't been outside in three-and-a-half months.

Women's rights and male license were traveling on similar tracks. Imagine asking an average *Playboy* reader during the Johnson administration to dictate a new sexual "constitution" that would replace the old one. His preconceptions and practical demands—on the oppressiveness of marriage, on the availability of birth control, on the desirability of mixing the sexes—would likely have overlapped with those of feminism, even if the ideals in the name of which those changes were sought were alleged to differ. In 1974, Virginia Slims found that women backed "most of the efforts to strengthen and change women's status in society" by a margin of 2 to 1 (57 to 26 percent) but that men backed them even more strongly—by 3 to 1 (64 to 20 percent).

Playboy readers and other sexual revolutionaries now demanded from sex the same variety, excellence, and convenience they had come to expect from their lives as consumers. Nothing wrong with that as a goal, of course. The Englishman Alex Comfort, an admired poet and novelist in his youth, wrote a book called *The Joy of Sex: A Gourmet Guide to Lovemaking* (1972). His conceit was that sex was exciting in the same way a really good meal was, and his book was organized like a menu, divided into four sections: Starters, Main Courses, Sauces and Pickles, and Problems. *The Joy of Sex* was so hastily assembled that its early editions retain on the inside an alternative subtitle, "A Cordon Bleu Guide to Lovemaking." That did not stop the book from selling 12 million copies.

In sex, as in coffee and beer, there was a trend toward connoisseurship. Billy Joel's 1977 song "Scenes from an Italian Restaurant" was a sad urban ballad about Brenda and Eddie, "the popular steadies and the king and the queen at the prom," who had foolishly married right out of high school, suddenly a low-class thing to do:

> *They got an apartment with deep-pile carpet*
> *And a couple of paintings from Sears,*
> *A big waterbed that they bought with the bread*
> *They had saved for a couple of years.*

That is, they squandered on a sex aid the money that couples of their parents' generation might have socked away for a down payment on a house. Waterbeds, which around that time were marketed as a magical tool for intensifying sexual pleasure to a dizzying meta-ecstasy, are here jammed together with two contemporaneous clichés of low-status consumption: shag carpets and department store paintings—as if undue preoccupation with sexual enjoyment were a proletarian indulgence. But just as connoisseurship was seeping down through the class hierarchy, crude ways of talking about sex in public were percolating up. Magazine advertisements for Trojan Kling-Tite Naturalamb condoms depicted them in front of a decanter full of what looks like rosé and an ancient bound copy of Hippolyte Taine's *History of English Literature*. "The touch of class," the ad informed those who might be slow to get the point.

People have always built their identities through choosing or, to use the old word, discriminating. On the one hand, feminism promised to give women access to the "higher" style of destiny-defining choices that men had seemed to monopolize, as heads of families and as swashbuckling soldiers, executives, and politicians. On the other hand, it threatened to drag both sexes down to a world in which petty, phony-baloney shopping decisions, carried out to the din of TV marketing pitches, were dressed up as matters of destiny and came to constitute the whole of one's identity.

Gloria Steinem, capitalism, and class

The journalist Gloria Steinem (Smith College, 1956), who on a journalistic assignment in 1963 went undercover as a scantily clad Playboy Club "bunny," saw women's liberation as patterned on black liberation. In 1969, two years before she founded the magazine *Ms.*, she wrote:

> Sex and race, because they are easy and visible differences, have been the primary ways of organizing human beings into superior

and inferior groups and into the cheap labor on which this system still depends. We [the supporters of Women's Lib] are talking about a society in which there will be no roles other than those chosen or those earned.

If earning was at the center of second-wave feminism, it is unsurprising that women's workplace fashions of the early 1970s were feminized male fashions: skirt suits, high-heeled wing-tips, scarves tied like bow ties. Women were being invited to "join" the male world in the same way blacks of the civil rights era had been expected to "join" the white one. This proved no more possible for the one group than for the other. In the 1970s, as feminism grew more strident and its program more ramified, it took on elements of illogic that had not been present in Friedan's original vision. Steinem, for instance, attacked capitalism as a system dependent on "cheap labor" and in the same breath enshrined it as the only legitimate source of values ("no roles other than those chosen or those earned").

Feminism was locked, from the start, in an intimate relationship with technology, management, and the market system. The power of feminism rested on advances in contraception and abortion, and on the spread of civil rights principles out of government and into the corporate world. It was, in its essence, an ideology of the innovative, entrepreneurial, and managerial classes, an ally of technocracy, modernity, progress, and wealth. Feminists wanted to integrate the Metropolitan Club, not the Elks. Steinem mocked "the house-bound matriarchs of Queens and the Bronx." She complained that, "to top it all off, the problem of servants or child care often proves insurmountable after others are solved"—and this at a time well before mass immigration had reintroduced household servants into American upper-middle-class life.

In the eyes of almost all men, women's liberation was not just by but *for* such women as Steinem. It aimed at improving the position of women in white-collar work. The question of whether blue-collar work—plowing, lifting, grinding, getting dirty—was appropriate to women came up much less often than one might have anticipated. Partly feminists were blinded to it by their own social background, but in hindsight we can see another explanation: The supply of well-paying blue-collar jobs had begun to shrink rapidly. It could not accommodate large classes of new entrants. The collapse of working- and middle-class economic security was one of the defining conditions of feminism's development.

It was also a consequence. Workplace feminism exacerbated inequality. It increased the number of intra-class marriages, and it undermined the New Deal culture of the "family wage"—the common-sense assumption among Americans of all classes that a wage paid to a "working man" went to support his wife and children as well. In its imperfect way, the family wage had compensated the housewife for her unwaged work. Whether she got sufficient control over the part of the wage that she flat-out earned is a separate, intra-familial question and potentially a genuine feminist grievance. Still, at the time feminism arose, it wasn't *much* of a grievance. The *Saturday Evening Post* had asked its female readers at the height of the Kennedy administration, "Would you like to see your husband work harder so that he could increase his income?" Five sixths (83 percent) of them responded no. Young Americans of the counterculture, who insisted that middle-class life ought to be about more than mindless striving, may have thought they were assailing American values. They were actually *expressing* them.

Feminism offered corporations an excuse (what the political philosopher Nancy Fraser called a "legitimation") for breaking the implicit contract to pay any full-time worker a wage he could raise a family on. It was feminism that provided, under pressure of the recessions of the 1970s, a pretext for repurposing household and national budgets. Instead of being used for reproduction (understood as both family-forming and investment), those budgets would now be *consumed*. The increment in the family wage that had been meant for the raising of children was withdrawn. Families were no longer entitled to it—mothers would have to enter the workplace to claim it. But they wound up getting only a small part of it, and their competition drove down their husbands' wages into the bargain.

Roe v. Wade and the Supreme Court

The cost-benefit calculation that had traditionally governed choices about love and destiny was shifting. In the early twentieth century, an unwanted pregnancy generally meant a woman would get stuck in a cramped village existence with the first man she fell in love with, which is probably what would have happened anyway. For more and more people by 1973, that was decidedly *not* what would have happened anyway. One risked missing out on an expanded roster of life choices involving education, travel, career advancement, class advancement, and sex.

But especially education. Between 1973 and the turn of the century, real income rose by 21 percent for Americans with advanced degrees and fell for everyone else: by 4 percent for college grads, 26 percent for high school grads, and 38 percent for dropouts. Now, getting stuck in a relationship due to an "accident" could mean the difference between an exciting life spent adventurously climbing the social ladder and bottom-rung drudgery.

The Supreme Court made abortion legal in 1973 with its 7–2 ruling in *Roe v. Wade*. The justices must have assumed that the future course of thinking on matters of reproductive rights was easy to discern. They were wrong. *Roe* was the most politically divisive Supreme Court decision in 116 years. Half a century later, its ultimate consequences are not yet clear. The polarization that faced Americans in the second decade of the twenty-first century had many causes. Most were long-developing economic and social shifts. *Roe* was an exception.

The decision was sloppily argued. It rested on a nonce right to "privacy" established in *Griswold v. Connecticut* that was only ever invoked for the ulterior purpose of defending abortion. In the countless important privacy cases that have come before the court in the half-century since, covering everything from internet surveillance of terrorists to GPS tracking of automobiles, the *Griswold/Roe* "privacy right" never came up. *Brown v. Board of Education* may not have been a forensic masterpiece, either, and the line of civil rights cases from *Katzenbach* to *Bakke* didn't exactly shine for its constitutional logic— but powerful political pressures were then bearing down on Americans regarding their historical responsibility for slavery, and these were enough to override majority misgivings. *Roe* was different. It pronounced on an issue on which Americans were divided, and froze those divisions in place. It laid down a fundamental moral and even religious order on a fickle and frivolous basis.

There did indeed seem to be a growing acceptance of abortion at the time of *Roe*, but it had no consistent political or ethical rationale. In 1967, three states had passed laws allowing abortion in the case of a permanent threat to the mother's health. Two were heavily Republican—Colorado and California, where the new governor, Ronald Reagan, signed the furthest-reaching liberalization of abortion in American history. But North Carolina, which had voted Democratic in the last nine presidential elections, passed similar laws. A presidential task force urged the repeal of abortion laws in 1968. New York, where Republicans controlled the governorship and both state chambers, legalized abortion in 1970; its legislature voted two years later to repeal the law, though the repeal was vetoed by Republican governor Nelson Rockefeller. Notably, there was also a belt of conservative Democratic states with brand-new laws permitting abortion under certain circumstances. They were all in the newly desegregated South. In the 1960s, every coastal Southern state from Alabama to Virginia legislated some kind of right to abortion, starting with a Mississippi law permitting abortion in the case of rape. By the time of *Roe*, half of the states with at least some abortion rights were south of the Mason-Dixon Line.

The upshot of *Roe* and an interlocking case (*Doe v. Bolton*, announced the same day) was an unlimited right to abortion at *any* stage in the nine months of pregnancy. For decades—until an uprising against so-called partial birth abortion in the 1990s—the United States would, alone among major industrialized countries, have no abortion laws, only *Roe*'s ramshackle mandate. Wherever they thought the winds of history were blowing abortion rights, a majority of Americans opposed this blanket deregulation. We can tell because they were evenly split on the question of the *least* controversial abortions, those in the first months of pregnancy. In the last poll Gallup took before *Roe v. Wade*, in December 1972, 46 percent said they would favor a law permitting abortions during the first three months; 45 percent said they would oppose it.

Polls taken in the days after *Roe v. Wade* show that Americans had a sense that abortion was bad, but lacked a moral framework that would allow them to think about abortion logically and confidently. They were concerned about dangers to a mother's health (for which they favored allowing abortion by 91 to 8 percent), rape (they favored abortion by 81 to 10 percent), and birth defects (abortion was okay by 82 to 15 percent). They wanted, it seems, to guard against "risk." But they understood that doing so could easily upset the rules of courtship, the balance of power between men and women, and what used to be called "the way of the world." They were divided on how to proceed. Suppose a married woman who doesn't want more children gets pregnant? Tough luck. People disapproved of abortion in that case, 51 to 46 percent. And a young woman who gets knocked up by her boyfriend? Tough luck to her, too. Forty-nine percent disapproved of abortion in that case, versus 47 percent who approved.

The hope that traditional sexual morality could survive the introduction and destigmatization of abortion was a vain one. Abortion brought changes in morality because it suppressed certain basic anthropological conditions. Female adultery had throughout history been a more serious trespass than male adultery, not because of any irrational sexism but out of a rational instinct for survival. When a man strays, he risks placing a child in some other household. When a woman strays, she risks introducing a creature with ulterior allegiances into the heart of her own. Such straying was the cause of a good deal of anguish and murder, and many of the best novels in the European tradition. But where contraception had reduced the incidence of such problems, abortion outright "solved" them. There need never be any progeny from an adultery. A certain rein on sexuality, particularly female sexuality, was snapped.

That in turn meant a new kind of society, one that would generate irresistible demands for further sexual freedoms. Just as Americans were getting comfortable with the things feminism had meant to Betty Friedan and her followers (liberation from household drudgery and loneliness, a fair shake in the workplace, equal dignity elsewhere), feminism began showing signs of what it would blossom into half a century later (gender studies, queer theory, a questioning of all rules about sex). In the wake of *Roe*, the magazine *Christianity Today* editorialized:

> Christians should accustom themselves to the thought that the American state no longer supports, in any meaningful sense, the laws of God, and prepare themselves spiritually for the prospect that it may one day formally repudiate them and turn against those who seek to live by them.

There would soon be hundreds of thousands of abortions a year. Many Americans were content to live with the legal void in which they occurred. But some were not, and that meant that everybody now had a dangerous constitutional problem.

Roe lacked the authority that had protected civil rights legislation from challenge. It was only a legal opinion and not a sturdy one—full of arguments that made it vulnerable to reconsideration and overturning. Those who found legal abortion repugnant naturally deplored *Roe*. But so did those who felt that legal abortion was an indispensable component of modern freedom and who assumed that, as such, it deserved firmer protection than the say-so of a 7–2 judicial majority, which could (and eventually would) become razor-thin. Now *Roe* could be

defended only by loading the Supreme Court with pro-abortion loy-
alists and bullying Americans into deferring to their power *as if* it were
legislative. Nationally, politicians began to sort themselves into a camp
that favored abortion rights and a camp that opposed them. In diamet-
ric contradiction to what one would have expected in 1960, the Democrats became the pro-abortion, the Republicans the anti-abortion party.

This reversal was a function of the new constitutional possibilities
in the Civil Rights Act. The Democrats were the party of new, court-
mandated rights—of all kinds. The habit spread to both parties—to
Democrats earlier than to Republicans—of promoting judges not for
their impartiality but for their political reliability, including on the federal
appeals courts, which are the "farm system" of the Supreme Court. From
time to time throughout American history, the Supreme Court had been
threatened by those who would use it as a weapon of partisan politics—
over-reaching decisions in the 1850s, court packing in the 1930s. But
those pressures had been episodic. The pressure the Court faced after *Roe*
was not. Within a decade-and-a-half, this small-looking problem would
begin to erode the constitutional legitimacy of the Supreme Court itself,
and the problem would turn critical in the following century.

Our Bodies, Ourselves

Feminism was potentially a rich intellectual current. It is close to that
part of Western philosophy that, since Rousseau, has speculated on
what is "natural" to humans and what has been conferred (or imposed)
on them by civilization. The first-wave feminism of the nineteenth century was built on the Bible and the Fourteenth Amendment. Second-
wave feminism was a moral work in progress. Happily it had no respect
for superstition. Less happily, it cast as superstition any tradition that
could not justify itself in one sentence. Very little that passed for sexual
common sense in the middle of the twentieth century would be left
standing by the end of it.

The extraordinary phonebook-sized health manual *Our Bodies,*

Ourselves was first mimeographed in Boston in 1969 by a collective of white, college-educated feminists in what would then have been called their childbearing years. It was published commercially in 1971. *Our Bodies, Ourselves* was a scientific self-help book, but there was an urgent ideological argument behind it. Women had become "alienated from their own bodies," the authors argued, and they must have been largely right, because almost immediately on its publication *Our Bodies, Ourselves* became a trusted reference work. By the twenty-first century it had sold 4 million copies in thirty languages.

The argument of the Boston Women's Health Book Collective was that doctors, the gynecological profession included, had been putting forward a mythological account of female sexuality that served society's moral needs more than women's medical ones. Consider venereal disease. "Our culture," the authors wrote, "has needed the fear of VD to limit sexual activity outside of marriage, especially the 'promiscuity' of young people and women. With the advent of widespread birth control, which eliminated the fear of pregnancy, fear of VD became the last effective deterrent against complete 'sexual license.'"

The editors put skeptical quotation marks around terms like "promiscuity" and "sexual license" because they did not believe there was any such thing. Those were parts of a moralizing view of sexuality that they rejected. Where doctors had withheld facts, *Our Bodies, Ourselves* would provide them. A woman worried about contracting venereal disease could use, for instance,

> the "short arm" inspection. This technique, known by prostitutes and in the military, involves examining the penis *before it becomes erect*. . . . You pull back the foreskin if he is uncircumcised, then squeeze the penis as in masturbation. . . . A drop or two of liquid indicates the presence of an infection.

Blecch! No one had ever talked to women that way before. Some version of the information, of course, could be found in urologists' handbooks, but to address it directly to women—and in such a prag-matic spirit, as if they had something to learn from prostitutes—was unheard of.

The editors had made a radical assessment: The male-dominated medical profession was so biased, so lacking in empathy, that a woman was safer seeking medical advice from her uncredentialed peers. This was the ethic the internet would be built on a quarter-century later. When it came to abortion, which at the time of the 1971 edition was il-legal in most states, the book described procedures, timing, and prices ($80 in Seattle if you were closer than ten weeks to your last period but $250 in private facilities in California). The authors went into such detail—even about such quack methods as infective catheterization, the "high douche," and pumping air into the uterus—because they were writing for women who might resort to an illegal abortion, an event that the book described with a kind of tragic poetry:

> When legal resources fail her and she cannot get to New York, the woman with an unwanted pregnancy starts asking friends of friends, nurses, and taxi drivers in a frightened and hysterical nos-ing around, which ends her up on a doctor's table if she is lucky, in the hands of some semi-medical quack if she is less lucky, at the mercy of her own mutilating hands if she is desperate, and in the emergency ward of a hospital if serious complications develop.

The book showed everything. There was no such thing as too much information. Since women often went into labor unsure of what de-livering a baby would involve, there was a series of close-in photos of babies "crowning" during birth, of the placenta emerging, and finally of the umbilical cord hanging free on a mass of afterbirth. It dealt with lesbianism, anal intercourse, and rape. ("If you're grabbed from the front, the most effective response is a fast and hard knee to the attack-er's groin.") It was, in short, a book of demystification.

There was a moralism behind *Our Bodies, Ourselves*: Sex was potentially a source of boundless pleasure for people, but crabby and envious older people, representatives of the old society, were conspiring to hide the truth about it. Those old crabs had to be fought and their mythologies discredited. The chapter on abortion came before the chapter on childbearing, as if the former were the norm and the latter the exception. Having children was an aspect of the quest for sexual pleasure, rather than the other way around. Skeptical about the maternal higher ends that had traditionally been ascribed to sex, the book was guileless and gullible about the hedonistic higher ends it proposed to replace them with.

There is a limit to how hard one can strain against a mythology. Sexuality, the font of human life, is fickle, mysterious, contingent. It is not always subject to will, to put it mildly, and sometimes seems to blow in like the weather. A mythology that moralizes sex may do something to shelter a delicate flame. It is hard to say exactly what, but there must be a reason that flourishing, fertile, creative societies tend to be conservative about sex.

The modern impulse to rationalize human relations undermined conservatism, and threatened to take the ground rules of sexual relations down with it. As early as the 1920s, the English philosopher Bertrand Russell had warned that the establishment of welfare states risked turning not just the economy but *everything* upside-down, because the state would replace the father as protector and provider. Breaking the traditional family structure might look rational, modern, and sensible. Nonetheless, Russell wrote,

> if this should occur, we must expect a complete breakdown of traditional morality, since there will no longer be any reason why a mother should wish the paternity of her child to be indubitable. . . . Whether the effect upon men would be good or bad, I do not venture to say. It would eliminate from their lives the only emotion equal in importance to sex love. It would make sex love itself more trivial. It would make it far more difficult to take an interest

in anything after one's own death. It would make men less active and probably cause them to retire earlier from work. It would diminish their interest in history and their sense of the continuity of historical tradition.

Here Russell, enthusiast for sexual freedom that he was, was willing to go out on a limb. Citing the ebb of paternal feeling in the Roman Empire and among upper classes in his own time, he warned that an *un*-superstitious attitude toward family formation would ultimately threaten Western countries with de-sexualization:

> My belief is, though I put it forward with some hesitation, that the elimination of paternity as a recognized social relation would tend to make men's emotional life trivial and thin, causing in the end a slowly growing boredom and despair, in which procreation would gradually die out, leaving the human race to be replenished by stocks that had preserved the older convention.

The idea that de-sexualization might be the result of scientific modernization seemed ridiculous in the flapper era, when Russell was writing, and even when *Our Bodies, Ourselves* was first published. The mass media was full of evidence that women were as sexual as they had ever been. In the late spring of 1962, the *Saturday Evening Post* had asked women what they thought the ideal age for marriage was. Their answers clustered around age 21, though a fifth believed in marrying younger. What is striking is that 99 percent of women listed age 27 or lower. There is no record in the responses of anyone suggesting a woman might not want to marry.

Russell was right: You can call sexual morality a mythology constructed by life-hating prudes, but they, too, serve an erotic function. Without an external source of sexual morality, people who would behave in a civilized way must produce their *own* prudery and carry it around inside them. He must de-masculinize; she must de-feminize.

As Ray Davies of the Kinks wrote in "The Good Life," his 1970 song about the absurd glut of sensual gratifications offered to a rock star, "I got so many women that I wish that I wasn't a man." It was a disturbing thought: Hyper-sexualization might be a mask worn by de-sexualization. What is thrilling, fulfilling, and functional about sexuality might be wrapped up in the very "complexes" about sexuality that crusaders for sexual freedom and other reformers insisted on getting rid of.

The Equal Rights Amendment

No ideology or belief system existing at the time of the 1960s counterculture would have allowed people to predict which facets of pre-counterculture sexual morality would flourish over the coming decades, and which die. One might have thought that prostitution would be validated (on grounds of freedom of choice and "entrepreneurship") and pornography scorned (on grounds of inauthenticity). That is how things were trending. In the winter of 1976, a convention of the American Bar Association came within two votes of endorsing the legalization of prostitution, while pornography was confined to disreputable red-light districts. It is a measure of how rare dirty movies were in 1978 that X-rated videocassettes sold in "men's magazines" for about a hundred dollars apiece.

But customs took a different turn. After some experimentation in the late 1970s, when the state of Nevada began licensing bordellos, the reputation of prostitution would suffer in ways it had not since the nineteenth century, when newspapers sensationalized it as the "white slave trade." (The equivalent twenty-first-century expression would be "human trafficking.") Meanwhile, pornography would, via the internet, find its way to the very heart of the nation's economic life and the world's. Martin Amis's *Yellow Dog* (2003) was one of the first novels to include a character, the pornography-addled tabloid journalist Clint Smoker, whose quest for imagined glory online winds up removing him from life altogether: "He knew that the distance between himself and the world of women was getting greater. Each night, as he entered the Borgesian metropolis of electronic pornography—with its infinities, its immortalities—Clint was, in a sense, travelling towards women. But he was also travelling away from them." By 2015, 45 percent of the men in Harvard's graduating class would be watching pornography multiple times a week.

The "objectification" of women, the grievance that had once seemed the primum mobile of all feminism, endured. Indeed, as the 1970s wore on, ads began to portray them as sex machines. "For those nights you want everything to be just right" ran a 1974 magazine spread for Electrophonic Stereos. The illustration showed a woman standing on a white shag rug behind various space-age stereo equipment, her head arced back in ecstasy as she is embraced from behind. "You'll let him know, too, that you're involved in the 'today' sound." When a shampoo called "Gee, Your Hair Smells Terrific" elicited the eponymous compliment, a young woman's thought bubble read "Jackpot!" The Mistress Collection, by Funky Fashions, advised sophisticated women to "own at least one pair of strategically cut out bikini panties." Women were being sold a sexuality more suited to adolescent males.

Americans wanted freedom from sexual rules, but they wouldn't be *really* free until they could be assured that no one would turn up his nose as if the old rules still obtained. That required imposing other kinds of rules. The title Ms.—a substitute for "Miss" and "Mrs." that implied nothing about marital status—was introduced into the national conversation when Gloria Steinem founded *Ms.* magazine in 1971. (Its ultimate source was a Marxist publication, *News & Letters*, which addressed its subscriptions that way. Steinem had heard it mentioned by a civil rights worker in a 1969 radio broadcast on New York's WBAI.) There was never much affirmative enthusiasm for Ms., even among feminists. In the spring of 1974, 14 percent of women and 12 percent of men said they liked the title. By the end of the decade, only 16 percent of women and 15 percent of men had taken it up. But the spread of Ms. was like a lot of other things after the 1960s. The lack of enthusiasm for it among the general public seemed to matter little. There was a moral certitude behind it, a missionary authority that could impose itself even in the face of resistance, though it was hard to tell where that authority came from. Over time, Ms. it was.

The biggest ambition was to alter the U.S. Constitution itself. A proposed Equal Rights Amendment held, quite simply, that "Equality of rights under the law shall not be denied or abridged by the United States or by any State on account of sex." Between 1972 and 1977, it was ratified by 35 of the 38 states necessary to amend the Constitution. Americans backed the ERA in polls, but their support was impressionistic and vague, broad but not deep. When state legislatures dragged their feet and five of them even rescinded their approval, no one particularly seemed to care. Despite a constitutionally dubious congressional extension of the term for ratification—from March 1979 to March 1982—the measure died.

The sudden collapse of support for the ERA shocked activists. Since the civil rights era, old understandings of the Constitution had seemed so antiquated and feeble that anyone speaking in the name of reform could knock them over with a breath. Now, it appeared, Americans didn't want the Constitution tinkered with. They had found ways to resist. The ERA promised to feminize public space just as the civil rights acts had promised to desegregate it. People didn't want that. As early as the spring of 1975, among those who blocked its passage, the reason most often cited was that "equal rights for women could eventually end up destroying the institution of marriage and family life." By the end of the decade, a majority of Americans had come to fear that, once women were given equal rights, "employers will have to hire admitted homosexuals." Nineteen percent even believed that "separate public toilets for men and women will not be allowed," though three quarters of the country dismissed that idea as fanciful.

In 1978, as Republican candidates were heading for big gains in midterm elections, women looked quite conservative in their views. The Roper Organization polled adults nationwide to ask whom they would vote for as "woman of the year." Anita Bryant led the field with 19 percent. Bryant had been Miss Oklahoma in 1958, a popular singer ("Paper Roses") in 1960, and a spokeswoman for the Florida citrus industry. What she was doing then, though, was leading a campaign called Save Our Children, aimed at reversing a Miami-area ordinance barring discrimination against gays. No other woman came close to her popularity. Only the president's wife, Rosalynn Carter, (13 percent) and the newscaster Barbara Walters (10 percent) even made it into double digits. That same month, the *Washington Post* found that only 39 percent of Americans believed "our society discriminates against women." Nonetheless, 58 percent favored giving them more rights. This was a common pattern with feminism, which looked in the light of certain polls like a solution in search of a problem.

President Richard Nixon, through an ambitious program of internal polling, had already made a discovery of more general application: Americans were happy to run their mouths about all kinds of experimentation, but they did not much like it up close. In this political sense, women's lib was very much like civil rights. Whenever you personalized the issue, rather than speaking in lofty abstractions, people got suspicious. Whatever pieties they might spout about helping the unfortunate, two thirds of Americans were outraged that "women getting welfare money are having illegitimate babies to increase the money they get." And although they *said* they liked the ERA, they had little respect for the people who were bringing it about. By the spring of 1977, Americans agreed (42 percent) as much as disagreed (42 percent) with the hard proposition that "advocates of the Equal Rights Amendment are mainly women's libbers who would totally change the traditional role of women, and that is wrong." They had come to identify the constitution-changers as a *class*—a new elite that had been formed in the crucible of protest against the Vietnam War.

4

—————

War

*The Vietnam War as an establishment undertaking—America's weak
rear—The Vietnam War generation and class—The counterculture—
Sources of Baby Boom power—Renaissance or decay?*

The war in Vietnam began in an act of presidential deceit.
Lyndon Johnson hustled the country into the conflict at the
height of the 1964 presidential campaign, winning congressional consent to bomb Vietnam in retaliation for a naval confrontation
with North Vietnamese vessels in the Gulf of Tonkin. That confrontation had been provoked, as Congress would discover only years
later, by U.S. and South Vietnamese naval incursions into the North.
The bombing, rationalized as an alternative to sending ground troops,
made ground troops necessary, once the elections were over, in order
to protect the perimeter of the South Vietnamese airbases from which
the bombers left. But then *those* troops were attacked. The "perimeter"
was gradually extended to most of South Vietnam, which over the next
decade became the temporary home of 2.7 million mostly non-college-
enrolled American youths.

The sudden victory of Ho Chi Minh's troops over the French in
1954 had led to a UN partition of the country into a communist North
and a pro-American South. But Vietnam was never as divided as it
looked. Ho's Communists would likely have won the national election
that the peace accords called for, had the United States permitted one.
Ho drew on broad nationalist and anti-colonial sentiments, however

big the eventual role of the Soviet Union in supplying weaponry (especially MiG fighters and anti-aircraft systems) and of China in supplying personnel (including troops after 1965) might have been. The South Vietnamese government, by contrast, would have crumbled without U.S. support. Its troops were battle-shy, outnumbered, and outgunned by a domestic (i.e., South Vietnamese) guerrilla insurgency, the so-called Viet Cong, which drew on local discontent as well as imported materiel. Eighty percent of the 5 or 6 million tons of American bombs dropped in the war fell on the South, not the North. The United States, in fact, would drop more bombs on the territory of its putative ally than it had dropped on all its World War II enemies. And then it would go on to do something from which American culture has still not recovered: It would lose the war.

The Vietnam War as an establishment undertaking

The top managers and "leading experts" were on the war's side. The war's prosecution had been placed in their hands, and for understandable reasons. For two decades America's bureaucratic and corporate experts had met every challenge they had been set, from a two-front war against Germany and Japan to the construction of an interstate highway system. Much as Johnson had revived Kennedy's stalled civil rights initiatives and turned them into a massive constitutional reform, he took Kennedy's inchoate plans to make a manly anti-communist stand somewhere in Southeast Asia (Laos had been the first country on which Kennedy's whimsy landed) and turned them into a focused military campaign.

President Kennedy had recruited Robert McNamara, the president of the Ford Motor Company, to be his secretary of defense. McNamara had won the esteem of the country's leaders, and the authority to manage its now-nuclearized armed forces, on the strength of his corporate career. McNamara was not a sadistic military strategist, like William

Tecumseh Sherman; he was a true believer in "systems management," like, in a later era, Mark Zuckerberg. He took certain techniques useful for managing corporations and grievously misapplied them. In 1967, at the height of the war, McNamara told a convocation at recently integrated Millsaps College in Jackson, Mississippi, that rational management, as he practiced it, was the only proper means of effecting humane change. "Management is, in the end, the most creative of all the arts," he said, "for its medium is human talent itself. What, in the end, is management's most fundamental task? It is to deal with change."

McNamara believed that, in war as in engineering, what could not be counted did not count. American authorities fell into line. They used statistics to convince themselves that they were winning. They claimed the percentage of the South Vietnamese population under control of the Viet Cong guerrillas had fallen from 60 percent to 40 percent. It was true, too—but only because U.S. bombing and search-and-destroy raids had depopulated the countryside. To this way of looking at the world, there was no difference between winning people's allegiance and turning them into refugees. The historian Theodore Roszak, in works such as his 1969 book *The Making of a Counter Culture*, described this way of thinking through oxymora like "mad rationality" and "lunatic realism." Vietnam did not introduce such irrationality into American life. It exposed it. As the social critic Loren Baritz put it, "*We* are what went wrong in Vietnam."

Johnson often claimed he feared Congress would use Vietnam as an excuse to underfund his Great Society programs. But he himself saw his two wars as complementary, not competitive. Since each took the same approach to an intractable reality, success in one was a warrant for success in the other. Johnson frequently described the war as a New Deal–style project and even launched a Mekong River Redevelopment Commission to industrialize, as far as possible, the vast, ramifying waterway that entered the South China Sea south of Saigon. "I want to leave the footprints of America in Vietnam," he said. "I want them to say, 'When the Americans come, this is what they leave—schools, not

long cigars.' We're going to turn the Mekong into a Tennessee Valley."
White House counsel Clark Clifford saw "a pattern for a kind of life
that the people of all Southeast Asia can begin to enjoy . . . So what
the president wants to make is a demonstration." The sociologist and
Johnson advisor Daniel Patrick Moynihan was eager to use the military draft as an engine of upward mobility for blacks and the poor.

By the summer of 1966, it was evident that the two Johnson
wars, on poverty and in Vietnam, were set to open up a vast deficit
that would make inflation inevitable. Johnson, with his cabinet's help,
bought time with various accounting tricks and falsifications. A year
later, McNamara, speaking privately to Tom Wicker of the *New York
Times*, was unrepentant. "Do you really think," McNamara asked, "that
if I had estimated the cost of the war correctly, Congress would have
given any more for schools and housing?" Such attitudes clarify the
Vietnam War's relation to the rest of Lyndon Johnson's agenda. It was
the war itself, and not the protests against it, that was the sister movement to the Civil Rights Act and the Great Society.

America's weak rear

General Vo Nguyen Giap, the lawyer, historian, and strategist of genius
who defeated the French army in 1954 and played a part in defeating
the Americans in 1973, was impressed with modern technology without being cowed by it. "A strong rear," he wrote, "is always the deci-
sive factor for victory in a revolutionary war." By rear he meant what
Americans would call the home front. For a long time, the Vietnam
War was not measurably unpopular in American opinion polls. Two
twentieth-century wars had been deeply resented—World War I,
during which opposition peaked at 64 percent of the population, and
the Korean War, which 62 percent came to oppose. Not until the final
years of the Vietnam War did opposition approach those levels. Nonetheless, the war effort's vulnerability to hostile public opinion was evident from the beginning. From the moment Johnson drew his country

into battle in Southeast Asia, Minh and Giap had him where they wanted him: He was fighting in a revolutionary war with a weak rear.

Americans, while giving their leaders the benefit of the doubt, worried that Vietnam would be a repeat of Korea. In 1950, Harry S. Truman, using a UN Security Council resolution as a substitute for declaring war, had committed the United States to defend the southern part of that nation, divided at the 38th parallel, after an invasion from the Communist North. He wound up paying for it with his presidency. General Douglas MacArthur swiftly recovered almost the entire country, South and North, from North Korean forces in a campaign of tactical mastery, but when he had driven the North Koreans almost to the Yalu River along the Chinese border, China entered the war with hundreds of thousands of troops. The Chinese and North Korean counterattack drove U.S. forces back to the other end of the peninsula and took tens of thousands of lives. The war ended in a stalemate, with a demilitarized zone back at the 38th parallel. It was a brave holding action in the war against communism. But it required a long and convoluted lecture to explain why it had been the business of Americans to fight and die there in the first place.

Vietnam was just as remote as Korea. Saigon lies at 106.625° E. longitude. If you wanted to go to the exact opposite side of the earth from there, you would be on 73.375° W., a line that makes landfall on Seymour Point at the mouth of Saugatuck River in Connecticut and runs past a half-dozen yacht clubs and golf courses in Norwalk and Westport. Vietnam was another partitioned, peninsular Asian country with a Chinese border, in which the United States was trying to use offshore bases (Japan in the case of Korea, the Philippines in that of Vietnam) to create a defensible southern enclave. It was a project that China could turn into a bloodbath at a time of its choosing.

Americans never expected Vietnam to be a cakewalk. In May 1965, Operation Rolling Thunder, the bombing campaign that would continue almost until Johnson left office, was only two months old. The Viet Cong had begun a series of decimating ambushes against

U.S.-backed South Vietnamese forces. The *Washington Post* asked Americans the loaded question of whether they were willing to "carry the ground war into North Vietnam at the risk of bringing Red China into the fighting." Only 22 percent were. And yet now that American prestige was on the line, only 31 percent were willing to withdraw from the conflict altogether. Almost half of respondents (47 percent) called for "holding the line." That may sound like a "rational" middle ground, but if so it was what Roszak would have called a mad rationality. U.S. forces were neither invading nor evacuating—they were immobilized, a bad thing to be in enemy territory. Giap and Vietnam's other generals were prepared to exact a steep price. The tripartite division in public opinion would remain roughly steady for the whole of the war. In August 1967, the *Post* asked again and found the numbers virtually unchanged. The percentage who wanted to fight for total victory had risen a smidgen to 24, and 34 percent wanted total withdrawal. Americans were trapped in a consensus for stalemate.

Though there was official optimism everywhere, in their hearts Americans could read the signs very early. If one could avoid using words that directly engaged national pride—words such as "surrender," "defeat," and "back down"—one could see the pessimism. In February 1966, just months into the war, Gallup asked voters whether they would favor "having the UN try to work out a solution." The answer was yes, by 78 to 7 percent. The following month, voters, by 67 to 16 percent, said they would be "more inclined" to vote for a congressional candidate who proposed a "compromise peace settlement."

An inward suspicion that the war was unwinnable, along with an inability to avow it, put Americans in a strange psychological state. Throughout the war, they proved comfortable with an escalation of violence, whether or not it was related to the war effort. When reports emerged in late 1969 that U.S. forces had massacred women and children in the villages of Songmy and My Lai, only 24 percent of Americans thought the soldiers should be punished, versus 48 percent who thought they should not. The mining of Vietnam's harbors in the spring of 1972 was approved of by a solid 59 percent majority. A slim majority approved of the all-out bombing of North Vietnamese cities at Christmas of that year. When Chicago police battered student anti-war protesters at the Democratic National Convention at the end of August 1968, 56 percent of Americans approved, versus just 31 percent who objected.

All the candidates running for the presidency in 1968 had a needle to thread. Americans were desperate to exit this lost war, but in a way that would permit them not to admit they had lost it. Richard Nixon found the right rhetorical formula when he spoke of "peace with honor." Usually that is a definition of a victory. Not this time. That Nixon left the public feeling they had secured anything resembling peace with honor was a triumph of political legerdemain. His own sophisticated internal polls, carried out by the Opinion Research Corporation just before the 1968 elections, held bad news. The bloody Tet Offensive, an all-out surprise attack by Ho Chi Minh's North Vietnamese and Viet Cong forces against southern cities earlier that year, had been a turning point. Though the American and South Vietnamese counterattack had crippled the Communist forces, the battle had raised the price of the war beyond what Americans back home were willing to pay. Two thirds (64 percent) were now willing to stop the bombing of North Vietnam "if there is any kind of sign whatsoever from North Vietnam that they are willing to reduce the fighting."

Any kind of sign whatsoever—the war had turned into a rout. Recall that, during the fight against racial segregation, one of the best ways to measure people's real views was to ask them whether the civil rights movement was going "too fast" or "too slow." Nixon began withdrawing troops in the first days of his presidency and by June 1969 was pulling them out at the headlong rate of 25,000 a month. The number of people who found this rate "too fast" was in single digits as soon as pollsters began inquiring and soon fell into the *low* single digits.

The administration insisted that its plans were not for an abandonment of Vietnam but for a "Vietnamization," a handover of fighting responsibilities to native forces. At least 60 percent of Americans favored Vietnamization. But they knew, at some level, that it was a pretense. A majority was convinced that the ARVN, the South Vietnamese army, would never "hold its own," as indeed it did not. The inability or disinclination of the non-Communist South Vietnamese to wage such a war was the reason Lyndon Johnson had committed the United States to Southeast Asia in the first place.

The only thing that now gave Americans pause was the protection of the country's fighting men. In December 1972, on the eve of the signing of the Paris peace accords, Nixon's internal polling showed that Americans—66 percent of them—would insist on the return of the country's POWs. It was an unusual worry. The return of captives is generally an essential part of a peace treaty. But the suspicion that some had been left behind would roil conservative politics for decades. By contrast, Americans seemed wholly indifferent to the lofty freedom-fighting rhetoric that had drawn the country into Vietnam a decade earlier. Only 7 percent wanted to insist on a removal of North Vietnamese troops from South Vietnam, only 5 percent on free elections in the South. What the United States was doing was surrendering.

Because of an extraordinary coincidence in American demographics and American politics, the surrender would mark an epoch. The U.S. military was, as we have noted, the template on which the whole civilian order had been patterned. As trust in the military plummeted, a lot of other things went down with it. All those congressmen honored for their service in the war, all that powerful civilian technology converted from wartime innovations, crew cuts, those TV shows that glorified cowboys and other gunmen, traffic, those uniform suburban subdivisions with their identical brick junior high schools . . . all of the things that had been taken as tokens of the sunny, can-do twentieth-century American Way now looked mediocre and tainted.

The power of reshaping the country's institutions would be hurriedly passed to the enormous generation of Americans born since the war. Those who were old enough (born in the late 1940s) and well connected enough (with an Ivy League education or the equivalent) would now take a grandiose role in national political life as tribunes of future generations. They would wag the American dog for the next half-century.

The Vietnam War generation and class

The Vietnam War generation was not made up of malingerers, agnostics, or cynics. Its battlefield heroism—from the four-day clash at Ia Drang in 1965, which began when a battalion of the 7th Cavalry was dropped by helicopter into an ambush in a rain forest, to the infernal multi-week siege of Khe Sanh in the wake of the Tet Offensive in 1968—matches anything in the annals of American combat. That heroism stuck in the popular imagination less than did "fraggings" (intentional maimings or killings of officers) and other incidents of indiscipline. Under the circumstances, one might have expected worse. Soldiers who had been told they were defending the freedom of the Vietnamese people arrived in-country expecting to be loved and supported. They weren't. One infantry lieutenant who had interviewed villagers day after day for a year recalled, "I never once heard a Vietnamese say, 'Don't go down that trail, there's a mine.'" The sense of betrayal must have been unfathomable.

But it dented the patriotism of the younger generation much less, and much more selectively and slowly, than later accounts would lead one to think. The top-selling single of 1966, according to *Billboard* magazine, was neither "You Can't Hurry Love" by the Supremes (which came in at number 8), nor the Troggs' "Wild Thing" (number 24) or the Beach Boys' "Good Vibrations" (number 33), nor anything by Simon and Garfunkel, the Rolling Stones, the Beatles, or Bob Dylan. It was Barry Sadler's martial "Ballad of the Green Berets." When, in November of that year, Robert McNamara made a visit to Harvard and found his car surrounded by a hundred protesting Students for a Democratic Society (SDS) members, one dean wrote to convey "our deeply felt apology for the discourteous and unruly confrontation forced upon you yesterday by members of the Harvard College community." A petition of apology quickly circulated among Harvard undergraduates, too, and within 48 hours more than half of them (2,700) had signed it. In late 1968, after the Tet Offensive and the riots at Chicago's Democratic convention, the war was opposed by a majority of those over 50 but supported by those younger.

But the leadership class that emerged out of the late 1960s was not a sociological cross section of the generation, the way the leadership class that came out of World War II had been. It was highly atypical, and that was a contingency that would warp American society and politics in the half-century that followed. For one thing, it was heavily selected for non-participation in, and even opposition to, the war. It had been mostly the working class and the poor who had fought overseas and mostly the university-educated elites who had protested back home. Enrollment in higher education had given the latter an automatic deferment from military service for as long as they could afford to study— an exemption that the Johnson administration eventually curtailed. An outraged editorial in the *Harvard Crimson* in 1968 called the end of such deferments "a bit of careless expediency—clearly unfair to the students who would have filled the nation's graduate schools next year."

They were protesting as much to keep themselves out of the war as to end it. In a diary he kept in 1966, the Harvard undergraduate Steven Kelman recorded the misgivings of a friend, who had said:

> I'm against the war, I guess, but I wouldn't want to fight in *any* war. . . . My brother had a friend who tried to get a four-F by eating a lot of sugar two days before he went for his physical and not pissing—so they'd think he had diabetes. They gave him the four-F, but that afternoon he fell into a sugar coma and died. . . . I could try freaking out—you know, coming in high on pot or doing the homo routine. But they put that kind of rejection on your record, and that can screw you up for life.

Years later Kelman's Harvard contemporary James Fallows would recall traveling on a bus to the Boston Navy Yard with draft-eligible classmates, who shouted pro–Viet Cong chants and threw their urine samples into the faces of orderlies. The Harvard students hoped that the "undesirable character traits" they manifested would keep them out of military service. Fallows himself got a medical exemption by dieting down to 120 pounds. As they left, a bus arrived with more draftees, whom Fallows described as "boys from Chelsea, thick, dark-haired young men, the white proles of Boston. Most of them were younger than us, since they had just left high school, and it had clearly never occurred to them that there might be a way around the draft."

In 1968, when 135 students affiliated with Students for a Democratic Society occupied Harvard's University Hall, the Harvard professor of Irish literature John Kelleher, a working-class Irishman from Lawrence, Massachusetts, called them "spoiled brats with an underdeveloped sense of history and a flair for self-protection." The occupation was broken up by policemen from surrounding cities, many of whom had sons and brothers in Vietnam. Scenes like this were happening all over the country. At Columbia University, SDS staged demonstrations against the building of a gymnasium in a nearby Harlem neighborhood. They morphed into larger protests against the Vietnam War and racial inequality, where police handled the kids roughly, too. "Part of the brutality," wrote the historian Todd Gitlin, ". . . reflected a kind of class war SDS had not reckoned with: working-class cops' resentment of the children of privilege."

As civil rights had divided the country by region into those who were heroically fighting for equality and those who could justly be assigned to receive moral instruction, Vietnam did the same by class. The defenders of peace and justice were disproportionately to be found at rich men's universities—and their innocence of military involvement would give them much more in common with those who came of age in the demilitarized decade or so that followed. The working class would wind up tainted by the popular culture's portrayal of the military as burners of villages and marauders in free-fire zones. Who would hire such a person to run a corporate department? Who would elect such a person to Congress?

The same "white proles of Boston" Fallows described would be subjected to the most high-handed carrying out of federal law in the decade to follow: the court-ordered "desegregation" of Boston's public schools, starting in 1974. The word *desegregation* belongs in quotation marks because most of the schools affected were within white ethnic (mostly Irish-American and Italian-American) neighborhoods. There had never been any black people there to segregate. The process involved two-way busing, transporting white students into poor and violent Boston neighborhoods and replacing them with bused-in black students.

When the whites of South Boston and Charlestown protested, their neighborhoods were put under military occupation. "Southie" had a curfew and laws against public assembly, enforced by 1,600 police officers, 100 federal marshals, 50 FBI agents, and 600 National Guard troops. Whites made up 60 percent of the public school system on the eve of busing, less than 20 percent when it had finally done its work, little more than a decade later.

Judge W. Arthur Garrity, a resident of the wealthy, 100-percent white suburb of Wellesley and the author of the court ruling that mandated busing, appointed a panel of "distinguished experts" to study the controversy, about whom William Bulger, for seventeen years the president of the Massachusetts Senate, quipped, "They were distinguished, as far as I could see, only in the sense that not one of them was the parent of a child who would be affected by forced busing."

Relative to their fellow citizens, privileged Americans took out of the Vietnam era a sense of their own moral authority that was not battered but strangely enhanced. The moral basis for overthrowing the egalitarian order established by Franklin D. Roosevelt had been laid. Whether one praised that order as fair or assailed it as Procrustean, New Deal liberalism had been built on one-size-fits-all rules: on uniformity.

The protests against Vietnam were a sign that the old mid-century rules were beginning to chafe. The novelist (later senator) James Webb wrote shortly after the war that America had shown itself "afraid to ask the men of Harvard to stand alongside the men of Harlem, same uniform, same obligation, same country." Now young men who as grade-school students had gasped when they learned that the Northern rich had been able to pay substitutes to fight and die for them in the Civil War were themselves seeking to carve out, in the middle of the so-called century of the common man, a niche that was worthy for elites to live in. "I am convinced that when the history of these decades is written 150 years from now," the columnist and critic Irving Kristol wrote in 1979, "there will be a chapter called 'The Aristocratic Impulse.'"

In April 1969, a member of Progressive Labor, a Maoist anti-war group at Harvard, wrote a soul-searching indictment of the more fashionable Students for a Democratic Society, accusing SDS of drifting toward elitism but explaining that drift in terms of temptations common to the entire student left:

> On the one hand we were angry about the war, about racism, about the countless vicious acts we saw around us. But on the other hand, we viewed America as one great wasteland, a big, monstrous, mechanized, air-conditioned desert, a place without roots or feeling. We saw the main problem, really, as: THE PEOPLE—the ways they thought and acted towards each other. We imagined a great American desert, populated by millions of similar, crass, beer-drinking grains of sand, living in a waste of identical suburban no-places. What did this imagined "great pig-sty of TV watchers" correspond to in real life? As "middle-class" students we learned that this was the working class—the "racist, insensitive people."

Things already going on at the time of the Vietnam War inclined privileged people to look on "average" Americans as the country's problem.

The counterculture

To many young Americans the war was traumatic not because it violated notions of what their culture was but because it conformed to them. It quite naturally produced a "counterculture." In popularizing that term, the scholar Theodore Roszak claimed that the mental habits of technocratic management had created a mechanistic "Myth of Objective Consciousness," which numbed and cheapened human relations. It seemed to explain not just Vietnam but a good deal more besides—from the sameness of suburbia to the insipidity of television. An important dimension was missing from American life. It seemed to be a religious or spiritual one. Perhaps Americans didn't think enough about their place in the universe. Perhaps they didn't love enough.

However much the generation of the 1960s and '70s may have been snickered at in later years for seeking spirituality and self-actualization in faddish programs (Hare Krishna, Esalen, Werner Erhard's est), young people were not wrong to believe their culture had lost its way. The problems they were so desperate to treat had been diagnosed by sober-minded institutions, too. At the Second Vatican Council between 1962 and 1965, the Catholic church had tried to wrestle with its parishioners' role in a modern, pluralistic world. The Harvard theologian Harvey Cox argued that secularization need not mean the trivialization of religion. For decades, reinvigorating Western religion and philosophy with a dose of Asian spiritualism had been a favorite project of Western intellectuals: Aldous Huxley, Alan Watts, F.S.C. Northrop, the Beat novelists and poets.

The generations that came of age in the 1960s and 1970s were, in this sense, religious. Until 1975 religion, measured by both professed belief and church attendance, had been falling off, but it then began a steep rise that would last two decades. The Harvard sociologist Robert Putnam classified the period as another in a series of what American historians call "great awakenings." Fundamentalism and evangelical Christianity would shape American politics, starting in 1976 with the election to the presidency of Georgia governor Jimmy Carter, himself a "born-again" Christian. It was a revival led by young people, not a remnant composed of a few geezers.

For a while, starting in 1963, when Timothy Leary was ejected from Harvard for his "demonstrations" of LSD, drugs were the spiritual solution with which that generation's protesters were most closely identified. "To arrive at the unknown by disordering all the senses," as the French poet Arthur Rimbaud put it, was a cause on a par with making love, not war. People used drugs with particular ardor for only about two decades until, around 1985, the government cracked down on them and young people decided they were not a liberty worth defending. In the years after that, the "head," the "stoner," faded out of the story of the 1960s, like some reprobate who enlivens the early pages of a gothic novel but whom the author loses track of as the action picks up.

Maybe the problem with drugs was that they were an affront to one vital component of countercultural thinking, religious or not: the idea of purity. Somewhere out there was the "real" America, unspoiled, unexposed to the influence of television and shopping, unmanipulated by politicians. Americans of the sixties and seventies sought out places where the twentieth century had not done its awful work on the national character: The University of Minnesota professor Robert Pirsig worked throughout the 1960s on *Zen and the Art of Motorcycle Maintenance* (1974), which mixed a memoir of mental illness and a reflection on occidental philosophy with a picaresque account of a long motorcycle journey with his son. For Pirsig, to exit from the federal highway system onto smaller roads was to enter another world:

> These roads are truly different from the main ones. The whole pace of life and the personality of the people who live along them are different. They're not going anywhere. They're not too busy to be courteous. The hereness and nowness of things is something they know all about. It's the others, the ones who moved to the cities years ago and their lost offspring, who have all but forgotten it.

A certain cultural environmentalism was the natural accompaniment of this rural hankering. It was not the mix of science, ethics, and politics that we call environmentalism today and which, back then, was only just emerging under the name of "ecology." It was more a Romantic way of life, in the sense that William Wordsworth ("Nature never did betray the heart that loved her") was Romantic. Drawing from Western culture's deep well of ideas about simplicity and authenticity, it was, while it lasted, something you could partake of even in a truck or on a motorcycle. It meant natural ingredients (author and dietician Euell Gibbons), home cooking (chef Alice Waters), family values as defined in some past era (not just *Happy Days* and other 1950s nostalgia but also *The Waltons*, a colossally successful 1970s television series about the Depression in Appalachia, almost never re-aired in the decades that followed), folk and country music, all kinds of crafts (macramé, latch-hook rugs, Quaker furniture), the grumpy novels of Edward Abbey, backpacking, and *The Whole Earth Catalog*.

When the Baby Boom rock critic Greil Marcus described The Band's eponymous second album (1969) as "a passport back to America," he meant it as a compliment. Turning back the clock was a shared societal yearning. Something linked, say, the New York University psychology graduate who joined a commune in Oregon, thinking America had been better before superhighways, with the rural Georgia native who moved to Arizona and joined a megachurch, thinking that America had been better when women stayed home. It was not a specifically political yearning, but politics, eventually, would come into it. When people came to distrust modernity as a kind of corruption, it was not just the corporate world's supermarkets and sitcoms and dandruff shampoos they resented. It was also Washington's dams and highways, regulations and bureaucracy. Over time it would be Johnson's Great Society, which expanded the welfare state to undreamed-of and undesired levels.

In certain lights, the 1960s counterculture looks like a reactionary movement disguised as a progressive one. Pirsig, for instance, may have been anti-war, anti-corporate, drug-friendly, and steeped in academia, but he was no "free spirit." What he liked about small-town America was its resemblance to the country of "a hundred or two hundred years ago," and he defended "political reactionaries" out to restore "individual worth." The mountain climber Guy Waterman had been a speechwriter for presidents Eisenhower, Nixon, and Ford, not to mention General Electric, before retiring to an electricity-less cabin in Vermont to write about nature. Illinois-born John McClaughry, who during the Reagan administration would begin calling for the revivification of small-town government from his Vermont log cabin near the Canadian border, had himself worked as an aide to Reagan. An important strand of 1960s "radicalism"—the individualistic strand—would wind up fitting 1980s "conservatism" like a glove.

Sources of Baby Boom power

The dominant American culture, for more than a generation after the Vietnam War, would be the culture of those who passed through universities during the war—that is, of the elite part of the so-called Baby Boom, the unusually numerous and politically hyperactive group born between the Second World War and the Kennedy assassination.

Baby Boomers were the first generation to inhabit as adults the America newly built out of experimental attitudes toward race, sex, and world hegemony. They were not the authors of the new constitutional understandings that, beginning in the 1960s, began to jostle with the traditional ones. Almost all of the ideas around which American life would be reformed were already in circulation by the early 1960s. By the time the oldest Boomers got to college in 1963, there were 16,000 troops in Vietnam and the March on Washington had already happened. When Martin Luther King and Robert Kennedy were assassinated in the spring of 1968, no Baby Boomer had ever voted in a presidential election. At the time of the countercultural music festival at Woodstock (1969) the youngest Baby Boomers were still too young for kindergarten.

The sources of this generation's dominance lay not in its exploits or ideas but in its sheer demographic might. The generation that grew into adulthood as the Vietnam War was being fought and civil rights law promulgated was the biggest in American history. Its peculiar demographics twisted the straightforward issues that confront every generation—inheriting, experimenting, rebelling, mating, standing on one's own two feet—into unfamiliar shapes.

The United States had a population below 140 million when World War II ended in 1945. It would add more than 70 million babies before 1964. At war's end there had been only one year in the nation's history when as many as 3 million babies were born. By the early 1950s, annual births were over 4 million and they kept rising into the 1960s.

It was not as big a leap in fertility as people often imagine. Sexuality had not been "pent up." Birth rates had been rising steadily *during* the war—since 1933, in fact. But over time, high fertility gave those born after the war an extraordinary preponderance. In the first years of the twenty-first century, there were about 80 million Baby Boomers in the United States. For a generation, they made up 37 or 38 percent of the voting population. By contrast, the generation born between 1930 and 1945 peaked at about 18 percent of the electorate. It produced no presidents. The Boomers' demographic weight allowed them to seize control of, enforce, and re-orient the social transformation their elders had inaugurated.

In a free-market democracy, population translates directly into political power, through votes. It translates indirectly into economic power, through market share. And it eventually translates into cultural power, because advertisers (and, less avowedly, artists) aim to titillate and flatter large audiences. From the get-go, no generation was more fussed over and pandered to.

"I know America's youth," said Richard Nixon in his first inaugural address in 1969. "I believe in them. We can be proud that they are better educated, more committed, more passionately driven by conscience than any generation in our history." In 1970, the Bendix Corporation, a maker of automobile brakes, carburetors, and starters, took out full-page ads featuring a business-suited executive looking with alarm at a bearded biker in a suede-fringed, fake–American Indian jacket. The company announced that it was more worried about poverty, crime, prejudice, injustice, and pollution than about the "generation gap" much spoken of at the time: "For one thing, we've got too much faith in today's young people," Bendix intoned. "They seem to be more concerned and less hypocritical than any generation in history." *Life* magazine that year tried to market itself to the youngest adults with flattery: "And we don't see anything silly about college students speaking their minds. We take what they say . . . about the war, about our cities, about our country . . . and print it. Because a lot of it makes sense."

Certain experiences cut a razor-sharp border between the experience of Baby Boomers and that of the generations before and after. Consider the difference between the pre–Baby Boom birth year of 1943, which included Vietnam War hero (later protester) and 2004 presidential candidate (later secretary of state) John Kerry; and the first Baby Boom cohort of 1946, which included onetime Texas governor George W. Bush, who defeated Kerry in the 2004 presidential election. (It is probably not a coincidence that 1946 is the only year in American history to have seen the birth of three presidents, all three, in fact, born in the summer months of that year.) In 1966, when 22-year-old Kerry got out of Yale, the war in Vietnam was still at an early stage. It was not yet unthinkable that the wealthy and privileged should serve in the military, and Kerry enlisted in the Navy. By the time the three future presidents finished college just two years later, the war had heated up, the Summer of Love had intervened, and better-off Americans were desperately seeking ways to avoid active service. None of the three went to Vietnam, though Bush served in the Texas Air National Guard.

The Baby Boomers were the last generation of Americans who would be taught in school that their country had "never lost a war." In most things, in fact, they would have more in common with their parents than with their children. They were educated for a pre-computer world. They listened to a combination of folk-rock and vaguely British-inflected rock, which, for their children, would be eclipsed by various kinds of rap. All Boomers were born into a pre–civil rights America, and they were the last generation to grow up wholly outside the shadow of what would be known as political correctness.

The Boom was split into two parts chronologically, in a way that would produce something like a class division within it. Those born at the front end of the Boom, in the late 1940s and early 1950s, were educated in a traditional America. Whether they cheered on the social experimentation of the time or looked aghast at it, they had a special role as emissaries of the "younger generation" to the broader culture. What we now think of as the culture of the Baby Boom was actually the culture only of its older age cohorts.

Those born at the tail end of the Boom, between, say, 1955 and the mid-1960s, had no such role. They were too young to fight either in or against the Vietnam War. By the time *they* were old enough to speak for the younger generation—in the 1970s and '80s—youth (as a subject) had gotten old. Society's institutions had already been reformed in accordance with the needs of "youth," as those needs had been understood during the Johnson administration: modular classrooms, non-traditional curricula, liberal politics, and lenient rules about premarital sex.

For three quarters of a century, other generations would be forced to share the preoccupations of their fellow citizens born in the late 1940s and early 1950s. The country was always "about" these older Boomers. It was built around carousing and sexuality in the 1960s and '70s and around "family values" and the acquisition of wealth in the 1980s and '90s. In the first decades of the new century, it was built around protecting the interests and fortunes of those who had prospered in decades past, according to rules they themselves had written—and around protecting the institutions and companies they themselves had established.

A burgeoning educational bureaucracy increased the leverage of the Baby Boom over other generations and shaped the ends to which it would exercise that leverage. The historian Eric Hobsbawm placed the rise of the Western university after World War II on the same level of demographic importance as the disappearance of the Western peasantry. Confining himself to Europe, he noted that "the number of students tripled or quadrupled in the most typical country, except where it multiplied by four to five, as in Federal Germany, Ireland and Greece; by five to seven, as in Finland, Iceland, Sweden and Italy; and seven to nine-fold, as in Spain and Norway." Although the United States started from a much higher baseline than those other countries, its college enrollment more than quadrupled, too, from about 1.7 million in 1940 to 7.5 million at the end of the 1960s. Earlier generations would have wondered what kind of clean-hands work could be found for all those bookish people to do—and they would also have asked who would do the dirty work now that education had unsuited much of the population to it.

The Baby Boom generation was the most culturally stable (or as we would say today, the "least diverse") generation in American history. The 1970 census, the first in which all the Boomers were present, was the only one since the founding of the republic two centuries before in which the foreign-born population was below 5 percent. Immigration still came largely from Europe. The three largest sources of foreign-born were Italy (1,009,000), Germany (833,000), and Canada (812,000). Twenty-first-century readers, accustomed to much higher numbers, might need to be told that those were total resident populations, not annual arrivals. There were only 760,000 Mexicans in the country, slightly more than the number of people from the United Kingdom, Poland, or the Soviet Union. Mexico and Cuba were the only non-European countries in the top ten. By 2010, there would be no European countries at all on the top ten list. Here it is: Mexico, China, India, the Philippines, Vietnam, El Salvador, Cuba, Korea, the Dominican Republic, and Guatemala.

Renaissance or decay?

Restaurants are generally the first immigrant businesses to take root, and decades after World War II there were still many states that did not have a single Mexican restaurant. New Hampshire did not get one until the 1970s, when the Acevedo family moved from El Paso to Manchester and opened Little Mexico on Elm St. Well into the 1970s, Americans understood themselves as they always had—as essentially a European country, displaced westward. Combining as it did wealth, cultural homogeneity, and relative equality of status and income, the America the Baby Boomers grew up in was more easily governable than it would be a generation or two later, as the country sought to absorb the largest wave of migration and settlement in the history of the world. Reforms conceived for a country that was provincial, dutiful, and 4 percent immigrant are not necessarily well suited to a country that is cosmopolitan, hedonistic, and 15 percent immigrant. The America of the 1960s had a leeway for safe experimentation that it would not regain.

This may be just as true in the arts as in government. The years from roughly 1968 to 1971, when, as noted, the American population was less "diverse" than at any time in its history, were also the high-water mark of the country's post-war culture, certainly of its popular music. In the four-and-a-half months of 1970 that separate the albums *Workingman's Dead* (June) and *American Beauty* (November), the Grateful Dead alone cranked out a dozen songs that have endured through the generations.

It was an impermanent flourishing, a transition. The rock 'n' roll stars of the 1960s and (to a degree) the 1970s had been trained to the old culture. They had mastered instruments and become real musicians, if only to play piano for guests in their parents' living rooms, or the organ on Sunday at church. Once rock was established, however, aspiring rock stars began modeling themselves on rock musicians, or even *non*-musicians. Paul Cook, the drummer for the pioneering punk

band the Sex Pistols, recalled the early punk music periodicals that
came out after 1976. "In one of the fanzines," he wrote, "there's even a
diagram showing you how to play three chords—C, D and A—with
the caption, 'Here's the chords. Now go and start a band!'" Similar
things were said by Rod Stewart and the musicians of Bachman–
Turner Overdrive.

The countercultural culture that lasted for a decade or two after the
1960s can seem a progressive reworking of old values, a drawing out
of new possibilities. Or it can appear a mere looting of the old culture,
a decadence, a spending down. In theory it could have been both at
the same time. But by the 1970s, Americans were drifting away from
the idea that they were in the middle of some kind of renaissance and
beginning to worry that their country was going down the tubes. This
was not just a reaction to a slowing economy. Certainly, in an economy
hemmed in by strong trade unions, new environmental regulation, and
newly expensive oil and gasoline, it seemed impossible to create jobs.
In December 1974 alone, the country lost 600,000 of them. But Americans were concerned more about the culture than the conjuncture.

American automobiles had once been a symbol of the country's
world-bestriding economy. Now their shoddiness was astonishing, embarrassing, no matter how obstreperously auto workers demanded to be compensated as the "best workers in the world." In
1977, Plymouth brought out a new "T-Bar coupe" called the Volaré.
"To the new generation of Americans who have never known the
driving pleasure of wind through the hair," the ads ran, "we proudly
dedicate our new T-Bar Volaré Coupe." It was a way for Chrysler to
avoid saying that it had lost the capacity to build convertibles at an
affordable price. Starting in 1978, General Motors began producing
station wagons—such as the Buick Century and the Oldsmobile Cut-
lass Cruiser—in which the rear windows didn't roll down. Magazine
ads for Ford and Cadillac depicted their new models against a dim
backdrop of historic ones, as if to console themselves that, if their
products were third-rate, they had at least once made better ones.

The prospects for government were, if anything, worse. It was not only that Richard Nixon had been forced from office in a scandal. The three great progressive endeavors of the preceding decades—civil rights, women's liberation, the attempt to impose a liberal order on the world militarily—had all been resoundingly repudiated by the public. Post–Civil Rights Act, violent crime and drug abuse in inner cities were at record highs. Post–*Ms.* magazine, legislatures were rescinding the ERA ratifications they had only recently passed. Post–Vietnam War, Soviet troops entered Afghanistan and revolutionary governments came to power in Nicaragua and Iran.

The mood was one of nostalgia and failure. The American public had come to see the political project of the 1960s as dangerously utopian. They brought California governor Ronald Reagan to power to put an end to it. Instead, in ways that neither his supporters nor his detractors have ever fully understood, he rescued it.

Part II

THE NEW CONSTITUTION

5

Debt

The counterculture in middle age—Reaganism: a generational
truce—Reaganomics: a political strategy—What did the debt buy?—
Immigration, inequality, and debt—Immigration and the failure
of democracy—The changing spirit of civil rights—"People of color"
and "African-Americans"—Immigration and inequality—
The quest for a new elite

The victory of Ronald Reagan in the presidential election of 1980 was not just the reaction of an older America against Baby Boom enthusiasms. On the contrary, it brought almost the whole of the Baby Boom generation into the electorate. It was the first major political event that everyone born in the 1940s and 1950s took part in as an adult. It was partly an answer by non-elite Boomers to the zeal of their activist contemporaries, partly an expression of elite Boomers' own changed priorities as the oldest of them entered middle age. "The cultural and Reagan revolutions," the historian Mark Lilla later wrote, "have proved to be complementary, not contradictory, events." The novelist Kurt Andersen shared this view of the relationship between the two eras. " 'Do your own thing,' " he wrote, "is not so different than 'every man for himself.' " The 1980s are what the 1960s turned into.

The counterculture in middle age

Historians differ on where to place the high tide of Reaganism. The first of two volumes in Steven F. Hayward's history *The Age of Reagan* starts in the Johnson administration and covers a decade or so of resistance to Great Society–type programs, ending in 1980 with Reagan's successful run for the presidency. For Hayward, Reaganism was an uprising that rallied a Middle American yeomanry to the project of shrinking an overweening government.

One such anti-establishment uprising had already been seen off, but only with the greatest difficulty. After squeaking into the presidency in 1968, Richard Nixon had governed in such a way as to turn his 1972 re-election campaign into a referendum on the Great Society. His vice president, former Maryland governor Spiro Agnew, specialized in erudite, alliterative, bomb-throwing oratory, much of it crafted by a crew of speechwriters that included the future columnists Patrick J. Buchanan and William Safire. They cast the struggle between the old ways of the World War II generation and the new values of the 1960s as a Manichean one. In Houston in January 1971, at an address to football coaches honoring the memory of Vince Lombardi, Agnew described the late Green Bay Packers coach as a symbol of the "early American ethic" that leftists meant to replace with a new order. That was dangerous to the survival of America as the GI generation understood it:

> For I doubt that many of us here tonight would be allowed to "do our thing." I have in mind the fact that in the New Left weekly rating of the people's enemies the institution known as Football Coach ranks high in the top ten—not far behind the Joint Chiefs of Staff, General Motors, the CIA, the FBI, John Wayne, and yours truly.

Whatever Agnew meant by a "New Left weekly rating of the people's enemies," most of the actual American people were on his side. Nixon won in 1972 by 18 million votes, the most overwhelming democratic mandate any American president has ever received, before or since. But the landslide wound up doing little to secure his presidency. Whether or not Nixon knew of the election season break-ins carried out by Republican campaign personnel at the Democrats' offices in the Watergate apartment complex, they snowballed into a scandal that gave his political foes an opportunity to destroy him. Nixon would be the first president hounded from office.

The Princeton historian Sean Wilentz also wrote a book entitled *The Age of Reagan*. It began where Hayward's first volume left off— with the first stirrings of a Reagan presidential run in the 1970s—and followed the story up to the 2008 presidential campaign of Barack Obama. For Wilentz, Reaganism was a style of policy making, built out of Reagan's own sunny Midwestern persona, that would protect the rich and narrow the scope of politics well into the twenty-first century.

Reagan's followers agreed with his enemies in calling his movement "conservative." In retrospect, that was the wrong word for it. Reaganism shared certain of the counterculture's deepest aspirations. The hippie agenda, as its most eloquent champions tended to lay it out, was often conservative. It defended tradition against progress. The mainstream, corporate, military-industrial culture built up since the war had sought "ruthlessly to cut the past away," wrote the Brandeis University classicist Philip Slater in *The Pursuit of Loneliness* (1970). What the new culture would seek instead was wholeness and continuity. "A community that does not have old people and children, white-collar and blue-collar, eccentric and conventional, and so on, is not a community at all," Slater wrote, "but the same kind of truncated and deformed monstrosity that most people inhabit today."

You can hear the echo of this kind of sixties talk in the most effective arguments President Reagan would make for cutting government. "The truth is," he said in the first months of his presidency, "we've let government take away many things we once considered were really ours to do voluntarily, out of the goodness of our hearts and a sense of community pride and neighborliness."

The return of power to communities that Reagan promised never happened. On the contrary, the world that his supposedly conservative presidency left behind was more indulgent of the anti-conservative impulse to "cut the past away," provided the cutting were done heedlessly by businessmen rather than purposefully by bureaucrats. American conservatism was something Reagan *tapped* rather than embodied. His version of it was oratorical, not constitutional. And conservatism's lack of a worked-out constitutional dimension would create the crisis out of which, decades later, a harder-edged "Tea Party" populism grew.

Post-war intellectuals had dismissed the prospects for conservative intellectual life in America. The literary critic Lionel Trilling had written in his introduction to *The Liberal Imagination* (1950):

> In the United States at this time liberalism is not only the dominant but even the sole intellectual tradition. For it is the plain fact that nowadays there are no conservative or reactionary ideas in general circulation. This does not mean, of course, that there is no impulse to conservatism or to reaction. Such impulses are certainly very strong, perhaps even stronger than most of us know. But the conservative impulse and the reactionary impulse do not, with some isolated and some ecclesiastical exceptions, express themselves in ideas but only in action or in irritable mental gestures which seek to resemble ideas.

Around the same time, Trilling's younger rival Irving Howe had described conservative thinking, not just in literature but also in politics, as fraudulent and unreal. He dismissed as a "mystifying pleasantry" the conservatism of the novelist Peter Viereck and kindred intellectuals. Howe added, "As for the 'conservatism' of the late Senator Robert Taft, which consists of nothing but liberal economics and wounded nostalgia, it lacks intellectual content and, more important, when in power it merely continues those 'statist' policies it had previously attacked."

Those of Reagan's supporters who called themselves conservatives snickered at such mockery, but time has vindicated Trilling and Howe. Like Taft, Reagan changed the country's political *mood* for a while, but left its structures untouched. Once he left office, Reagan's adversaries and bogeymen recovered their ambitious projects from receivership. His supporters were left outside to warm themselves by the embers of Reaganite rhetoric. It was as if the conservative political wave of the late 1970s and early '80s had never happened. Indeed, Reagan raises the perennial question of whether conservatism is possible at all in a political culture that has the "pursuit of happiness" written into its founding documents.

Reagan came to power amid a din of rebellion and radical democracy—and not just among hippie holdovers. The mid-1970s saw a craze for citizens band radio, which allowed long-haul truck drivers to communicate the whereabouts of state police speed traps and evade enforcement of the 55-mile-an-hour speed limits imposed in the wake of the 1973 Arab oil embargo. It was by CB that truckers communicated when, in December of that year, J. W. "River Rat" Edwards started a nationwide "blockade" outside Lamar, Pennsylvania, to protest gas prices and highway regulation. The slang the truckers used to disguise their identities (for they were breaking the law) was romanticized in the film *Smokey and the Bandit* (1977) and in songs so numerous that there were whole LP-length anthologies of them.

The popularity of truckers' slang was reminiscent of the way nineteenth- and twentieth-century English novels had romanticized Cockney thieves' rhyming slang: Even readers who had never met a Cockney acquired a degree of fluency in their dialect. By 1975, when Cledus Maggard & the Citizen's Band released their hit "White Knight," most Americans would have understood that its lines

> *When, wall-to-wall, I got a call*
> *from my front-door big-bear trapper*
> *He said, Breaker one-nine, good buddy o' mine,*
> *I got a Smokey in a plain white wrapper*

meant that a trucker had, thanks to good reception, just picked up a warning on CB channel 19 from a driver ahead of him that a state policeman was traveling in an unmarked vehicle.

Truckers were heroes to a broad public in a way that striking union laborers often were in Great Britain and France but seldom in the United States. C. W. McCall's country gag song "Convoy," which climaxed with a band of truckers smashing through a tollbooth in New Jersey, became the best-selling single in the country just before Christmas 1975.

That was the year President Gerald Ford signed the Metric Conversion Act, pledging considerable funding and all the powers of the federal government to the project of converting Americans from English measures to the more sensible-sounding decimal system of meters and liters and grams. In England itself, "metrication" had been going on for a decade, with only mild grumbling. Americans met it with scorn and non-compliance. The measure was soon abandoned.

But by the middle of the Reagan administration, the romance had gone out of that kind of law-breaking and resistance. A program launched in Boston in 1983 urged citizens to inform on any suspicious-looking neighbors. They might, after all, be drug dealers. "Drop a dime, stop a crime," the billboards read, a dime being what it cost to make a call to the local police station from a public phone booth.

Reaganism: a generational truce

Reaganism was, like most political movements, a mix of high philosophy and low tactics. It cut deadwood out of the New Deal economy and guided American institutions as they began using computers, junk bonds, non-unionized labor, and outsourcing to re-establish the economy on different bases. It secured for another generation of Americans the exorbitant privilege of using the U.S. dollar as the world's reserve currency and getting to write the rules of international commerce, an outcome that had seemed uncertain when Reagan took office. It helped end the Cold War. And it began a process that by the early years of the following century would render American society unrecognizably inegalitarian, even oligarchic.

Reagan's decades as a partisan and a politician overlapped with the period in which a subculture developed around the Russian émigrée Ayn Rand, whose business boosterism was of the sort that some Americans have perennially mistaken for a philosophy. Rand laid out her libertarian worldview in *The Fountainhead, Atlas Shrugged,* and other turgid, two-dimensional novels in the 1940s and 1950s. Her characters were all domineering, headstrong, the inheritors of big companies and good genes, and above all didactic, even when they were discussing cigarettes ("I like to think of fire held in a man's hand. Fire, a dangerous force, tamed at his fingertips."). They liked sex, which in certain circumstances could be so thrilling it resembled business management ("his hand moving over her breasts as if he were learning a proprietor's intimacy with her body").

Rand's main obsession was socialism. That was the only conservative thing about her. For the most part her zeal for liberating businessmen from red tape and taxation drew its intellectual consistency and philosophical panache from a larger program: "freeing" citizens from historical rationales, traditional institutions, vernacular frames of reference, homespun ideas of moral responsibility, and habits of respect.

But in the 1970s, when rebellion held a monopoly on prestige, the vituperation of authority in which Rand's anti-socialism came wrapped was an immense morale boost for a certain kind of conservative. All authority, from Jim Crow to speed limits, from the Gulag to the IRS, could now be cast as a depredation of "big government." The 32-year-old stockbroker who spoke out against the high taxes he paid was, along this narrow Randian axis, comparable to his more dashing classmates who had marched for civil rights in Alabama or smoked weed at Woodstock. He, too, was an individual brave enough to stand up against the system.

For at least two generations, Rand's thinking would win the loyalty of conservatives, intellectual ones disproportionately. William F. Buckley, Jr., the founder and editor of *National Review*, was impressed with Rand, but he described future Treasury secretary Alan Greenspan as having been "absolutely bewitched" by her in the early 1950s, when he attended her salons at 36 East 36th Street in New York. Decades later, the future Republican speaker of the House, Paul Ryan, was similarly smitten as a high school student in Wisconsin. "I give out *Atlas Shrugged* as Christmas presents, and I make all my interns read it," he would later say. In 1991, when the Book of the Month Club and the Library of Congress asked readers to name the book that had most influenced their lives, *Atlas Shrugged* ranked second only to the Bible.

Reagan professed himself an "admirer" of Rand. The feeling was not reciprocated. Rand spent the last months of her active life traveling from college campus to college campus, denouncing Reagan in increasingly purple language for his electoral courtship of Christian voters and others on the religious right who had misgivings about abortion. That was a subject of the very last speech she gave, to the National Committee for Monetary Reform in New Orleans in November 1981. "The appalling disgrace of his administration is his connection with the so-called Moral Majority and sundry other TV religionists," she said, pausing to acknowledge applause, "who are struggling, apparently with his approval, to take us back to the Middle Ages, via the unconstitutional union of religion and politics."

At the time, a credo that mixed untrammeled capitalism (deemed "conservative") with untrammeled sexuality (deemed "liberal") seemed self-contradictory. It was not. It was logical and powerful. It would come, a generation later, to seem invincible.

But Rand's enmity toward Reagan on that account was short-sighted. That he learned to sound certain conservative notes about sex in the 1970s, and even gave a barn-burning speech against abortion in 1983, should not distract from his pre-eminence as a sexual progressive. In 1967, as governor of California, he signed the furthest-reaching liberalization of abortion in American history. In 1969 he introduced no-fault divorce statewide with his Family Law Act. By the time of his campaign for the presidency in 1980, it would have been fair to say Reagan had done more than any politician of either party to build up the institutions of post-feminist sexual liberation.

Reagan's stress on "family values"—a strange term that was being used twice as frequently by the end of his term as it had been at the beginning—disguised his acquiescence to modern ways. Values were presented as equivalent to institutions, but they were not. A homosexual couple, a single mother, a couple cohabitating outside of marriage might be challenging an important family institution—but they were no threat to anyone's values. At a time when new institutions were at odds with old ones, talking of values was a way of pretending that no one had any real grievance or interest worth arguing over.

Reagan's libertarian vision had as much of Martin Luther King's "dream" in it as it did of Ayn Rand's capitalism. It was sunny and it was progressive. It assumed that an untrammeled thriving was possible, if only a few hardened sticks-in-the-mud and pessimists could be kept from undermining it. Skepticism was the equivalent of oppression. Bearers of bad news were indistinguishable from enemies of the people. This vision did not appeal to all minds, but it seemed to strike a chord in all hearts. That is why Reagan won every state but Minnesota when he ran for re-election in 1984.

The expression "American Dream" is not an ancient one and has had its ups and downs. It was invented only in 1931 by the historian James Truslow Adams and caught on a bit in that decade, only to fall out of fashion in the 1940s. It owes its near-omnipresence in today's political discourse to two periods when it was very much in fashion. In the seven years between 1963 (the year King gave his "I have a dream" speech and the first Baby Boomers left high school) and the end of the decade, its usage more than doubled. In the seven years between 1986 (the year the last Baby Boomers left college) and 1993 (the year Bill Clinton, the first Baby Boom president, took office after twelve years of Reaganism), its usage went up by nearly 50 percent.

Dreams were where Americans lived. An unwillingness to recognize the limits of reality and common sense in any walk of life became the signature of their political rhetoric, of their corporate marketing, and even of their national culture. The editor of *Cosmopolitan*, Helen Gurley Brown, published a manifesto in Reagan's second year in office called *Having It All: Love, Success, Sex, Money—Even If You're Starting with Nothing*. The tax-cutting congressman Jack Kemp derided as "root-canal economics" the traditional idea that tax cuts would have to be accompanied by spending cuts if the budget were to be kept in balance. Bill Clinton, when he took office, dismissed as "false choices" any assertions that existing programs might need to be cut to pay for his more ambitious new ones. Nike promised "No Limits" to those who bought its sneakers, and a generation later almost every information-age startup made similar pledges. By 2008, Alaska governor Sarah Palin would run for the vice presidency promising an "all-of-the-above energy strategy"—and the Obama administration would pay her the compliment of adopting the policy (or at least taking the name) for its own.

The rhetoric of smashing limits was necessary to Reagan's own greatest achievement: He arranged a truce between the World War II generation and the Baby Boomers, whose interests had, until his campaign, appeared irreconcilable. The demographers William Strauss and Neil Howe described "an implicit deal in which G.I.s achieved economic independence (and spent the post-Vietnam fiscal 'peace dividend' almost entirely on themselves) while Boomers asserted their social independence."

For a while at the end of the twentieth century, this deal appeared to have brought an idyll. The United States combined the best of both worlds—the aristocratic rule-breaking of the 1960s with the working-class solidarity and stability of the 1940s. Reagan held off for roughly a quarter-century the work of institutional dissolution that seemed to be under way when he was running for president in the late 1970s.

The problem came from how he managed it. In social life, questioning limits means not bowing down to anything. In economics, questioning limits means not paying for anything. At first, the American Baby Boomers appeared to be doing with little effort what other generations had only managed to do by the sweat of their brow. But that was an illusion. What they were doing was using their generation's voting power to arrogate future generations' labor, and trading it to other nations and peoples for labor now. Reaganism meant Reaganomics. Reaganomics meant debt.

Reaganomics: a political strategy

"The national debt tripled under Reagan"—to understand this six-word sentence from a sympathetic biography would be to understand much about the last half-century of American politics. Reagan's economic advisors claimed to be skeptical of the "Keynesian" framework of economic policy that governments had been pursuing since Roosevelt's New Deal. Under that earlier dispensation, Washington had fought unemployment by spending money on roads, dams, and other infrastructure programs, and in so doing had rescued the country from the Great Depression, or so the country believed. Lyndon Johnson thought the welfare programs he launched in the 1960s were in the spirit of Roosevelt's dam-building and road-building and mural-painting. They would pump money into the economy just as effectively, and stimulate things.

But Johnson was wrong. By the mid-1970s, unemployment and inflation were rising in tandem, confounding familiar models. Economists who had cheered LBJ's welfare experiments, such as Harvard's John Kenneth Galbraith, lost the ear of elected officials. Skeptics, such as Milton Friedman, came into vogue.

The first measures to scale back taxation and spending were passed under Democratic president Jimmy Carter in the 95th Congress, in which Democrats held over two thirds of House seats, and it was Carter's appointee to head the Federal Reserve, Paul Volcker, who determined to wring inflation out of the economy by pitilessly tightening the money supply, starting in October 1979.

It is hard to say precisely what so-called Reaganomics had to do with these developments. The only consistent feature of Reagan's economic views over the years was an enthusiasm for cutting taxes. The rationale shifted. Often it rested on an assumption that, once tax levels were set, the budget would come into balance spontaneously. "The answer to a government that's too big is to stop feeding its growth," Reagan told Congress in the spring of 1981. If one shared the opinion that government was too big, then tax cuts were laudable at all times and in all contexts.

But there was an even harder-line position. It was based on the logical-sounding assertion that tax rates, if they got sufficiently high, retarded productive activity. Capitalists, bereft of the profit motive, would withhold their irreplaceable creativity. In effect, the elites would go on strike, like the cabal of Promethean industrialists who alternately sermonize and taunt a starving world in the later pages of Ayn Rand's *Atlas Shrugged*.

Keynesian economists had believed that higher taxes could make the economy not only fairer but also more efficient. Rich people tended to sock their money away as savings. A progressive government could dislodge it via taxes and invest it in big projects, pumping up demand as it did. But this argument became harder to defend after FDR's infrastructural state gave way to LBJ's welfare state. "Supply-side" economists now argued, with considerable cogency, that when government collected too much from "the rich," potentially productive concentrations of investment capital were eroded, and spooned back into society in bites of welfare too small to be used for anything but immediate consumption.

One night in the autumn of 1974, when the top income tax rate stood at 78 percent, the business economist Arthur Laffer of the University of Southern California sketched out a graph with a felt-tip pen on a cocktail napkin. He was having dinner at the Two Continents restaurant, across the street from the White House, with *Wall Street Journal* opinion writer Jude Wanniski and two aides to President Gerald Ford, Richard Cheney and Donald Rumsfeld. Laffer was claiming that, on top of the collateral inefficiencies they provoked, high tax rates could actually cost the government money.

The "Laffer Curve" was not terribly rigorous. Its origins in a restaurant rather than a classroom are evident from the napkin itself, which is now in the possession of the National Museum of American History. It shows the independent variable—the tax rate—on the y, not the x, axis, as would be normal in academic economics. But if it was even remotely plausible that tax cuts might unleash enough economic activity to "pay for themselves," then Laffer had discovered the political equivalent of a magic lamp.

Wanniski would become the great salesman and impresario of so-called supply-side economics. He urged it on Republican politicians as a political strategy two years before he laid it out as an economic theory. With the toastmaster's language that was his trademark, he argued in 1976 that Republicans kept losing elections because Democrats forced them to "embrace the role of Scrooge," while Democrats played the role of Santa Claus. "The first rule of successful politics," he wrote, "is Never Shoot Santa Claus." Democrats had claimed an identity as the party that generously offered benefits and security, leaving Republicans the responsibility of announcing which taxes they would raise to keep the budget balanced. Wanniski was alerting Republicans who stood behind the Reagan revolution that they could play this trick in reverse. They could bring the good news of tax cuts and let Democrats scramble to announce what services they planned to trim. His article was widely read on Capitol Hill.

In 1978, Wanniski came out with *The Way the World Works*, a global history focused single-mindedly on marginal tax rates and entrepreneurship. It was high taxes that caused the fall of Rome, tax moderation that President Warren Harding was talking about when he promised a "Return to Normalcy," and tax cuts that spurred Japan's post-war boom. The book sparkles with aphorisms, but scarcely a page passes in which the reader does not feel a pang of doubt about whether Wanniski knows what he is talking about. He writes that a Soviet collective farm would "permit the workers to keep 10 percent of the value of their production. The marginal tax rate is thus 90 percent." But if the whole increment between workers' wages and the "value of their production" is a tax, then where do profits come from, which supply-siders assumed were the motor of an economy?

Wanniski's ideas were at odds with those of most economists, both liberal and conservative, as well as most historians. Economies throughout history had grown rich and remained stable without necessarily licensing the very richest to make money hand over fist. But the Wanniski vision jibed with the have-it-all culture at large. By this time, he had won over Jack Kemp. Beloved in the suburbs of Buffalo as the longtime quarterback of the American Football League's Buffalo Bills, Kemp won a congressional seat there in 1976, campaigning on a version of supply-side economics he had been teaching himself since his retirement from football. Faced with the prospect that Kemp might make tax cuts the centerpiece of a rival presidential campaign, Reagan endorsed the cuts Kemp had championed.

Clearly Reagan bought Wanniski's political insight about the advantages of playing Santa Claus. It is less clear that he bought Wanniski's economics. As president he would stress how painful the measures needed to cut deficits would be. In an autumn 1981 economic address, he urged cutting most agency budgets by 12 percent, eliminating others, laying off 75,000 workers, and slashing federal loan guarantees. That was not the program of a politician who believed his tax cuts would "pay for themselves."

Reagan's tax cuts never forced Congress to balance the budget. The supply-side windfall never happened, either. By the autumn of Reagan's first year in office, it was evident the government was growing apace, and the deficit along with it. "We cut the government's rate of growth nearly in half," he told Congress, but it was a weak boast—for it was the size of government, not the velocity of its growth, that he had promised to reduce. Government would continue to grow by 2.5 percent a year throughout his administration.

The difficulty of shrinking government led nobody in the president's entourage to reconsider his tax cuts. A means had become an end. "Even if Congress manages to pass the usual boondoggles," wrote the journalist George Gilder in his 1981 book *Wealth and Poverty*, "we should not abandon the drive to retrench taxes." Having railed against the "Keynesian" demand-side stimulus of his predecessors, Reagan wound up presiding over nearly a decade of full-throttle stimulus himself, along with the overheated private-sector economy and large annual deficits that are its hallmark.

Some good came of Reagan's economic policies, certainly. The federal government's share of GDP fell from 20.2 percent to 19.2 percent during his term. Reagan indexed tax rates to inflation, putting an end to the "bracket creep" that had steadily ratcheted Americans into higher rates even as their real wages stalled out. Bracket creep had posed a novel constitutional problem: a mechanism for expanding revenue (and thus government) without the direct consent of Congress. It was taxation-without-representation in the strictest sense.

Today Reagan's defenders credit him with having prepared the country for the competitive conditions of the global economy. He did, but that was no part of his vision. A former spokesman for General Electric, Reagan did not win two elections by promising to close more plants, outsource more jobs, and lay off more industrial workers. The Reagan administration, according to his aide William A. Niskanen, erected "more trade barriers than any administration since Hoover."

Reagan's critics, for their part, saw a redistribution from the poor to the rich. That may have been a long-term consequence, but at first the transfer was not from one social class to another but from one government program to another. The transfers went, according to Niskanen, "from discretionary domestic spending to defense, entitlements and interest payments." Reagan took money from bridge building, park tidying, and arts funding and used it to pay for a military buildup and the very Great Society programs he had come to office promising to dismantle. That required borrowing.

What did the debt buy?

Dwight Eisenhower warned in his 1961 farewell address, "We—you and I, and our government—must avoid the impulse to live only for today, plundering, for our own ease and convenience, the precious resources of tomorrow."

By then the country had known massive borrowing, but only in wartime. To fight World War II, the federal government had added $200 billion to its debt—an amount that by war's end was about the size of the gross domestic product. Although the size of the total credit market (including private individuals) would expand every single year from 1947 to 2008, in the first thirty-five years after World War II the trajectory of government debt (measured as a percentage of gross domestic product) had steadily declined. Under Reagan it began to rise. That opened a new chapter in American fiscal history.

Looking at numbers and charts, it is easy to miss the most basic question: Why on earth, at the height of the Baby Boom generation's productive years, did the government need to borrow in the first place? What did this binge of debt *buy*? What emergency did it extricate the country from?

From an actuarial and from a human-capital perspective, the quarter-century after Ronald Reagan's election should have been the easiest time to balance the budget in the history of the republic. The entirety of the vast Baby Boom generation, making up 38 percent of the population, was in its productive years. There were relatively few retirees and dependent children to tend to. The country was (until the Iraq War after 2003) at peace. It set the rules for the global economy. But since Baby Boomers were due to leave the workforce between 2010 and 2030, big obligations for Social Security and Medicare loomed. Those would go unmet.

The borrowing power of the Baby Boom generation was invested in avoiding the choices that the confrontations of the 1960s had placed before the country. What the debt paid for was social peace, which had come to be understood as synonymous with the various Great Society programs launched by Lyndon Johnson in the two years after the Kennedy assassination. We should understand the Great Society as the institutional form into which the civil rights impulse hardened, a transfer from whites to blacks of the resources necessary to make desegregation viable. Desegregation was, as we have said, the most massive undertaking of any kind in the history of the United States. Like any massive undertaking, it required endurance, patience, and prohibitive expense. Almost everyone who did not benefit from it was going to be made poorer by it. Now it was being presented to the public as the merest down payment on what Americans owed.

The best evidence we have is that it was too much for most Americans from the beginning. The rhetoric that brought Reagan two landslides was, among other things, a sign that Americans were unwilling to bankroll with their taxes the civil rights and welfare revolution of the 1960s and the social change it brought in its train.

In retrospect, we can see that by acquiescing in the ouster of Nixon after the *previous* landslide, those who voted for him had lost their chance to moderate the pace of that change. With the impeachment of Nixon, promoters of the Great Society had bought the time necessary to defend it against "backlash," as democratic opposition to social change was coming to be called. In the near-decade that elapsed between Nixon and Reagan, entire subpopulations had become dependent on the Great Society. Those programs were now too big to fail.

They were, as we have said, gigantic. Once debt was used as a means to keep the social peace, it would quickly run into the trillions. One of Johnson's lower-profile initiatives from 1965, the Higher Education Act, created the so-called Pell Grants to help "underprivileged" youth go to college. Their cost had risen to $7 billion by the time Reagan came to Washington. Although their effectiveness was disputed, there was an iron coalition of educational administrators and student advocates behind them. So Reagan didn't touch them. They would swell to $39 billion by 2010. And they were not the whole story of federal support for education. According to one sympathetic account, federal grants and loans to college students, adjusted for inflation, were $800 million in 1963–64, $15 billion in 1973–74, and $157 billion in 2010–11.

Such grants didn't just finance individual educations. They provided a pool of billions in investment capital that spawned new for-profit universities set up largely to collect them. In the twenty-first century, the largest collector of Pell Grant tuition would be the University of Phoenix, a nationwide open-enrollment "university" founded in 1976. Its students owed $35 billion in taxpayer-backed federal loans. Their default rate was higher than their graduation rate. More and more the vaunted Reaganite "private sector" was coming to operate this way. It was a catchment area set up to receive government funds—usually by someone well enough connected to know before the public did how and where government funds would be directed.

Reagan stinted on none of the resources required to construct Johnson's new order. Having promised for years that he would undo affirmative action "with the stroke of a pen," lop the payments that LBJ's Great Society lavished on "welfare queens," and abolish Jimmy Carter's Department of Education, he discovered, once he became president, that to do any of those things would have struck at the very foundations of desegregation. So he didn't—although Democrats and Republicans managed to agitate and inspire their voting and fundraising bases for decades by pretending he had. Meanwhile, his tax cuts provided a golden parachute for the white middle class, allowing it, for one deluded generation, to re-create with private resources a Potemkin version of the old order.

Those losing out had to be compensated. Consider affirmative action—unconstitutional under the traditional order, compulsory under the new—which exacted a steep price from white incumbents in the jobs they held, in the prospects of career advancement for their children, in their status as citizens. Such a program could be made palatable to white voters only if they could be offered compensating advantages. A government that was going to make an overwhelming majority of voters pay the cost of affirmative action had to keep unemployment low, home values rising, and living standards high. Reaganomics was just a name for governing under a merciless contradiction that no one could admit was there: Civil rights was important enough that people could not be asked to wait for it, but unpopular enough that people could not be asked to pay for it.

Reagan permitted Americans to live under two social orders, two constitutional orders, at the same time. There was a pre–Great Society one and a post–Great Society one. Paying for both soon got expensive. The cost can be measured roughly by the growth of the debt, public and private, over the decades after Reagan's arrival in the White House. By 1989, the year Reagan left office, according to an estimate by the economist Roy H. Webb of the Federal Reserve Bank of Richmond, the government's unfunded liabilities (mostly for Social Security, Medicare, and veterans' benefits) had reached $4–5 trillion, and would rise exponentially if nothing were done. Nothing was done. By the time of the 2016 election, a calculation of those liabilities similar to Webb's ran to at least $135 trillion.

Ronald Reagan saved the Great Society in the same way that Franklin Roosevelt is credited by his admirers with having "saved capitalism." That is, he tamed some of its very worst excesses and found the resources to protect his own angry voters from consequences they would otherwise have found intolerable. That is what the tax cuts were for. Each of the two sides that emerged from the battles of the 1960s could comport itself as if it had won. There was no need to raise the taxes of a suburban entrepreneur in order to hire more civil rights enforcement officers at the Department of Education. There was no need to lease out oil-drilling rights in a national park in order to pay for an aircraft carrier. Failing to win a consensus for the revolutions of the 1960s, Washington instead bought off through tax cuts those who stood to lose from them. Americans would delude themselves for decades that there was something natural about this arrangement. It was an age of entitlement.

Periods of fiscal irresponsibility are often not immediately recognizable as such. Outwardly they can even look like golden ages of prosperity, because very large sums dedicated to investment are freed up for consumption. That is exactly what the standard Solow growth model and other economic descriptions of investment predict. Societies can even go through periods of extraordinary material and cultural radiance when they are on the verge of bankruptcy.

A writer can only marvel at the beauty and variety of electric typewriters that were available to the American public in the 1980s, just before word processing programs would doom them forever: Underwood, Smith-Corona, Royal, Remington, Olivetti, and the IBM Selectric, elegant, immovable, authoritative. A reader can only marvel at the quality of newspapers available in the 1980s, 1990s, and 2000s, before almost all newspapers gave way to ranting opinion websites. They were thick. The biggest *New York Times* ever, published on September 14, 1987, was 1,612 pages long and weighed 12 pounds. They were thorough, as filled with articles on everything from poetry to politics to philately to philandering as they had been throughout the twentieth century, but by the turn of the twenty-first most of them were in color!

Using resources taken from future generations, the Baby Boom generation was briefly able to offer the vision of an easy and indulgent lifestyle, convincing enough to draw vast numbers of people to construct it, like the pyramids or the medieval cathedrals or the railroads.

Immigration, inequality, and debt

Draw people it did. Collectively, American Baby Boomers cashed out of the economy their forebears had built, shifting the costs of running it not just to different generations but to different parts of the world, through outsourcing and immigration. These, too, are a form of borrowing. Low-wage immigrants subsidize the rich countries they migrate to, and this is especially true of illegal immigrants. They are low-wage precisely because they are outside the legal system. Ultimately, natives pay some kind of "bill" for such labor. Either they invite the laborers into their society, and the costs to natives take the form of overburdened institutions, rapid cultural change, and diluted political power; or they exclude the laborers, and the costs take the form of exploitation, government repression, and bad conscience. Until that bill comes due, immigration must be counted among a country's "off-balance-sheet liabilities."

These liabilities are difficult to quantify. Mass immigration can help a confident, growing society undertake large projects—the settlement of the Great Plains, for instance, or the industrialization of America's cities after the Civil War. But for a mature, settled society, mass immigration can be a poor choice, to the extent that it is a choice at all. Reagan was tasked by voters with undoing those post-1960s changes deemed unsustainable. Mass immigration was one of them, and it stands perhaps as his emblematic failure. Reagan flung open the gates to immigration while stirringly proclaiming a determination to slam them shut. Almost all of Reaganism was like that.

The Hart-Celler immigration reform of 1965 is sometimes overlooked amid the tidal wave of legislation that flowed through Congress that year. It overturned the "national origins" system, passed under the Immigration Act of 1924 and reaffirmed in 1952, that had aimed to keep the ethnic composition of the United States roughly what it was. Even in the mid-1960s, immigrants from Britain and Germany made up more than half of national "quota" immigration—and those countries plus Ireland, Italy, and Poland accounted for almost three quarters. It is hard to say exactly what the bill's backers believed they were doing. On one hand, they sang of an America that was triumphing over its historic racism. On the other, they promised even more ardently and solemnly that doing away with national-origin quotas would do nothing to change the American ethnic mix. "Quota immigration under the bill is likely to be more than 80 percent European," said its House sponsor, Emanuel Celler.

Once the bill passed, Johnson summoned the Congress to a signing ceremony hundreds of miles away at the foot of the Statue of Liberty, an extravaganza at odds with his soft-pedaling of its importance. "This bill that we will sign today is not a revolutionary bill," he said. "It does not affect the lives of millions. It will not reshape the structure of our daily lives, or really add importantly to either our wealth or our power." He did protest too much. The Hart-Celler bill would alter the demography of the United States. It would also alter the country's culture, committing the government to cut the link that had made Americans think of themselves for three centuries as, basically, a nation of transplanted Europeans.

"The American Nation returns to the finest of its traditions today," Johnson said. "The days of unlimited immigration are past." In fact, those days were past only because of the restrictive laws of 1924—which Johnson was now striking from the books. Johnson's new attorney general, Nicholas Katzenbach, shared the president's naïveté. Katzenbach had claimed, more likely from innumeracy than from any intent to deceive, that the new kind of migration would account for precisely "two one-hundredths of one percent" of future population growth. "Without injury or cost," he proclaimed, "we can now infuse justice into our immigration policy."

Senator Edward "Ted" Kennedy, younger brother of the slain president, thought this way, too. In shepherding the Hart-Celler bill through the Senate, Kennedy had been just as reckless as Katzenbach and just as wrong as LBJ. "The ethnic mix of this country will not be upset," he had said. He even named the nine countries that would be the principal beneficiaries of the new open system: China, Greece, Hungary, Italy, Japan, Poland, Portugal, Spain, and Yugoslavia. (Of these, only China would figure among the top ten sources of immigrants half a century later.) "The bill will not aggravate unemployment, nor flood the labor market with foreigners, nor cause American citizens to lose their jobs," he said. "These are myths of the first order."

But Kennedy added something new to his appeal. Barely a year after his brother's assassination, he cast the bill's opponents as unpatriotic and un-American:

Responsible discussion is expected on the provisions of any bill. The charges I have mentioned are highly emotional, irrational, and with little foundation in fact. They are out of line with the obligations of responsible citizenship. They breed hate of our heritage, and fear of a vitality which helped to build America.

Like Katzenbach, who believed that justice could be secured "without injury or cost," Kennedy had a hard time distinguishing between America's morals and its interests. It is a confusion that puts one on the road to strife. If morals and interests always coincide, then the person who opposes your interests is probably evil. In Kennedy's swagger we can see a harbinger of America's twenty-first-century political culture.

Immigration and the failure of democracy

Not only did every promise of the Hart-Celler bill's sponsors wind up wrong. Even the warnings of the bill's detractors—excitable pamphlet-pushers like the American Committee on Immigration Policies—underestimated the sea change it would bring. In the three-and-a-half centuries between its discovery and 1965, the United States had received 43 million newcomers (including a quarter-million slaves). In the half-century that followed Hart-Celler, it would get 59 million.

From that perspective, the migration problem that confronted Reagan early in his presidency was still relatively minor. An unintended consequence of the 1965 law was to favor disorderly over orderly immigration. Low-volume European migration had not required a vast rural and border enforcement apparatus, but by the mid-1970s a new kind of immigration was under way. Roughly 3 million illegal immigrants, most of them Latin American agricultural workers in the Southwest, were overburdening public services and making natives uncomfortable.

Even after the Reagan "revolution," the political parties differed

little on immigration. That is how Ted Kennedy, a driving force behind the Hart-Celler law, ended up playing a powerful role in Reagan's
attempts to fix it. In the waning days of the Carter administration,
Kennedy proposed a Select Commission on Immigration and Refugee
Policy, chose Notre Dame president Father Theodore Hesburgh to
head it, and selected the reading materials that would guide it. Two of
the Kennedy commission's members, Republican senator Alan Simpson of Wyoming and Democratic congressman Romano Mazzoli of
Kentucky, sponsored the legislation that would become the 1986 Immigration Reform and Control Act (IRCA).

Simpson-Mazzoli aimed at a bold compromise. It legalized and offered American citizenship to illegal immigrants who could prove they
had been resident in the United States for even the briefest of stays.
A Special Agricultural Worker (SAW) program gave permanent resi-
dency to workers who could show they had done 60 days of farm work
between May 1985 and May 1986, regardless of whether they knew any
English or had any understanding of American civics. A quarter-million
were estimated to be eligible for the program, but the documentation
and testimonials it required were easily counterfeited: 1.3 million
wound up using it. Those admitted came to well over 3 million in total.

To keep this easy mass legalization from incentivizing future immigration, the bill proposed shutting down illegal immigration almost
entirely. It contained documentation requirements, $123 million in
new security funding, and ferocious-looking penalties for businessmen who knowingly hired illegals. Simpson-Mazzoli brought with
it the single largest expansion of federal regulatory power since the
establishment of the Occupational Safety and Health Administration
in 1970.

There was something disquieting about this level of intrusion into
the decisions of business owners, even if it had precedents in the New
Deal's National Recovery Administration and in the Civil Rights Act,
particularly in affirmative action, which had by then been up and running for more than a decade. That turned out to be the core of the

problem. The parts of the law that encouraged immigration—the amnesty, the processing of working papers—were unpopular, but their introduction went smoothly. They were real. The parts that retarded immigration—the border controls, the employer sanctions—were popular, but they proved impossible to enforce. They were fake.

Opponents of mass immigration were inclined to see IRCA as an outright fraud perpetrated on the public. The truth was more complicated. It had to do with a change in the country's constitutional culture.

The changing spirit of civil rights

To do away with illegal immigration, Americans would have had to send a strong message, not just in their statutes but in their enforcement practices and their day-to-day behavior, to the effect that illegal immigration, and therefore illegal immigrants, were not welcome. Every poll from the time tells us that Americans intended to convey just such a message. In June 1986, those who wanted less immigration outnumbered those who wanted more of it by 7 to 1 (49 to 7 percent). Historically, whenever social change began to move too fast, this kind of gruff, coarse, reactionary plurality would "come out of the woodwork." Doris Meissner, later the commissioner of the Immigration and Naturalization Service, said of the migrants who were in the country illegally, "Everyone assumed they would just leave, that the new employer restrictions would push them out." That approach to overheated immigration might have worked in a pre-1964 America, but the country had changed. Now there *was* no woodwork.

Immigration was one of many subjects that were becoming harder to discuss openly. As late as 1975, the *Los Angeles Times* could still report on economic competition from immigrants, headlining a story "Employers Prefer Workers Who Can Be Exploited, Paid Minuscule Wages, US Officials Say." That year, 47 percent of news stories about immigration mentioned its dampening effect on wages. By the turn of the century, only 8 percent did. In 1976, the Texas Democrat Ann Richards reportedly said, in the course of a campaign for the Travis County commissioners court, "If it takes a man to hire non-union labor, cross picket lines and work wetbacks then I say thank God for a woman or anyone else who is willing to take over." It was a sentiment that most Texas liberals of the time would have been proud to avow. By 1990, when Richards made a successful run for governor, "wetback" was an inadmissible slur and the report of the old speech jeopardized her campaign.

In late amendments, the 1986 IRCA bill was filled with language stressing that an employer could be held liable for discriminating on account of national origin. This looked like window dressing, but in the new, post–Civil Rights Act judicial climate, it became the heart of the bill. It turned inside-out the penalties against employers for hiring illegal immigrants. However harsh the "employer sanctions" had originally looked on paper, they required employers to act in ways that civil rights law forbade. An American boss now had more to fear from obeying the immigration law than from flouting it. An INS official sent in 1987 to investigate a factory on Long Island suspected of using illegal labor stressed that he was there "to explain the new immigration law's provisions on employer sanctions, 'not enforce them.'" As housing secretary three years later, Jack Kemp sought a waiver that would permit the city of Costa Mesa, California, to offer welfare benefits to the newly arrived, circumventing a legal ban.

In policy terms IRCA is usually described as a mix of successes and failures. In constitutional terms it was a calamity. Presented as a means of getting immigration under control, IRCA wound up mixing explicit incentives to immigrate (via amnesty) with implicit ones (via anti-discrimination law). It provided courts and federal civil rights agencies—both of them staffed with law school graduates and other highly credentialed professionals at the very apex of the American social pyramid—with new grounds for overruling and overriding legislatures and voters on any question that could be cast as a matter of discrimination. That was coming to mean all questions. Every law was turning into an expansion of civil rights law.

In a 1994 referendum, 5 million Californians sought to deny welfare benefits to illegal immigrants, giving the state's Proposition 187 an 18-point landslide at the polls. But district court judge Mariana Pfaelzer decided they were wrong—on the grounds that limiting state welfare payments amounted to setting immigration policy, which was a prerogative not of the states but of the federal government. And that did it for Prop 187.

The wave of immigrants interacted with the country's changing legal regime in a way that would make this migration different from the last. The rags-to-riches stories of people from the most desperate corners of Asia were similar to those of early immigrant groups. Those stories, often repeated and widely publicized, reunited Americans with the pride they felt in the European melting pot of the early twentieth century. In 1983, four years after she had arrived in the United States speaking no English, the Cambodian refugee Linn Yann, whose father had been killed by the Khmer Rouge, won the Zone V spelling bee in Chattanooga, getting "exhilarate" and "rambunctious" right and losing the Chattanooga–Hamilton County finals only when given a word she had not come across in Tennessee: "enchilada."

But even when it was working best, immigration introduced tensions into the system being built up around civil rights. For one, the success of new immigrants, Nathan Glazer noted, provoked "unspoken (and sometimes spoken) criticism" of blacks for their relative slowness to rise. For another, the new migrants were being shepherded into the civil rights system as potential *victims* of discrimination, not as potential perpetrators of it. Illegal immigrants were attractive to employers because they had fewer rights in the workplace. They were unattractive to the general public because they had more rights in the courtroom. Immigrants' American-born children would have not only citizenship but also privileges that white natives' children lacked. They would be "people of color."

"People of color" and "African-Americans"

The phrase "people of color," which crept into vogue sometime during the Reagan administration, was a linguistic Rubicon. On the other side of it, an entirely new and harder-line spirit of civil rights would prevail. It is hard to say where it came from. Martin Luther King used the term "citizens of color" in his "I Have a Dream" speech, but it scarcely appeared in newspapers before 1990.

"People of color" was a harbinger of what later came to be called "intersectionality," a philosophical-sounding term for the political strategy of bundling different minorities into a coalition. Almost everyone other than white heterosexual males could benefit in some way from civil rights laws. Vast, hitherto unenvisioned coalitions, perhaps even electoral majorities, could be formed by rallying other non-white groups.

The advancement of people of color was a project different from the one that the National Association for the Advancement of Colored People had first proposed a century before. The old project had aimed at fixing an unfair system. This could best be done by talking about justice rather than race, and these were two distinct things. To impute the American race problem to anything explicitly racial, in fact, risked reproducing the old racial ways of thinking under a different name.

The politics that emerged as the twentieth century ended, by contrast, were zealously racial. They grew out of a pragmatic international solidarity against white rule that King had invoked in his 1963 letter from Birmingham City Jail. A wicked if moribund white colonialism and a world still run along Western European lines—for King, these provided a context in which the misfortunes of the American black man could be better understood:

Consciously and unconsciously, he has been swept in by what the Germans call the *Zeitgeist*, and with his black brother of Africa and his brown and yellow brothers of Asia, South America and the

Caribbean, he is moving with a sense of cosmic urgency toward
the promise[d] land of racial justice.

King's literary gift was for showing the race problem as larger and
more "cosmic" than people might have realized, but also as somehow
simpler. White people had a lot of prerogatives they did not deserve.
Fighting racism now meant attacking white privilege.

The French philosopher Jean-Paul Sartre had anticipated this
change in 1948. He described the subjugation of colonial blacks as an
exploitation analogous to that of the white working class but insisted
that their means of liberation must be different and more explicitly
race-based. "The unity which will come eventually, bringing all op-
pressed peoples together in the same struggle," Sartre wrote, "must be
preceded in the colonies by what I shall call the moment of separation
or negativity: this anti-racist racism is the only road that will lead to the
abolition of racial differences."

That turned out to be wrong. As the French sociologist Christophe
Guilluy remarked two generations later, the multiculturalism of the new
century would steadily intensify the consciousness of racial differences:

> Unlike our parents in the 1960s, we live in a multicultural society, a
> society in which "the other" doesn't become "somebody like your-
> self." And when "the other" doesn't become "somebody like your-
> self," you constantly need to ask yourself how many of the other
> there are—whether in your neighborhood or your apartment
> building. Because nobody wants to be a minority.

It was quite natural, under the circumstances, that the question of
non-white immigration should move to the dead center of American
politics. It would be what the spread of slavery in the western territo-
ries had been in the two decades before the Civil War—an issue that
could be used by one side or the other to connive at a position of permanent political dominance.

Shortly after "people of color" came into vogue, whites were given another sign that more deference would be required of them than they had anticipated in 1964. On December 20, 1988, the civil rights activist Jesse Jackson held a news conference in a Hyatt Regency hotel near Chicago's O'Hare Airport to announce that "African-American," not "black," would henceforth be the term of preference. "To be called African-Americans has cultural integrity," he said. "It puts us in our proper historical context."

There was nothing false about that, and a writer in *Ebony* magazine in 1967 had even made similar points. There had already been one nationwide change of nomenclature, in the late 1960s and early 1970s, from "Negro," the term favored by Booker T. Washington and W.E.B. Du Bois, to "black." But this new one was urged in a different spirit and brought about in a different way. The problem was a sociolinguistic one. It is true, as Jackson said in defense of his neologism, that there existed a word "European-American," but it was a scientific term. It had never been used in casual conversation, nor could it be, for the simple reason that it had eight syllables. The term "African-American" had seven—which was seven times as many as the word it replaced. People simply don't talk that way. As a linguistic matter, the word resonated as an elaborate formula of deference, like "Your Excellency" or *"radi allah tala 'anhu!"* and other not-to-be-abbreviated Arabic callings-down of peace upon scholars and companions of the Prophet.

A change in the spirit of civil rights was visible. If we think of Lyndon Johnson's Great Society as a revolution, then all of the political energies of the 1970s had been counterrevolutionary. But although no one had voted to make it so, the social changes of Reagan's late 1980s were all suddenly going *with* the grain of the Johnson revolution. The waning of a conservative quarter-century was clear by 1987, when the newly arrived Democratic majority in the Senate rejected the Yale Law School professor Robert Bork, a towering figure in American legal philosophy, for a seat on the Supreme Court.

Their discomfort was understandable. Bork had had misgivings about the constitutional basis for civil rights law, noting its potential to endanger First Amendment freedoms, and he had argued this case powerfully, not just in law reviews but in the pages of the *New Republic*. Also, as Richard Nixon's solicitor general, he had fired the Watergate special prosecutor in 1973 when his superiors refused to. But the opposition to Bork sounded immoderate and unhinged, never more so than when Ted Kennedy opened the hearings on July 1 by casting Bork as a positively Satanic figure:

> Robert Bork's America is a land in which women would be forced into back-alley abortions, blacks would sit at segregated lunch counters, rogue police could break down citizens' doors in midnight raids, schoolchildren could not be taught about evolution, writers and artists would be censored at the whim of government, and the doors of the federal courts would be shut on the fingers of millions of citizens for whom the judiciary is often the only protector of the individual rights that are the heart of our democracy.

While Kennedy's oratory still has the whiff of sulfur about it, it is clear in retrospect that he understood the stakes of the Bork nomination better than his more moderate Senate colleagues did. The Supreme Court would now be fought over with the same rancor and no-holds-barred partisanship that once marked democratic politics, because, since the legislative revolution of 1965, the courts and the bureaucracy had *replaced* democratic politics.

Kennedy asked that a joint statement by civil rights leaders Benjamin Hooks and Ralph Neas of the Leadership Conference on Civil Rights be read into the *Congressional Record*. "This is the most historic moment of the Reagan presidency," they wrote. "Senators will never cast a more important and far-reaching vote. Indeed, this decision will profoundly influence the law of the land well into the 21st century." That was a sober assessment. Every word of it was correct. Bork would be rejected in a Senate floor vote, and the vacancy occupied by a little-known Sacramento lawyer from Reagan's political circle whom Reagan himself had recommended for a judgeship a few years back: Anthony Kennedy.

An admirer of Reagan would say he accomplished something extraordinary: He tamed a furious populist movement and harnessed it to his own statesmanlike (because very different) ends. A more skeptical view of Reagan is that he was put at the command of a victorious insurgency and handed away its victories. He abused the trust of a democratic movement and created conditions under which the next populist movement that arose would be satisfied only with deeds, not words.

Immigration and inequality

A big problem with immigration was that it bred inequality. Its role in doing so was as significant as that of other factors more commonly blamed: information technology, world trade, tax cuts. In 1995, the economist George Borjas, writing in the *Journal of Economic Perspectives*, modeled the actual effects of immigration on Americans. He found that while immigration might have caused an increase in economic activity of $2.1 trillion, virtually all of those gains—98 percent—went to the immigrants themselves. When economists talk about "gains" from immigration to the receiving country, they are talking about the remaining 2 percent—about $50 billion. This $50 billion "surplus" disguises an extraordinary transfer of income and wealth: Native capitalists gain $566 billion. Native workers lose $516 billion.

One way of describing mass immigration is as a verdict on the pay structure that had arisen in the West by the 1970s: on trade unions, prevailing-wage laws, defined-benefit pension plans, long vacations, and the power workers had accumulated against their bosses more generally. These had long been, in most people's minds, excellent things. But Republicans argued that private business, alas, could not afford them, and by the 1980s they had won the argument. Immigration, like outsourcing and tighter regulation of unions, allowed employers to pay less for many kinds of labor. But immigrants came with other huge costs: new schools, new roads, translation (formal and informal), and health care for those who could not afford it. Those externalities were absorbed by the public, not the businessmen who benefited from immigration.

Naturally businessmen preferred this arrangement to the old one, which had involved paying expensive benefits to an entitled, querulous, native-born, and sometimes unionized workforce. Investment bankers preferred it, too. Their decisions on what to fund and what not to fund added impetus to the transformation of the economy. Sectors in which low-wage newcomers dominated (restaurants, landscaping, construction) began to crowd out sectors in which they did not (mostly manufacturing and local retail). Now immigration *was* the economy.

It was an extraordinary subsidy. Extraordinary things were done with it. For the class of people in the lee of immigrant competition—a class to which, at the time, virtually all politicians, business owners, financiers, and journalists belonged—the changes brought by low-cost service labor and low-cost imported goods seemed like an outright miracle. Immigrants caused a revolution in the way Americans ate—more because of the new savings that could be had from immigrant labor than because of the cuisines immigrants brought. (That is, Starbucks is as much a creation of the immigrant economy as El Taco Rico.) Inexpensive landscape gardeners made possible an explosion of golf courses and an extraordinary beautification of the country's suburbs. The drab lawns of the 1970s, treeless and bordered by cracked cement driveways and boxy, scratchy hedges—these were now replaced, even in middle-class neighborhoods, by bowers of shady willow and laurel, hydrangea bushes in half a dozen colors, and thousands of varieties of daylilies.

Outsourcing was a similar windfall. Sending manufacturing jobs abroad offered consumers all the advantages of heavy industry and none of the pollution. Americans could now have blue herons plashing and pecking in their streams and hawks swooping off their rooftops as if the Industrial Revolution had never happened—and no one would have to give up the power mower in his garage. Pollution continued at the same rate, of course: It just involved deforesting Brazil instead of pouring bilge into Lake Erie. And it would be years before people began paying attention to the cost of permanent underemployment outside the country's globalized cities.

The country outsourced repression along with jobs. Americans could get goods from authoritarian China more cheaply than from Western societies, with their trade unions and wage laws and workplace regulations. Many of the so-called developing countries did handsomely under globalization.

If we were judging open immigration and outsourcing not as economic policies but as U.S. aid programs for the world's poor, we might consider them successes. But we are not. The cultural change, the race-based constitutional demotion of natives relative to newcomers, the weakening democratic grip of the public on its government as power disappeared into back rooms and courtrooms, the staggeringly large redistributions of wealth—all these things ensured that immigration would poison American politics right down until the presidential election of 2016.

The quest for a new elite

Once inequality reaches a certain magnitude, those who have, rule. Not everyone is troubled by that. "Observe Reagan's futile attempts to arouse the country by some sort of inspirational appeal," said Ayn Rand in one of those college speeches she made in the last months of her life, when she was so nervous about the future of capitalism that even backwoods religion struck fear into her.

> He is right in thinking that the country needs an inspirational element, but he will not find it in the God-family-tradition swamp.

The greatest inspirational leadership this country could ever find rests in the hands of the most typically American group: the businessmen. But they could provide it only if they acquired philosophical self-defense and self-esteem.

At the time, the idea that anyone might look up to entrepreneurs and captains of industry sounded like a joke. If you asked before the Reagan administration who the greatest seers into the soul of mankind were, even a young man in business school would probably have replied: Poets. Or: Philosophers. The world's moguls were unbalanced, insane, and unenviable. Who would want to be Howard Hughes or John Paul Getty?

But in the 1980s, economic titans began to write autobiographies again, as if they had lessons to teach the public. They were mostly corporate executives, like Lee Iacocca and Jack Welch. One was a New York real estate developer who described his calling as "the art of the deal." And some were bankers. *Time* magazine ran a notorious cover in February 1999 describing Treasury secretary Robert Rubin, his assistant, Lawrence Summers, and Federal Reserve chairman Alan Greenspan as the "Committee to Save the World."

Society took on a Roman aspect. The very rich were held to be cool (Steve Jobs), prophetic (George Soros), or saintly (Warren Buffett). Wealth has never been without its appeal and its power. But it was striking that, more than any generation for a century, and in sharp contrast to its own declared youthful values, the Baby Boom generation *revered* wealth.

For people without a foothold in the new service and financial businesses, it was harder to make ends meet. At the start of the 1970s, homeowners—often in single-earner families—generally spent two-and-a-half years' worth of their income when they bought a house. That number began to rise and rise. By 2010, it had nearly doubled. Buying a house now took almost four-and-a-half years of a family's earnings. People could sense the deteriorating relative position of the working class even before it showed up in the statistics. Wealth was being more openly signaled, and consumers were warned that they were being sorted and tiered. A smugness that had been alien to American culture made a triumphant return. "All it takes is success," ran an ad for the Gold MasterCard in 1987.

The rich had become different once again. Upper-middle-class people stopped drinking the water that came out of their taps and began buying it bottled, from stores. The Jeep Cherokee was brought to market in 1984 as the first modern "sport-utility vehicle." SUVs would be regulated not as cars but as "light trucks," allowing them to circumvent regulations drawn for a more democratic age. Other than SUVs, domestic cars outright disappeared from the wealthiest American neighborhoods. Rich people drove BMWs, Audis, and Lexuses. You could tell you were among hoi polloi when you saw a lot of Pontiacs and Fords and Chevys parked on the street.

A culture of ambition and striving was developing. People learned from business gurus about how to take "power naps" and "power walks." Businessmen wore two-toned, white-collared shirts (which they called "power shirts") with pink, margarine-yellow, and salmon-orange ties (which they called "power ties"). What made those ties power ties was that they were effeminate. They displayed that the men who wore them were too high up the corporate or social pecking order to be safely snickered at.

The Reagan administration's model of deficit financing was like the business deals that were going on at the same time. Leveraged buyouts, which spread across the business world in the 1980s, involved borrowing against the assets of a company you didn't own in order to buy it—at which point the borrowed money could be paid back by a combination of superior efficiencies (which often did not materialize) and pitiless sell-offs (which always did).

This meant that financiers had to become more like politicians. They had to tell a story to convince the public they were advancing progress, not stripping assets. The economist and businessman Louis

Kelso, who, like Lewis B. Cullman and many others, claimed to be the inventor of the leveraged buyout, always described his financial innovation as a kind of shareholder democracy. Boardrooms were now the place for "activists"—fighters and crusaders who wanted to earn billions, fix world hunger, or preferably both at the same time.

Corporations, too, began to campaign for themselves as politicians always had. Apple rolled out its IIc model in 1984 with a series of two-page magazine ads that were longer than the articles they interrupted. "The newest member of the Apple II family," one began, "has its own reasons for being." But such ads were now explicitly political, too. Increasingly they presented the company under discussion as being in the Making-the-World-a-Better-Place Business. "Barbie: The Doll Dreams Are Made of," ran one 1986 ad showing the doll in an astronaut suit. It would be sexist *not* to buy it.

Companies were even ready to do some of the regulatory work that had heretofore been thought government's business. "Starting April 23," announced one 1988 ad, "only Northwest Airlines will prohibit smoking on all flights starting in North America." The ad ended with what, to the culture of ten years before, would have been a bizarre spectacle: a planeful of rich-looking businessmen with their power shirts and owl eyeglasses, applauding and guffawing as if they were people whom Americans might envy and emulate.

Up-and-coming businessmen like these were seldom Reaganites. They didn't appear even to *like* Reagan. Why should they? Those profiting most in the 1980s were not, as Reagan's oratory implied, government-hating small-town loners dreaming big. Nor were they cigar-chomping robber barons, as his detractors would have it. Increasingly, they were highly credentialed people profiting off of financial deregulation and various computer systems that had been developed by the Pentagon's Defense Advanced Research Projects Agency (DARPA) and the NASA space program. They were not throwbacks to William McKinley's America but harbingers of Barack Obama's. They were the sort of people you met at faculty clubs and editorial-board meetings.

Their idea of what constituted a shining city on a hill was different from the one held by the president who enriched them.

Political engagement and economic stratification came together in an almost official attitude known as snark, a sort of snobbery about other opinions that dismissed them as low-class without going to the trouble of refuting them. Why offer an argument when an eye roll would do? Snark existed before Reagan—it is visible in the mockery that intellectuals in Woody Allen's *Manhattan* (1979) aimed at their imaginary "Academy of the Overrated" (Gustav Mahler, Isak Dinesen, F. Scott Fitzgerald). And it existed after. A string of magazines in New York—*Spy, Wigwag, Egg*—embodied snark for a few months at the turn of the 1990s before folding.

But the targets of elite condescension could be roughly identified as those Americans who made up the Reagan electorate, minus the richest people in it. A new social class was coming into being that had at its disposal both capitalism's means and progressivism's sense of righteousness. It would breathe life back into the 1960s projects around race, sex, and global order that had been interrupted by the conservative uprisings of the 1970s.

6

Diversity

Computers: homogenization, dehumanization, atomization—
The truce with technology—Postmodernism: the authenticity of
Banana Republic—Bakke: Diversity begins—The Martin Luther
King holiday—The exemplary destruction of Al Campanis—
Political correctness—Diversity and the Pax Americana—
The war for the soul of America—Heather Has Two Mommies:
Diversity spreads

The decades after Ronald Reagan's arrival in power were a time of globalization and globalism. Globalization means the internationalization of the division of labor. Globalism means the political promotion of globalization, and the breaking and remaking of institutions to facilitate it. Starting in the 1980s, American businessmen freed themselves from the customs that had bound them to their country's labor force. They established a new and more profitable symbiosis with immigrants and less empowered, less well-compensated workers overseas.

It is common to lament that no means has been found to restore American laborers to the advantageous position they occupied in the 1960s. But talking workers into surrendering the advantageous redoubts they once occupied was the whole point of post-1960s economic reforms, at least for politicians, the businessmen who funded them, and the economists who advised them. Working-class prerogatives constrained innovation, it was held. They were also incompatible with government efforts to use civil rights law to reshape the labor market from above.

The security of the working class had provided a margin for error for all the social experiments of the last half-century. By 2016, that margin was gone.

Computers: homogenization, dehumanization, atomization

Computers were involved in this change—partly as cause, partly as pretext. Every newspaper editor and junior high school science teacher had been predicting for decades that the importance of computers would grow. Long before the average American had any experience of computers, they were the stuff of dystopic science fiction movies and "This does not compute!" jokes on Saturday-morning cartoons. Until well into the Reagan era, typefaces like Gemini (1965), Amelia (1967), Computer (1968), Data 70 (1970), and Orbit-B (1972) imparted a "Space Age" look to books of technological prediction, Alvin Toffler's *Future Shock* (1970), for instance. Those fonts were all patterned on E13B, designed by engineers at Stanford and General Electric in the mid-1950s for magnetic-ink check-reading machines. That an Eisenhower-era innovation looked like "futuristic" technology for three decades was a sign of complacency. Despite their long advent, the extent of change wrought by computers in the 1980s, 1990s, and 2000s caught by surprise everyone but a few well-connected industrial and financial titans.

Technology was Janus-headed. It had its good side and its bad. It could bring speed, power, comfort, and longevity but also smog, DDT, and the languor of the inveterate TV watcher. In the year after the Kennedy assassination, the University of Chicago historian Daniel Boorstin warned about the way "we have used our wealth, our literacy, our technology, and our progress, to create the thicket of unreality which stands between us and the facts of life." Computers were part of the thicket of unreality. If not kept in their place, they would deaden souls and turn people into robots. Martin Luther King, Jr., spoke of our "computerized plans of destruction" in Vietnam, and even when computers weren't dealing death they were a kind of death. As Ray Davies of the Kinks sang in "Muswell Hillbilly" (1971):

> *They're putting us in identical little boxes,*
>   *No character, just uniformity.*
> *They're trying to build a computerised community,*
>   *But they'll never make a zombie out of me.*

This was, in the 1960s and '70s, the consensus view.

What Americans liked about technology was the speed-and-power part. It was routine in the 1960s for fathers to regale their sons with stories about "the Year 2000," when jet packs and airplanes would have replaced cars. ABC-TV's first color program was *The Jetsons*, a cartoon that aired in prime time in the autumn and winter of 1962–1963. (You would hardly know from its long afterlife that it had been on the air for only a few months.) *The Jetsons* envisioned the exciting world of a century thence, in 2062—glassed-in and antiseptic but high-speed.

John F. Kennedy was then promising to do considerably more by the end of the 1960s than put a man on the moon. In a graduation speech to the U.S. Air Force Academy in Colorado Springs, then less than a decade old, the president announced to the young airmen a public-private initiative to build commercial jets that would move at twice the speed of sound: "Some of you will fly the fastest planes that have ever been built," he said. "We are talking about a plane in the end of the '60s that will move ahead at a speed faster than Mach 2 to all corners of the globe." A year later, Lockheed was projecting a supersonic transport that would go at *three* times the speed of sound.

That never happened. American capabilities in the area of transportation steadily declined. Great Britain and France collaborated on a short-lived experiment in supersonic flight, the Concorde, but fewer than two dozen were ever built. The United States, more focused on military applications, never participated. Its SR-71 "Blackbird" reconnaissance plane, developed in secret after 1964 in the Lockheed "skunk works" by engineer Kelly Johnson, set the world air speed record in 1976—a record that was still standing four decades later.

By the 2016 presidential election, the quickest flights from New York to London took 6 hours and 40 minutes, almost three quarters of an hour *longer* than they had taken during the Nixon administration. The train trip from New York to Washington, D.C.—a mere 2 hours and 15 minutes when the Beatles made it on their first American tour in 1964—now took half an hour longer on the very fastest trains. A few years into the new century, not only had the United States lost the trick of landing a man on the moon—it did not even have rockets capable of sending scientists to orbiting space stations, relying on Russian generosity for that. The "abolition of distance" was not the advance it seemed. The breakthrough was not in travel but in communications. The distance abolished was the kind that is in people's heads.

Looked at this way, computers have been not so much an expression of America's historic ingenuity as an alternative to it. In his history of economic growth in the United States, the Northwestern University economist Robert Gordon found no special productivity boost from the computer age. Outside of Silicon Valley, according to the economist Edmund Phelps, American innovation "would narrow to a trickle" after the 1960s. In 1969, U.S. Industries, Inc., had promised that within a decade the 1960s would seem like the Dark Ages, once Americans got used to "automatic highways—computerized kitchens—person-to-person television . . . food from under the sea." That would not happen for more than a generation. In the 1970s, corporations were casting about for readily marketable consumer gadgets. The Presto Meat Toaster, the Dymo Label Maker, the Hot Beverage Machine, the Hot Lather Machine: the decade seemed to promise some life-transforming invention that never appeared.

The breakthrough, when it came, would arise from attempts by Western Electric and various phone companies after the 1960s at "crossing a telephone with a TV set." The first harvest of innovation came from Japan, starting with the Panasonic Toot-a-Loop AM-radio-and-bracelet, and culminating in the Sony Walkman, the great bridge product from the industrial to the information economy, released in the final weeks of the 1970s.

Artists were generally as blind as anyone else to the upshot of computers, even as the computer age approached. Stanley Kubrick's *2001: A Space Odyssey* (1968) correctly anticipated both voiceprint security identification and, seemingly, the end of the Cold War. Kubrick, however, viewed twentieth-century American corporations as immortal, placing a Howard Johnson's motel in a space station that could be reached by a Pan Am moon shuttle.

In the Reagan years, the writer of science fiction novels Isaac Asimov praised "the logical approach to computers" espoused by the manufacturer/retailer Radio Shack. "Instead of making one computer try to do everything," he said, "Radio Shack makes many computers." Asimov was wrong. Radio Shack eventually went bankrupt pursuing that strategy, which was diametrically opposed to the one Silicon Valley's investors favored. The computer revolution, when it came, focused on all-purpose machines that could carry out a variety of functions by swapping software in and out (or switching it on and off).

Paul Verhoeven's movie *Total Recall* (1990), a futuristic depiction of the loss of freedom that information technology might someday bring, looked quaint and tame by the end of the twentieth century. The brutalist concrete buildings where the movie's characters work and meet were presented as an architecture of the future, even though architects had stopped designing buildings that way in the 1970s, a decade-and-a-half before the movie came out. Surveillance technologies, presented in the movie as the wild dystopian possibilities of a century hence, arrived in the next decade. The construction worker Douglas Quaid (Arnold Schwarzenegger) was able to remove the bulky transmitter that had been surgically placed in his nose, but he would not be able to do the same with an implanted twenty-first-century microchip.

His attempts to hide from government investigators would be doomed in an age of retinal scans and facial-recognition software. In *The Truman Show* (1998), a movie about surveillance and technological artificiality that dates from the era of email, none of those possibilities appeared—and only rarely did computers.

One is reminded of the English writer Somerset Maugham's remark that the nineteenth-century American novelist Henry James had missed one of the great episodes of world history—the rise of the United States as a great power—so he could report on the tittle-tattle of English tea party conversation. Computers appeared only rarely in art and literature and, as late as the late 1980s, it was possible to graduate from an excellent university with ambitions for a career in which computers figured not at all.

The truce with technology

The computer was a machine that was very good at *keeping track* of things. That was its main use. Keeping track of, say, automobile parts or gourmet coffee roasts in a just-in-time inventorying system. Keeping track of booty in one of those hypnotic shoot-'em-up video games like *Grand Theft Auto* (1997) or *Call of Duty* (2003), to which a large part of a generation of boys born in the 1980s and 1990s would sacrifice all the sunlit afternoons of their youth. Eventually computers would keep track of people themselves—whether following their movements along a highway in order to shorten their routes (Waze) and collect their tolls (E-ZPass), tallying their clicks and likes for the building of customer profiles, or alerting the government that they were being drawn into political radicalism. The French word for the device—*ordinateur*—captured much better what it actually did than the various cognates of "computer" in different languages. It sorted, reordered, and rearranged things.

The internet did not create this sorting function, but it offered the biggest pile of profits in history to those who could exploit it. The Brandeis University classicist Philip Slater, mentioned earlier, had predicted this development in 1970. "The gross national product will reach its highest point," he wrote, "when a material object can be interpolated between every itch and its scratch." It is enough to make one reconsider whether rich Western countries really have shifted to an immaterial or even "post-materialist" economy, as the University of Michigan sociologist Ronald Inglehart long argued. Information technology actually *introduced* materiality—an exploitable materiality—into areas that had previously been immaterial. Befriending people was once life's profoundest joy, and it was free. Friending people required buying a machine and paying Mark Zuckerberg.

There was a mystery surrounding this process: After the 1990s, which saw the internet-ization, the wiring, the data-fication of everything, the familiar complaints that technology was dehumanizing were no longer to be heard. Technology had gone from a mixed blessing to an ideal: *Honi soit qui mal y pense* (Shame on him who thinks ill of it). Steven Soderbergh's movie *Sex, Lies, and Videotape* (1989) and Sam Mendes's *American Beauty* (1999) both featured protagonists who recorded life on cheap, hand-held video cameras. Both were garlanded with awards (the Palme d'Or in the former case, the Academy Award for Best Picture in the latter) and critical praise that would mystify later generations of watchers. Both heralded the video camera as a new way of capturing the "language really spoken by men," or at least the gestures made, that was supposed to transform film in the way that William Wordsworth and Samuel Taylor Coleridge had transformed poetry in 1798 with their collection *Lyrical Ballads*—except that now another expensive appliance was to be interposed between the itch of creative inspiration and the scratch of the poem or film.

By the turn of the century, high tech was indistinguishable from the American Way. "Data," said Lawrence Summers, who was secretary of the Treasury at the end of Bill Clinton's administration and president of Harvard after that, "is the ultimate public good." When a dictatorship deserved to be toppled, its benightedness was often illustrated through its ignorance of technology. During the U.S.-led war on Serbia in 1999, stories circulated that soldiers of the rump Yugoslavia who had raided a Belgrade opposition radio station had ordered journalists to "hand over the internet." By contrast, any twenty-first-century uprising—from Cairo to Qom to Kiev—that could be presented as the work of young people communicating via social media received the benediction of pundits and the State Department.

Congress in 1998 passed a law cheekily called the Internet Tax Freedom Act, which banned the taxation of internet access, as well as special taxes on internet companies. Since state politicians were no more knowledgeable than anyone else about how to levy sales taxes on computerized transactions they never saw, the government had effectively conferred tax exemption on the new online book emporium Amazon, and with it a multi-percentage-point pricing advantage over brick-and-mortar stores that would allow the company to crush all of the country's nationwide book chains and major independent stores within two decades.

Some people with a low opinion of the 1960s blamed the tech culture for institutionalizing the ideals of that decade. "The personal computer, and its offshoot the internet," wrote the French journalist and historian Eric Zemmour, "would amplify the revolutionary potential of the 1968 gospel: individualistic, cosmopolitan, anti-hierarchical, and anti-state." Others blamed the tech culture for doing just the opposite. It had *undermined* the ideals of the 1960s, making the world more hierarchical, not less. It was "evil," according to the independent historian Kirkpatrick Sale, "that computerization enables the large forces of our civilization to operate more swiftly and efficiently in their pernicious goals of making money and producing things." Certainly it would have surprised a pot-smoking, natural food–eating skinny-dipper at Woodstock to be told that the single greatest achievement of his generation would be to bring computers into corners of American life unimagined then—to put a television screen in everyone's jacket pocket.

Even if pessimists like Sale had the better of the political argument, twenty-first-century citizen/consumers were focused less on politics than on esthetics. Kevin Kelly, the editor of *Wired* magazine, insisted that the industrial technology, with its uniformity and regularity, was being superseded by "technology that's decentralized, that plays on differences, that's irregular on demand, that's nonlinear, and that's very interactive." Such technology had been an aspiration of the counter-culture, too. When Robert Pirsig was riding his motorcycle around in the late 1960s preaching against low-quality technology, a plethora of personalized, democratic, and "empowering" products, such as the Polaroid instant camera, were already winning the country over. In *Zen and the Art of Motorcycle Maintenance*, Pirsig held out hope. When technologists embrace quality, he preached, "the specter of technology ... becomes not an evil but a positive fun thing."

By the 1990s, a revolution in ergonomics, convenience, and utili-tarian design was under way. It was Steve Jobs and the designers of var-ious Apple products who were most associated with it, but the change was visible even in the most primitive industrial-age forms. Oxo's smooth-handled can opener would not hurt your hand the way the old ones did, nor would its whisks collect egg yolk. A twenty-first-century Carrier air-conditioning window unit had rounded plastic corners, not the sharp, rustable metal ones that had filled the country's emergency rooms with inattentive children in the 1960s and '70s. A Miele vacuum cleaner might not wake up the whole house if switched on downstairs on a Sunday morning. Americans left for another day the question of whether the country was getting more or less free. For consumers who remembered the late 1970s, it was enough that the country was getting less crappy.

Postmodernism: the authenticity of Banana Republic

As Americans' new machines were recording reality with ever more precision, irrationality and even superstition were on the rise. This is not as paradoxical as it sounds. Acquired knowledge obeys a

Malthusian logic: Each new fact brings a handful of new questions, which, when answered, bring a handful more. Facts grow arithmetically, but questions grow geometrically. The result is a deterioration of certitude. The closer we get to the truth, the less confident we are in our possession of it.

The old word for this state of affairs was *relativism*. The French adage *Tout comprendre, c'est tout pardonner* ("To understand is to forgive") summed it up. The new word for it was "postmodernism." "Postmodernist" was coined, most likely, by the architect Charles Jencks in 1968, applied to politics by the French philosopher Jean-François Lyotard in 1979, and developed into an almost coherent philosophy by the critic Fredric Jameson in the 1980s and '90s.

But there was a difference between relativism and postmodernism. Relativism was a kind of tolerance. Postmodernism was a kind of insurgency. Postmodernism described narratives, from communism to mainline Christianity, that—interesting though they might be as myths—were losing their power to bind people into communities and spur them to action. Postmodernism also vied with those narratives: It was a project to delegitimize them. Every institution it penetrated, it politicized.

A burden of proof fell on conservatives. Nothing was taken for granted, given the benefit of the doubt, or grandfathered in. By early in the twenty-first century, there were dozens of books in print with a title or subtitle in the form "Why [Something] Matters"—*Why Writing Matters, Why Gender Matters, Why Wall Street Matters, Why Orwell Matters*—as if to pre-empt mockery. It was natural that, when one thing was held to be as good as another, the adjective "compelling" became literary critics' all-purpose synonym for "good." By the year 2000, the word was being used twice as frequently as it had been during the Eisenhower administration.

Postmodern writers and critics naturally took up one of the great obsessions of the 1960s and '70s: authenticity. Back then, the counterculture had been divided into many bickering currents, but there was one viewpoint that all of them shared: a dismay that the United States was so fake. Uniform housing developments that either made claims to be what they were not ("Heritage Boulevard") or purported to celebrate what they had actually destroyed ("Oak Meadows"), a Procrustean educational culture (although worse was still to come), factory-made food—these were powerful symbols of the dishonest basis on which the culture was built. The postmodernists' way of addressing these issues was the one that artist Andy Warhol had pioneered in the 1960s: They saw that, most of the time, Americans not only tolerated fakeness but embraced it.

In the late 1970s, a San Francisco couple set up a company called Banana Republic to sell "authentic safari & expedition clothing." Whether the clothes were authentic or imitation was unclear even in the mind of the company's co-founder Patricia Gwilliam when she was interviewed for its catalog in 1978. "Authentic bush garments are nearly impossible to find," she said. "So I figured that somewhere in this world there had to be authentic safari clothes, and I decided I would find them." Having learned that the military surplus of foreign nations was the best source of "safari-style" clothing, she set off around the world. She also had "friends and buyers, scouting surplus for us from Iceland to the tip of Africa." They often came up with items of high quality, according to Gwilliam, and, if not, no worries. "What I couldn't find, I'd design, using original fabrics if I could find them, and if not I would find natural fabrics that were as good as the originals."

It was an extraordinary elision: a promise of authentic merchandise, with a codicil permitting the seller to substitute something inauthentic and even scrambled up. It was impossible to tell from the early Banana Republic catalog description whether the "Israeli paratroopers messenger bags" had been bought in bulk from some newly demobilized sabra quartermaster in Haifa or whether it was just some Bay Area executive's idea of a comely tote bag, contracted out to a factory in Thailand. As for whether the company's cotton backpack had really been "slightly used by British soldiers serving in the tropics," you would have to give it a sniff to find out.

Only a minor adjustment was required to turn a countercultural project promising a more direct and authentic way of dressing into a run-of-the-mill American clothing corporation. Once you began thinking about it, the categories of real and fake seemed contingent and hard to set apart. What were "original fabrics"? The customer was supposed to let his skepticism go and content himself with inhabiting the dream. Just as the 1950s had had synthetic wood, the 1970s and '80s would bring "pre-washed" jeans and the '90s "distressed" furniture. If they were imitations, they were authentic imitations.

The seller had the leeway not just to embroider the description of his product but to come up with a new identity for himself. In 1980, the Häagen-Dazs ice cream company accused a competitor, Frusen Glädjé, of ripping off Häagen-Dazs's "unique Scandinavian marketing theme." One of the grounds for the suit was that Frusen Glädjé, like its older competitor, was "a two-word germanic-sounding name having an umlaut (¨) over the letter 'a.'" At first glance that seemed a preposterous claim: A Scandinavian ice cream company stood accused of violating someone else's copyright on being Scandinavian. Well, there was nothing authentically Scandinavian about Frusen Glädjé, it turned out, except the more or less Swedish-sounding name. The ice cream was made in Pennsylvania by a guy named Richard E. Smith. But it was still just as Scandinavian as Häagen-Dazs, which had been named with a Nordic-looking nonsense word by its founder, Reuben Mattus of Brooklyn, and was manufactured in New Jersey.

Over the same period the age-old, verbless American question "Where you from?" changed its meaning. In the middle of the twentieth century, it was an inquiry as to one's birthplace or native city or state. The answer did not change in the course of a person's life. By the early twenty-first century, the question had become an oblique and pretentious way of asking "Where do you live?" There was something illegitimate in curiosity about birthplace, with its assumption that any aspect of identity could be ineluctable. Dealt fates were being crowded out by chosen identities.

No one wanted to be pinned down any more than he had to be. The astonishing growth in so-called self-storage facilities reflected an indecisiveness about moving house and throwing stuff out. Those huge rentable hangars with their rows of garage doors hadn't even existed before 1964, when two friends in Odessa, Texas, opened A-1 U-Store-It U-Lock-It U-Carry-the-Key. By 2015, there were almost 50,000 of them, four times as many as there were Starbucks, adding up to 21 square feet of storage space for every American household.

Something deeper was at work. Introducing the 1962 lecture by Leo Strauss, "Why We Remain Jews," that we mentioned earlier, Strauss's friend and collaborator, the political theorist Joseph Cropsey, confessed himself fascinated by the way Strauss's question, in the light of modern science and politics, "can easily be transformed, with some modifications, into the question of why anybody should remain *anything* he happens to be to begin with."

Understanding this is necessary to understanding the political anxiety that overtook the United States in the second decade of the twenty-first century. Fascinating though the paradoxes of postmodernism are to intellectuals, they are not principles for living. Most people hate them. If all arguments and narratives were "unstable" or "contingent," who would take the trouble to learn the facts on which they are based? On what basis would respect for truth rest? On what basis respect for other human beings? Such questions were not low-stakes at all. The collapse of old absolutisms was supposed to open up space for diversity. It opened up space for something of that name, which soon showed signs of becoming an absolutism itself.

Bakke: Diversity begins

"Diversity"—the governing principle, as distinct from the abstract noun—was introduced by the U.S. Supreme Court, almost accidentally, in 1978. It was a moment of mortal peril for affirmative action, the main avenue through which civil rights law was changing the country's public and private institutions.

Allan Bakke's application to the medical school at the University of California, Davis, had been rejected twice. The school blamed his age. Bakke, who had served in Vietnam as a Marine captain and worked as a NASA engineer, was 33 when he applied. He himself blamed the university's "task force program," an affirmative action program that set aside spots for 16 minority students in every class of 100.

Bakke's scores on the multi-part Medical College Admission Test (MCAT) would normally have won him admission to even the most elite medical schools. They were in the 96th, 94th, 97th, and 72nd percentiles. The averages for Davis admittees were 69, 67, 82, and 72. The averages for minorities admitted through the university's set-aside program were 34, 30, 37, and 18.

California judges ordered Bakke admitted and the special program scrapped as racially discriminatory. The university appealed the case to the Supreme Court. Eight of the nine justices voted to uphold Bakke's admission. But the court deadlocked on political lines when it came to the affirmative action program that had deprived him of admission. That such programs discriminated, by reallocating opportunities from whites to blacks and other minorities, was obvious. It was their whole point. The justices were concerned with *how* the programs discriminated, and on what grounds. Four accepted the California court's view that affirmative action had turned into an upside-down Jim Crow— something repugnant to American conceptions of equality. But four accepted Lyndon Johnson's description of American society as a footrace to which one runner had arrived shackled—on that basis, they could countenance some infringement on whites' individual rights in order to fix a society-deforming wrong.

Justice Lewis Powell wrote a decision that tried to reconcile the two sides. He accepted the logic of his colleagues who found affirmative action appalling but voted with his colleagues who found it appealing. He thought it was wrong to penalize an individual like Bakke as a means of "compensation for past discrimination." He thought admitting people on the basis of racial quotas was wrong. But he thought it would be okay for UC Davis to achieve the same result by filling its slots the way Harvard's undergraduate admissions program did—not through quotas but through a "new definition of diversity" that allowed administrators to use race as a "plus factor."

Powell's suggestion that Harvard College's experience of affirmative action might serve as a model for provincial public professional schools was, to put it mildly, confused. The basic problem that affirmative action existed to solve was a shortage of blacks qualified to fill leadership positions. With its wealth and prestige, Harvard would have an easier time attracting and forming such people than any other institution in the world.

Affirmative action's most ingenious defender, the Anglo-American legal philosopher Ronald Dworkin, saw immediately that Powell had mistaken a constitutional question for an administrative one. "The handicap [used in the diversity-based admissions system that Powell proposed] and the partial exclusion [used in the quota-based one he overturned] are only different means of enforcing the same fundamental classifications," Dworkin wrote. "In principle, they affect a white applicant in exactly the same way—by reducing his overall chances—and neither is, in any important sense, more 'individualized.' "

Powell's opinion, in short, did not eliminate quotas. It just dressed them up as something else. It required all schools that used racial preferences to recast them as programs to promote their interest in the diversity of their student bodies. That was an interest that many universities had not realized they had. Yes, some liberal-arts schools had gone out of their way to admit, say, musicians and athletes—but it was not something that professional schools did. Nor was it the kind of diversity the justices meant. Admitting blacks on this basis was now a legal requirement.

Until then, most social thinkers in the Western tradition had considered diversity of the sort Powell contemplated not a condition of citizens' rights but rather an obstacle to them: "Free institutions are next to impossible in a country made up of different nationalities," wrote John Stuart Mill in his *Considerations on Representative Government*. Mill would have expected that the more loudly a country professed its commitment to diversity, the less tolerance it would have for actual dissent.

Title VI of the Civil Rights Act of 1964 had permitted the federal government to withhold funding from school boards and other entities found to have discriminated. The Office for Civil Rights (OCR) in the Department of Health, Education and Welfare (later the Department of Education) had been tasked with deciding when such cutoffs were justified. But within a decade it had invented a new task for itself that was at some remove from the one the statutes had given it. The OCR was now writing detailed standards for racial balance that courts accepted as grounds for ordering injunctive relief. Those standards were called quotas in 1970 and diversity after 1990. What is more, the OCR model was "cloned" in one federal agency after another. Since repairing race relations was taken as an emergency, the safeguards that had been in place to prevent abuses in regulation writing—from traditions of "notice and comment" to newer applications of the Administrative Procedure Act—were never applied.

That innovation caused civil rights law to work in a very different way from laws in the past. For instance, no law required busing to desegregate schools, and the 1964 Civil Rights Act seemed to forbid it. But after 1966, the Justice Department's OCR issued guidelines that set percentage targets for black student populations and opened the door to busing. Federal courts treated these guidelines as if they were law itself, and called on lower courts to follow *future* guidelines, which could only embolden the OCR. So without the participation—or even the knowledge—of the broad, non-lawyerly public, progressive legal projects ricocheted from bureaucrats to judges and back, growing more ambitious and onerous with each bounce. A net of regulatory power soon constrained "the conduct of nearly every employer, school and unit of state and local government in the country," as the political scientist R. Shep Melnick put it.

Affirmative action was unpopular. As most Americans saw it, it was unfair. But until *Bakke* it had at least been morally intelligible to a broad public: It sought to atone and compensate for slavery and Jim Crow. No lesser task would have justified giving the government such powerful, arbitrary, and constitutionally dubious tools. *Bakke* altered that rationale. Racial preference was meant to remedy not past but *present* discrimination. If there was no evidence of such discrimination, it could only be because the whites who held power were hiding it. They were practicing racism deviously, underhandedly—or, at the very least, unwittingly.

This was not the glorious role white Americans had envisioned for themselves when they came bearing what they saw as the gift of civil rights in 1964. And to look at the evidence from the *Bakke* opinion, the case that they were systematically denying opportunities to black people seemed weak. A white man rejected with scores in the 97th percentile while minorities got admitted with scores in the 18th!

The range of things that had to be explained away was broadening considerably. It would have been futile to admit blacks to college, and to prestigious jobs, on easier terms than whites if people were free to say that, for instance, the degree of a black woman admitted to Princeton in the *Bakke* era did not measure the same things as the degrees of her white classmates, impressive though that woman might be on her own terms. Or if people were free to ask why it was that immigrants who had spent their early-childhood years hunted by the Khmer Rouge were outperforming American blacks in schools.

In 1978, the year of the *Bakke* decision, Nathan Glazer could still write:

The fundamental challenge to the requirement that work forces should reflect availability is that the differences among ethnic and minority groups, and men and women, are real differences, deeply based, and that requiring any fixed proportions of one group or an- other to be hired or promoted inevitably means that employers must act as if these differences do not exist. . . . The most crucial point about the occupational distribution of ethnic groups in the United States is that this distribution is only in part—and probably for most of the protected groups in small part—owing to discrimination.

This sort of talk became, for all intents, illegal. Civil rights, as it de- veloped after the *Bakke* case, required censorship. The imputation of free-standing, spontaneously arising racism—racism with no cause or justification, like some force of nature, and which no reference to history or custom could mitigate or justify—was the only logical chan- nel for the exercise of power that the "diversity" doctrine had dug. If people were permitted to take positions like Glazer's, to argue that any part of the difference in outcomes between the races was attributable to anything other than racism, the entire logic of civil rights law would break down. So now the government got into the business of promul- gating attitudes about race.

The Martin Luther King holiday

When Ronald Reagan arrived in office, a handful of states had a holi- day celebrating Martin Luther King, Jr. Many more had chosen not to have one. Reagan signed a federal King holiday into law in 1983. Glo- rious and tragic though King's life was, the felt need to commemorate it was waning in the 1980s. The city council in San Diego had changed the name of Market Street to Martin Luther King Way in 1986, only to see voters reverse the change by a landslide margin in a referendum a year later. Young and politically active blacks were themselves not sure that King was the civil rights hero most deserving of commemoration. The more confrontational strategies of Malcolm X, assassinated three years before King, were more popular.

Though many whites saw the King day as a "black holiday," there was a case for white people to honor him as well. It was like the case that the abolitionist Charles Francis Adams, Jr., writing decades after the Civil War, had laid out for calling Robert E. Lee an American hero and not just a Southern hero—that he had forsworn violence even as many of his allies were urging it. King, similarly, had created a middle ground where the two races could meet.

Now, though, it was a different world. Immigration was beginning to create a country with several races, not two. King's vision of deseg-regation had been one in which his children would "not be judged by the color of their skin, but by the content of their character." The insti-tutions of desegregation set up by the courts rejected that approach. They took account of race as never before.

The more distant King's vision of race relations became, the more imperative it became to advertise it as if that were the vision of race relations the country had gotten. By the end of the 1980s, there were only three states left that did not have a King holiday: New Hampshire, Montana, and Arizona. Each commemorated civil rights in its own way, but the idea of states' going their own way was now intolerable. It was not enough that everyone have some kind of holiday celebrating racial harmony—every single state must now honor King, and affirm its delight in doing so.

This was deemed more important than respecting democratic forms. In May 1986, when the Arizona state legislature rejected a bill creating a King holiday, Governor Bruce Babbitt declared one by exec-utive order. The sequel hinted at the politics America would fall into three decades later. A gauche Air Force veteran and Pontiac salesman named Evan Mecham complained about the new holiday. "It has the effect of elevating King while demoting Washington and Lincoln," he said, "which I think is a disgrace." A stickler would say Mecham was wrong, but he had a point: The federal Uniform Monday Holiday Act, passed in 1968, had moved the celebration of George Washington's birthday (February 22) to the week before, where it often falls in the same week as Lincoln's (February 12) but never on Washington's birth-day itself. Most states renamed the moved holiday Presidents' Day, al-though its official federal name remained (and remains) Washington's Birthday. Mecham was arguing that that consolidation had somehow "made room" for a King day.

Arizonans would probably have let the matter go, had Mecham not been able to paint Babbitt's move as a constitutional usurpation. Mecham was zealous about the Constitution; on such matters he professed himself the follower of a firebrand fellow Mormon named W. Cleon Skousen. Behind a Republican coalition, unusual at the time, of retirees and the less educated, Mecham won the governorship and canceled the holiday.

The movement for a King holiday now became a movement to oust Gov. Mecham by any possible means. A recall drive was launched against him in his first days in office. (He was eventually impeached for misuse of campaign funds, though no crime was ever proved against him.) A gay insurance millionaire named Ed Buck led the drive, elic-iting invidious bumper stickers ("Queer Ed Buck's Recall") from Me-cham's supporters. Once it was apparent that Babbitt's executive order would not stand, vast resources were devoted to diverting Arizona's democracy from the channels in which it had flowed. Two referenda were held in 1990 to restore the holiday, under a threat from the NFL to move the 1993 Super Bowl, scheduled for Phoenix, if an MLK hol-iday did not result. Voters rejected both referenda, giving one of them less than a quarter of their votes. The NFL made good on its threat within hours. Trade associations canceled a quarter-billion dollars' worth of conventions.

Voters eventually passed the holiday in a 1992 referendum. Some-how the passage of a holiday honoring King in one state had turned out to be a vital matter for boardrooms not just in Phoenix but ev-erywhere. Corporations and businesses put up almost all of the un-counted millions behind the Yes campaign. (The No campaign raised only $6,000.) Whatever it was that stirred business about the holiday, it was not King himself. Consultant Paul Mandabach, whose public relations firm, Winner/Wagner & Mandabach, marketed the campaign, later said that the key to passing the holiday had been "messages emphasizing American values—not Dr. King's life." Businessmen rallied behind the King holiday in the name of those values, arguing not so much in political terms as in religious ones. It was a "battle for Arizona's soul." Political activists were coming to relish this kind of theological talk. The adjective "iconic" was creeping into American English as a replacement for "famous" or "significant"—it would be used ten times as frequently in the early twenty-first century as it had been at the end of World War II.

Now there were sacraments of both adoration and anathema. Bono Hewson (as he was then called) and his band, U2, were scheduled to play two concerts at Arizona State University in early April of 1987, three months into the controversy over the King holiday. Activists made contact with them. Their manager offered to cancel their shows if that was the "mood of the community." But this was not what the holiday campaigners wanted. Instead, U2 agreed to a deal by which they would contribute money to a Recall Mecham committee and read a denunciation of Mecham onstage—in a controversy of which U2 had had no knowledge when they landed at Sky Harbor.

Paul Eckstein, the Phoenix lawyer who led the impeachment proceedings against Mecham, explained that King was to be celebrated because he had "brought an end to our national shame." Eckstein was wrong. He misunderstood and underestimated King and his method. In a 1963 interview on a Massachusetts public television station, King had been questioned about Malcolm X's criticism that his non-violence played "into the hands of the white oppressors." King replied that no one who had the slightest familiarity with the dynamics of Southern protest would say such a thing:

I think it arouses a sense of shame within them often. In many instances, I think it does something to touch the conscience and

establish a sense of guilt. . . . This approach certainly doesn't make
the white man feel comfortable. I think it does the other thing. It
disturbs this conscience and it disturbs this sense of contentment
he's had.

People whose contentment has been disturbed are not usually
grateful. For many white Americans, particularly outside the South,
the King holiday did the opposite of what Eckstein said it would. It
marked not the end but the beginning of shame, of an official culture
that cast their country's history as one of oppression, and its ideals of
liberty as hypocrisies. The official understanding of the American race
problem now came to resemble in almost every particular the *Vergangenheitsbewältigung* (coming to terms with the past) through which
Germans had for decades been confronting their responsibility for
Nazism and the Holocaust.

Certain whites, however, far from feeling the shame of racism, stood
in a newfound moral effulgence as fighters against it, sharing a little bit
of Martin Luther King's glory. It seemed coincidence at first that they
were generally society's leaders. CEOs, lawyers, professors, and other
rich and well-educated people who had allied with civil rights activists to prevail against Arizona's uncooperative democracy—these were
now the custodians of America's conscience, the priests of the nation's
repentance.

As we have noted, this was a "postmodern" era, when all narratives
of religion, patriotism, material progress, scientific objectivity, and
gentlemanly virtue were under suspicion. But the narrative of racial
justice that had motivated the activists of the 1960s was an exception. Alone among historical accounts, it was above suspicion. As the
unique surviving narrative, it became a moral beacon. When President
Gerald R. Ford first officially recognized Black History Month in 1976,
calling upon the public to "honor the too-often-neglected accomplishments of black Americans," it seemed a negligible development, a perfunctory bit of officialese. The *New York Times* gave the story two small

paragraphs at the bottom of the fifth column on page 33 of a Wednesday morning paper. Yet by the twenty-first century, black history was
far from neglected. It was fair to say that ethnic studies had taken over
not just college curricula but even primary and secondary school history teaching. In 2008, education professors from Stanford and the
University of Maryland asked 2,000 eleventh and twelfth graders to
name the ten most significant Americans who had never been president. Three standbys of Black History Month—Martin Luther King,
the anti-segregationist protester Rosa Parks, and the escaped slave
Harriet Tubman—ranked 1, 2, and 3, far ahead of (for example) Benjamin Franklin, Emily Dickinson, Mark Twain, Thomas Edison, and
Henry Ford.

The exemplary destruction of Al Campanis

At the start of the 1987 baseball season, Ted Koppel, the host of ABC's
Nightline, invited Los Angeles Dodgers executive Al Campanis to discuss the fortieth anniversary of Jackie Robinson's rookie season as the
first black player in the major leagues. Perhaps Campanis was expecting
a sleepy chat. Koppel confronted him with the question of why baseball had been so slow to hire blacks as managers and general managers.
"I really can't answer that question directly," Campanis said. There *were*
black managers, he explained, and perhaps the most prominent former
players had found better opportunities elsewhere.

"Baloney," Koppel replied. "Is there still *that much prejudice* in baseball today?"

Campanis suddenly found himself in an awkward position—
defending his employers and his colleagues against a charge of bigotry.
He responded with a string of clumsy answers. "They may not have
some of the necessities to be, let's say, a field manager, or perhaps a general manager," he said. Then, perhaps as a way of parrying any sinister
interpretation that might be put on the word "necessities," he started
blurting out his thoughts, which grew more and more tangled. "Why

are black men not good swimmers?" he asked, before answering his own question. "Because they don't have the buoyancy."

Dodgers owner Peter O'Malley tried to defend Campanis, but there was pointed rage from baseball hero Hank Aaron, the NAACP, the Urban League, and prominent black politicians in Los Angeles, including mayor Tom Bradley. Assemblywoman Maxine Waters came up with an activist innovation. She demanded that the Dodgers cut all ties with Campanis, who had been working for the Dodgers since 1943. O'Malley gave in to this demand, making clear to the *Los Angeles Times* that Campanis "will not be given another position in the organization, nor will he serve as consultant." Discouraging or disciplining racist attitudes was no longer enough—it had become necessary to destroy the life and livelihood of anyone even suspected of harboring them.

To understand Campanis's position, one must understand his role in Jackie Robinson's life. The two had been teammates with the Montreal Royals in 1946, at a time when Robinson was the target of ostracism by rival players and hostility from fans. Campanis became Robinson's roommate in the middle of that controversy, and would remain his friend until Robinson's death in 1972. Well after Campanis and Robinson's time, until the turn of the 1970s, in fact, blacks and whites rooming together was almost unheard of. "That's why you'd usually see an even number of blacks on teams," Robinson's teammate Carl Erskine later recalled. Robinson never had a white roommate in the major leagues.

Campanis, that is, had been invited to the interview that would end his career because he was a hero of racial integration. Interviewed twenty years later about the incident, Koppel, admitting to knowing "nothing" about baseball, said: "Al Campanis must have been a pretty extraordinary guy."

His humiliation was a watershed. Half a year later, the CBS on-screen football bookmaker Jimmy "the Greek" Snyder, drunk at a Martin Luther King Day lunch at Duke Zeibert's bar in Washington, D.C., tried to address the issue before a black journalist and a cameraman for WRC-TV. "If they take over coaching like everyone wants them to, there's not gonna be anything left for the white people," he said. Then he baldly stated that "the black is a better athlete to begin with" and made a few speculative comments about how blacks had been bred for strength during "the Civil War." (He was not a historian.) His friendships with the football stars Walter Payton, Ahmad Rashad, Irv Cross, and Gene Upshaw, all of whom later vouched for his character, were insufficient to rescue him. CBS did not merely fire Jimmy the Greek. It denounced him, terming his remarks "reprehensible."

Such episodes showed the double-edged nature of civil rights. The major leagues established an affirmative action program within days of Campanis's disgrace and hired a sociologist to lead an executive search. Retired first baseman Bill White became the first black president of the National League. The young ABC producer who had first booked Campanis, while admitting to feeling "slightly tinged by guilt," consoled himself that all this activity on behalf of diversity was "not a bad legacy."

That is uncertain. The price of that legacy was a system of censorship. People resisted calling it by its name, but censorship it most certainly was—government censorship, adapted for an age in which all sorts of government functions, from troop provision to prison construction, were being outsourced to private entities. It worked through a civil court system that had seen its scope and punitive capacities enhanced by civil rights law. Litigation could make it embarrassing, expensive, and potentially fatal to an organization like the Los Angeles Dodgers or CBS to have anyone in their employ speculating, woolgathering, or talking off the cuff.

It was an institutional innovation. It grew directly out of civil rights law. Just as affirmative action in universities and corporations had privatized the enforcement of integration, the fear of litigation privatized the suppression of disagreement, or even of speculation. The government would not need to punish directly the people who dissented from its doctrines. Boards of directors and boards of trustees, fearing lawsuits, would do that.

Campanis and Snyder were both in their seventies: old men. "What a shame," their contemporaries would have muttered. But you can imagine the effect that their disgrace would have had on a 29-year-old in the Dodgers' front office who was still five promotions away from occupying Campanis's position. Americans in all walks of life began to talk about the smallest things as if they would have their lives destroyed for holding the wrong opinion. And this was a reasonable assumption. Over the decades, one hapless white after another would see his career brought to a sudden stop when a tantrum, a drunken slip, or some imperfectly calibrated phrase revealed wrong attitudes about race, gender, or sexuality. Cant was the only way a sensibly self-protective person would talk about race in public—and when it came to civil rights, every place was public.

Because there was no statutory "smoking gun" behind it, this new system of censorship was easily mistaken for a change in the public mood, although it remained a mystery how a mood so minoritarian could be so authoritative. The system itself came to be called political correctness.

Political correctness

Never did a movement seem more assured of history's derision. Political correctness, or P.C., as it was called by everyone except its adherents, was a grab bag of political stances descended from queer theory, critical race theory, critical legal studies, post-colonial studies, and various other new academic schools of thought. It aimed at the redesign of institutions and philosophies so that they might recognize, accept, vindicate, validate, and console groups deemed disadvantaged: blacks, women, gays, immigrants. The intellectual signature of P.C., wherever it appeared, was an unwillingness to distinguish between institutions (which could be oppressive) and opinions (which could only be misguided).

But the origins of P.C. were political, not intellectual. They lay in feminist and anti-racist activism. Of all the battles that pitted students against forces of order in 1968—from demonstrations against administrative high-handedness at Columbia University to clashes with police at the Chicago Democratic convention—the most consequential, in retrospect, was the five-month strike launched by the Black Student Union and the Third World Liberation Front (TWLF) at San Francisco State University that fall. At the end of it, the university established the first ethnic studies departments in the United States. Thus began a process that would saturate the national culture with racial and gender politics.

These ethnic studies departments, which had spread to virtually all universities by the end of the 1970s, aimed not so much at understanding power relations among ethnic groups as at transforming them. Another purpose was to provide a welcoming landing spot for students admitted under affirmative action programs. By the end of the 1980s, the spirit of "teach-ins" had taken over entire colleges. Antioch in Ohio instituted a policy, designed by a group called Womyn of Antioch, requiring explicit verbal assent at every stage of an escalating romantic encounter and establishing the on-campus position of "sexual offense advocate." The Modern Language Association gave its academic conferences over to such panels as "The Muse of Masturbation."

At City College of New York, the Afrocentric scholar Leonard Jeffries laid out theories of how his own people ("sun people") had invented virtually everything worthwhile in Western philosophy and culture. They had been robbed of the credit, though, by "ice people," as Jeffries called the "slick and devilish and dirty and dastardly" people descended from Europeans. Jeffries meant that eighteenth-century classicists denied Egyptians credit for the columned temples they ascribed to Athens and that modern historians wrote black inventors like Benjamin Banneker and Granville Woods out of their narratives, the better to glorify Alexander Graham Bell and Thomas Edison. Running blacks down, he said, was the aim of a "conspiracy, planned and plotted and programmed out of Hollywood" by "people called Greenberg and Weisberg and Trigliani and whatnot."

Armed with such anecdotes, P.C.'s enemies presented it as an enthusiasm of radical, intemperate, and disreputable scholars. But that was not the heart of P.C. at all. The heart of it was a set of sober procedures promulgated by cautious academic administrators and government regulators frightened of civil rights law. The University of Maryland reprimanded students flying American flags out their dormitory windows, on the grounds that "this is a very diverse community, and what may be innocent to one person may be insulting to another." The University of Connecticut banned "inappropriately directed laughter." Disciplinary or counseling programs for those with conservative views were set up at Stanford, Wisconsin, and Michigan.

Traditionally there had been extraordinary expressive freedom in the United States. "Free speech, free press, free exercise of religion are placed separate and apart," wrote Supreme Court justice William O. Douglas. "They are above and beyond the police power; they are not subject to regulation in the manner of factories, slums, apartment houses, production of oil and the like." This conception of First Amendment freedoms was being eroded.

Douglas's warning came in the form of a dissent in *Beauharnais v. Illinois* (1952), in which the Supreme Court asserted that it was possible to libel a group. The case involved an activist who had handed out pamphlets defending racist housing practices in metropolitan Chicago. Douglas didn't endorse the man's opinions, but they didn't strike him as a reason to narrow the First Amendment, either. He wrote:

Today a white man stands convicted for protesting in unseemly language against our decisions invalidating restrictive covenants. Tomorrow a Negro will be haled before a court for denouncing lynch law in heated terms. Farm laborers in the West who compete with field hands drifting up from Mexico; whites who feel the pressure of Orientals; a minority which finds employment going to members of the dominant religious group—all of these are caught in the mesh of today's decision.

How strange that passage sounds in our day. Douglas not only considered all these positions legitimate ones to argue over, he implied that only a tyranny would restrict them. By the end of the Cold War, all these opinions, save that of the black man denouncing lynch law, would have been dangerous to express in public.

Diversity and the Pax Americana

National newspapers and magazines started raising alarms over political correctness during the 1990–91 academic year, shortly after Nina Wu was expelled from the University of Connecticut. Wu had put a sign on her dorm room door to the effect that "preppies," "bimbos," "men without chest hair," and "homos" were to be "shot on sight." Although she assured the university authorities she had not intended it literally, they accused her of violating a student behavior code that banned "making personal slurs or epithets based on race, sex, ethnic origin, disability, religion or sexual orientation." This was not a behavior code of the sort that colleges had traditionally drawn up and passed down. It contained no ancient campus lore. It recapitulated the language that ran through the Civil Rights Act of 1964, punctiliously including the collectivities that had been brought under its protection in the years since. The speech code's purpose was to demonstrate a good faith that might shield the university from the tornado of public prosecution and private litigation that civil rights law had unleashed.

We have discussed this before: The goal of the civil rights laws, at least as they were understood by a sentimental public, was to short-circuit the sham democracies of the American South, to bring them into conformity with the Constitution. But it turned out to be harder than anticipated to distinguish between the South's democracy and everybody else's. If the spirit of the law was to humiliate Southern bigots, the letter of the law put the entire country—all its institutions—under the threat of lawsuits and prosecutions for discrimination.

What made political correctness different from other persecutory interludes in twentieth-century America, including McCarthyism, was its direct access to the courtroom. By Nina Wu's time, national university-accrediting bodies, themselves operating under the fear of litigation, had begun to use "diversity" as a criterion in their deliberations. The University of Connecticut would be better positioned to defend itself in court against a charge of discrimination if it could show it had come down on Nina Wu like a ton of bricks.

In early press accounts, the enforcers of P.C. appeared as hate-filled and totalitarian. They reminded the Berkeley philosopher John Searle, who covered various campus battles for the *New York Review of Books*, of Nazis. "The objective of converting the curriculum into an instrument of social transformation" he wrote, ". . . is the very opposite of higher education. It is characteristic of the major totalitarian regimes of the twentieth century—leftist and rightist." The correspondent for *New York* magazine called P.C. "more frightening than the old McCarthyism" and likened it to apartheid. Others brought up the Spanish Inquisition.

But the fall of communism in Eastern Europe in 1989 and its repudiation everywhere made the rise of P.C. hard to take seriously. Campus radicals must just have been the last to get the news of leftism's demise. Political correctness was unpopular. By 59 to 24 percent, Americans considered it a "bad thing." But above all, it was absurd. Pointing out its fallacies, its ignorance, and its intolerance was like shooting fish in a barrel. It would be a fad, *New York* magazine predicted. Closing its account of the fate of Harvard historian Stephan Thernstrom, hounded for his failure to include more slave narratives in his "Historical Studies A-25 (The Peopling of America)," the magazine reassured its readers, "Resistance to this sort of robotic sloganeering is beginning." Searle, assuming that the biggest risk from P.C. until its inevitable demise would be "silliness rather than catastrophe," saw signs that "the tide is turning." By 1993, newspapers were writing obituaries for P.C. "Trendy Movement Is on Its Last Legs," ran one headline.

At a time when people were still naming airports after Ronald Reagan, few thinkers understood how tenacious identity politics had become. But the writer Paul Berman did. He made the bold suggestion in *A Tale of Two Utopias* that Western progressives not only had not gone down with the communist ship—they had emerged from the Cold War triumphant and even strengthened. Berman looked at the dissident circle around the Czech playwright (later president) Václav Havel. He found them to have been more inspired by rock musicians, by Frank Zappa and the Velvet Underground, than by any Reaganite talk about the virtues of capitalism. Most countries shaken by student activism in 1968, he wrote, had undergone a "two-step evolution— from a dream of orthodox social revolution to a movement for personal liberation." By the former Berman meant socialism; by the latter he meant civil rights.

The politics of civil rights proved America's most successful late-twentieth-century export. European political advisors who had attended American law schools, or were at least familiar with the American style of "rights talk," sought to tap into its power. By the 1990s, Berman noted, virtually all the leaders of gay rights movements in non-Western countries had spent time in the West. The United States was still the rich countries' rule maker and enforcer, as it had been during the Cold War. But now its diversity mission also gave it the Cold War role of the Soviet Comintern—as a repository of hope for many of those who would overturn the world order's injustices.

The task that civil rights laws were meant to carry out—the topdown management of various ethnic, regional, and social groups—had always been the main task of empires. At the turn of the twenty-first century, the real place of the Vietnam War in the history of American diplomacy became much clearer. It had not been an aberration, the blunder of a handful of militarists allowed too much power—no, it had merely been one of the less successful of the experiments in global "governance" that the United States was doomed by its imperial position to make. It laid the groundwork for the "humanitarian invasions" of the 1990s and beyond. All the country's interests and incentives remained in place, but they were now buttressed by a new set of universalist justifications for intervening.

The war for the soul of America

Patrick J. Buchanan, the former speechwriter to Nixon and Reagan, was alone among conservative political figures in correctly assessing the power of political correctness. In 1992, he challenged George H. W. Bush for the Republican nomination and won a stunning 38 percent in the New Hampshire primary. Nostalgic, protectionist, isolationist, often misunderstood, Buchanan argued on behalf of the declining American "woodwork," and warned that there was a "war for the soul of America" going on. His campaign was about globalization, which his friend and supporter Samuel Francis defined as "the managed destruction of the nation, its sovereignty, its culture, and its people."

Americans were not thinking about globalization yet—or at least not a presidential majority's worth of them. "If Buchanan loses the nomination," Francis wrote when Buchanan ran again four years later,

> it will be because his time has not yet come, but the social and political forces on which both his campaigns have been based will not disappear, and even if he does lose, he will have won a place in history as an architect of the victory those forces will eventually build.

Buchanan's supporters aside, conservatives were confident to the point of exuberance. Republican National Committee chairman Rich Bond belittled a group of liberal protesters outside the Houston convention in the summer of 1992, saying "We are America! These other people are not America!" How disorienting the end of the Cold War must have been for people like Bond. Republicans would lose that election to Bill Clinton, who had spent his college years protesting Vietnam. The Republican party's Cold Warriors would get nothing from their Cold War victory, nor would its culture warriors get anything from a decade of Reaganism. The Reagan era had in retrospect marked a consolidation, not a reversal, of the movements that began in the 1960s.

In the quarter-century after Reagan, conservatives lost every battle against the substance of political correctness. Almost no claim made for expanded rights or recognitions for women or minorities would be deemed to have "gone too far." Already in 1988, Stanford had replaced its Western Culture requirement with a more flexible, multicultural rubric called "Culture, Ideals and Values." The five hundred mostly minority students who on January 15, 1987, had marched with Rev. Jesse Jackson down Palm Drive in Palo Alto, chanting "Hey, hey! Ho, ho! Western Culture's got to go!" were snorted at on campus and mocked in newspapers from coast to coast. Then they won. Change spread beyond the universities to corporations, foundations, and government offices. CNN founder Ted Turner ordered his company's personnel to refer to things outside the United States as "international" rather than "foreign," threatening to levy fines (which he would donate to the United Nations) on those who disobeyed. Political correctness was not a joke after all. It was the most comprehensive ideological capture of institutional power in the history of the United States.

Those who pooh-poohed P.C. assumed that the partisan arrangements that had governed Western thinking in the Cold War would last forever. True, the "conservative" "hawks" had outlasted the "liberal" "doves" and the anti-communists the communists. And true, most of the groups now clamoring for rights and recognition had belonged, in one way or another, to the dovish side in that conflict. But that had been a matter of expedience. Campaigners for civil or women's or gay rights had never had any particular affinity for Marxist ideas of economic organization and the Soviet state that defended them.

Now, in fact, it was possible for people who had wanted a different racial or sexual order to demand it of the American system without incurring the suspicion that they were working against the country's national security. To blacks and women, immigrants and gays, it was exhilarating. This minority coalition, pursuing a more or less unpopular set of programs, racked up victories as if it were a righteous majoritarian crusade. In the course of it, these minorities discovered, perhaps to their own surprise, that civil rights law gave them an iron grip on the levers of state power.

A radical understanding of race and gender arrived on campus at the same time as Baby Boom professors. It has thus been tempting to trace P.C. to a "takeover" of the universities by 1960s radicals. That is not exactly how it worked. In 1990, Baby Boom professors were between their late twenties and their mid-forties. They were not, as we noted earlier, the makers of the 1960s revolution. They were what the sociologist Max Weber called "successors"—a generation that undertakes the routinization, the bureaucratization, of the charismatic movement that preceded it.

In the academy, the Baby Boomers never enjoyed the demographic veto that they did in the voting public at large. By 1990, in fact, they were as under-represented on college faculties as they were over-represented everyplace else, making up only about a quarter of professors. The under-representation had a natural cause: a logjam of now tenured professors who had been hired to teach the Boomers in the 1960s. A calcified corporate structure thwarted efforts to transform the university right away. At the dawn of political correctness, American faculties, even humanities faculties, were not particularly progressive. A 1991 poll found that 58 percent of professors considered themselves either moderate or conservative, against 42 percent who called themselves leftist or liberal.

Universities may have been radicalizing not because radical Baby Boomers were entering the faculty but because conservative Baby Boomers were exiting the student body. In their place was a different population, on the other side of a generational razor's edge. In 1983, no Harvard undergraduate had a computer; in 1986, as the youngest Baby Boomers graduated from college, practically no one did not. That was also the year the high-tech developer Oren Etzioni was granted the first Harvard undergraduate degree in computer science. A year later, the Chicago philosophy professor Allan Bloom published *The Closing of the American Mind*, which spent four months atop the *New York Times* bestseller list and ushered in a climate of worry about ideologized teaching in universities that has never lifted since. Hip-hop, or rap, as it was then always called, began with the Sugar Hill Gang's "Rapper's Delight" (1979), a hit just as the first post-Boomers entered high school, and imposed itself on a national radio audience with Grandmaster Flash's "The Message" (1982), just as they were heading off to college. Searle noted that by 1990, more than half of the students at Berkeley were non-white.

There was no clamor in the general public to suppress heterodox thinking. Americans' views on free speech had been remarkably consistent. In 1955, in the immediate aftermath of McCarthyism, the Harvard sociologist Samuel A. Stouffer published a classic study called *Communism, Conformity and Civil Liberties*. His goal was to figure out how willing people *really* were to let communists do three things: make a speech in their community, teach in a university, or have a book kept in the public library. After 1972, the National Opinion Research Center added several scenarios to Stouffer's to test communities' tolerance for speech that insulted their sensibilities on race, religion, and democracy. On no issue did the eagerness to ban speech rise significantly in the decades preceding political correctness. In fact, the percentage of people who would permit a library to lend a racist book rose slightly, from 60 percent in 1972 to about 63 percent in 1990.

Political correctness was a top-down reform. It was enabled not by new public attitudes toward reactionary opinions but by new punishments that could be meted out against those who expressed them. The power of political correctness generally derived, either directly or at one remove, from the civil rights laws of the 1960s. "Subversive" became a term of praise in academia around then—but it was deployed in an unusual sense. "Subversive" scholars were supporting the very same things the government was mustering all its budgetary and enforcement power, and the corporate and foundation sector all its funding and ingenuity, to bring about. Rarely did professors now seek to subvert (as they had in the past) promiscuity or atheism or pacifism. Today's "subversive" opinions—that there ought to be more blacks in positions of authority, that a gay relationship is just as good as a straight one—were given special protection by civil rights laws, and there were now hundreds of thousands of people at all levels of government and business who had been trained to impose them.

Heather Has Two Mommies: Diversity spreads

In part because it worked to purge and punish dissident opinions, the governing system built up around civil rights was much more efficient than waiting for Congress to require, or for society to undergo, a moral regeneration. Activists eagerly replicated its lawsuit-driven model in other areas of public life, from women's rights to education in immigrant languages. By the dawn of the public uproar over political correctness, the same legal framework was being used to advance gay rights. In the school year of 1992–93, Joseph Fernandez, chancellor of the New York City public school system, was implementing a "Children of the Rainbow" initiative developed by his predecessor. It aimed to bring the powerful disciplinary and interpretive tool of diversity to bear on questions of the family. "What I am requiring," Fernandez said, "is that diverse family structures be recognized and that each is acknowledged as a loving, caring household."

A book called *Heather Has Two Mommies* came to symbolize the controversy. It had appeared on Fernandez's list of recommended first-grade readings. The school board in the Queens neighborhood of Middle Village understood the list (correctly) as an attempt to normalize not only single motherhood but also homosexuality and the idea of gay people as parents. The local board refused to adopt the curriculum. Fernandez suspended the local board. The city board overruled him and reinstated the board.

It was striking that the two sides had no common language in which to speak to one another. They had two different conceptions of political legitimacy, as if they were operating under two different constitutions. "I don't know what they're upset about," said one of the curriculum's designers. "I keep looking but I can't find it." The curriculum was greeted, not just in the cheap tabloids but also in learned journals, with cynical laughter and you-couldn't-make-this-up ribaldry. Such responses were familiar from similar discussions about campus race politics. So was the certitude that this novel social experiment would die of its own preposterousness. A journalist predicted that an incisive and caustic speech by Board of Education vice president Irene Impellizzeri, a Rainbow foe from Brooklyn, "may eventually stand as a turning point in New York's cultural wars." That view was delusional. The controversy over "rainbow families" in New York's outer boroughs would be resolved the same way questions of race and gender had been on college campuses: The wildest utopian suggestions of the "radicals" turned out to be only the smallest down payment on the system-overturning change they would eventually get.

What was playing out, as arguments shifted from race to sex, was an old problem, one of the oldest. Human beings, as individuals, require flexible institutions for the sake of their sexual fulfillment. Human beings, as a society, require uniform and even somewhat rigid institutions for the sake of order and self-perpetuation. This conflict is what *Romeo and Juliet* is about, and it accounts for the universalizability of the "gay" works that make up such a large part of our twentieth-century literature, from the Nobel Prize–winning French novelist Roger Martin du Gard to the Thatcher-era rock lyricist Morrissey. The situations they described were tragic. They were part of the human condition. They were not political.

But now, with the tools provided by civil rights law, they appeared

quite political. One defender of the Rainbow curriculum, a member of
the Lesbian and Gay Teachers Association in Brooklyn, explained the
problem this way: "A curriculum that was designed to promote tolerance has instead revealed an astonishing level of homophobia. It has
prompted bashing of lesbians and gays, bigotry and purposeful lies."
This language of "-bashing" and "-phobia" and "bigotry" and "lies" was
new. No longer was the irreconcilability of individuals' and society's
sexual priorities a tragedy or a disagreement. Recast in the categories
of civil rights law, it was a crime, a crime that was being committed
against a whole class of people. The customs and traditions in the name
of which it was being committed were mere alibis.

All institutions were now under the purview of civil rights laws.
Aggrieved minorities no one had considered in 1964 had access to a
mysterious set of passwords and procedures that would require government and business to drop everything and respond to their demands.

Politicians were slow to notice that the change rendered a good
deal of their traditional work irrelevant. Georgia congressman Newt
Gingrich arrived as Speaker of the House of Representatives in 1995,
after a landslide election victory that "social" (i.e., sexual) controversies like the Rainbow curriculum had done much to bring about. He
spent his first weeks mulling over the correct balance between individuals' sexual needs and society's and how to address them legislatively.
In his mind it might as well have been 1963. He worried about the
encouragement of homosexuality ("You have had, clearly, examples of
what is in effect recruitment in so-called counseling programs."). He
put his foot down on the question of protecting sexual orientation in
the federal civil rights laws ("Does that mean a transvestite should automatically have the right to work as a transvestite? I don't think so.").

Republicans kept winning elections with this kind of rhetoric.
More than that: They could whip the electorate into a frenzy in a way
that brought even Democratic politicians to heel. In 1996, Gingrich
rallied the country behind a Defense of Marriage Act (DOMA), which

Bill Clinton signed. So overwhelming was the consensus against gay marriage, so unlikely seemed the outcome that the bill aimed to prevent, that many Republicans worried the legislation was overkill. It expressed an unseemly triumphalism. Yet the world that conservatives sought to "conserve" kept receding. The world they mocked on the campaign trail kept encroaching. Republican triumphs were won in a "legacy" system from which real political power had been withdrawn. As a matter of common sense, both tradition and diversity had claims that needed to be respected. As a matter of law, only diversity did. Heather was not having an argument. She was laying down the law.

Republicans, again, were blind to this. They saw political correctness as little more than a series of jokes. *Getta loada this!* Bank of America puts Braille on the keyboards of its drive-through automatic teller machines! *True story!* The Appalachian Mountain Club's Galehead Hut, five miles up a mountain from the nearest road, is wheelchair-accessible! The congressmen pontificating about proper sexual conduct, the editorialists snickering at Heather and her mommies—they made no distinction between voluntary initiatives and government compulsion and seemed not to realize that their own chances of prevailing on matters of law had fallen to nil. Once social issues could be cast as battles over civil rights, Republicans would lose 100 percent of the time. The agenda of "diversity" advanced when its proponents won elections and when they lost them. Voters had not yet figured that out. As soon as they did, the old style of democratic politics would be dead.

"Political correctness" was a name for the cultural effect of the basic enforcement powers of civil rights law. Those powers were surprisingly extensive, unexpectedly versatile, able to get beneath the integument of institutions that conservatives felt they had to defer to. Reagan had won conservatives over to the idea that "business" was the innocent opposite of overweening "government." So what were conservatives supposed to do now that businesses were the hammer of civil rights enforcement, in the forefront of advancing both affirmative action and political correctness?

Corporate leaders, advertisers, and the great majority of the press came to a pragmatic accommodation with what the law required, how it worked, and the euphemisms with which it must be honored, even if Gingrich had bet that such an accommodation would be impossible. All major corporations, all universities, all major government agencies had departments of personnel or "human resources"—a phrase five times as prevalent in the 1980s as it had been in the 1960s. "Chief diversity officers" and "diversity compliance officers," working inside companies, carried out functions that resembled those of twentieth-century commissars. They would be consulted about whether a board meeting or a company picnic was sufficiently diverse.

The Rainbow curriculum that Joseph Fernandez was advancing in the early 1990s in Queens, for instance, had been laid out by his predecessor, Richard Green, in 1989 as a full-spectrum overthrow of everything in the New York school system, including its personnel. In Green's words, "The commitment to multicultural education will permeate every aspect of educational policy, including counseling programs, assessment and testing, curriculum and instruction, representative staffing at all levels, and teaching materials." Things were starting to work that way in the private sector, too. CNN founder Ted Turner announced he would no longer hire smokers, even if they didn't smoke at work.

At a time when political conservatism was alleged to be triumphant, politics came under the dominance of progressive movements that had been marginal the day before yesterday: questioning the Western literary canon, arguing that gays ought to be able to marry and adopt, suggesting that people could be citizens of more than one country, and so on. These disparate preoccupations did not spring up simultaneously by coincidence. They were old minoritarian impulses that could now, through the authority of civil rights law, override every barrier that democracy might seek to erect against them.

Almost everything carried out in the name of civil rights, for good or for bad, wound up irrevocable. Voter outrage could once in a while oust someone like Fernandez and delay his work for a bit—but never reverse it. Controversy could even help entrench it, by creating the illusion of democratic consultation. Consider "bilingual education," which, though never written into law, had been mandated by the Supreme Court in *Lau v. Nichols* (1974) and sketched out in various federal Office for Civil Rights guidelines between 1970 and 1975. By the 1980s, bilingual ed was so widely despised in public opinion polls, had been so often discredited in academic studies, and had led politicians into so many embarrassed apologies and backpedalings that most Americans were under the impression it had been abolished. It had not. Almost all of the programs set up in the 1970s survived intact into the twenty-first century, as New York mayor Michael Bloomberg discovered in 2004 when he tried and failed to end the bilingual ed program there.

Only with the entrenchment of political correctness did it become clear what Americans had done in 1964: They had inadvertently voted themselves a second constitution without explicitly repealing the one they had. Each constitution contained guarantees of rights that could be invoked against the other—but in any conflict it was the new, unofficial constitution, nurtured by elites in all walks of life, that tended to prevail.

This was a recipe for strife. Republicans and others who may have been uneasy that the constitutional baby had been thrown out with the segregationist bathwater consoled themselves with a myth: The "good" civil rights movement that the martyred Martin Luther King, Jr., had pursued in the 1960s had, they said, been "hijacked" in the 1970s by a "radical" one of affirmative action, with its quotas and diktats. Once the country came to its senses and rejected this optional, radical regime, it could have the good civil rights regime back.

None of that was true. Affirmative action and political correctness were the twin pillars of the second constitution. They were what civil rights *was*. They were not temporary. Affirmative action was deduced judicially from the curtailments on freedom of association that the

Civil Rights Act itself had put in place. Political correctness rested on a right to collective dignity extended by sympathetic judges who saw that, without such a right, forcing the races together would more likely occasion humiliation than emancipation. As long as Americans were frightened of speaking against civil rights legislation or, later, of being assailed as racists, sexists, homophobes, or xenophobes, their political representatives could resist nothing that presented itself in the name of "civil rights." This meant that conflict, when it eventually came, would be constitutional conflict, with all the gravity that the adjective "constitutional" implies.

7

Winners

*Outsourcing and global value chains—Politicized lending and the
finance crisis—Civil rights as a ruling-class cause—Google and
Amazon as governments in embryo—Eliot Spitzer, Edward Snowden,
and surveillance—The culture of internet moguls—The affinity
between high tech and civil rights—The rise of philanthropy—
Obama: governing without government—Nudge and behavioral
economics—From gay rights to gay marriage—Windsor: the
convergence of elites—Obergefell: triumph of the de facto constitution*

I t took a long time for Americans to realize that the New Economy
was a *new economy*. They were accustomed to marketing hype.
When politicians used the term "New Economy," it was easy for
voters to assume it was only a jazzed-up way of describing the process,
familiar for centuries, by which mechanization was introduced into certain industrial tasks, creating limited short-term sectorial disruptions
but offering rewards to those trained in the new technology.

The globalization of the division of labor that gathered speed in the
1980s was more thoroughgoing. Different things would be made in
different places and by different people altogether, and the American
social structure would be upended. Certain things would no longer
be made in America at all. The country would therefore become an
economic part rather than an economic whole, rendering nonsensical,
at least for a while, all kinds of inherited cultural and political beliefs
about sovereignty, national independence, and social cohesion. In this

sense the New Economy was like the new constitution. Over the fifty years leading up to the election of 2016, those who found ways to use the newly unleashed powers flourished. Those who continued to believe they could trust in old traditions, or vote their way to the country they wanted, lost ground.

Outsourcing and global value chains

The high wages of industrial workforces in Western countries had once been invulnerable, because the capital-owning part of an economy was bound by the laws of the land and the laws of economics to the fate of its workforce. The workers who made any given product needed to be near one another and near their bosses. Competition in the market for goods was, as the economist Richard Baldwin explains, "the only way international competition could get into an economy." Foreign auto workers could never threaten American auto workers' wages until lower-wage countries had built the factories, along with sundry support industries, to pump out American-quality cars. Americans found it unsettling when Japan and Korea managed, in the 1970s and 1980s, to do just that. But competing required those countries to undergo a thorough industrialization, and by the time Asian car companies could sell into Western markets, their workers were approaching Western wage levels.

Computers broke that invulnerability. They enabled Western corporations with access to a cheap labor source to assemble individual components remotely. Once that became possible, even pre-industrial societies could compete with the United States. Any country that could master a primitive assembly-line task—as Vietnam, to take a real-life example, did with auto-body wire harnesses—could take that task, and all the jobs that went with it, from a high-wage country, without ever industrializing at all. Corporations began to exploit these "global value chains."

In the work of *New York Times* columnist Thomas Friedman and other global economy boosters of the 1990s, you find value chains described as kaleidoscopic and complex: Nandan Nilekani, the CEO of

Infosys, holding "virtual meetings" across eight time zones, at which "American designers could be on the screen speaking with their Indian software writers and their Asian manufacturers all at once."

But really there was less to global value chains than met the eye. They were not symphonies of specialist craftsmanship conducted by some boardroom maestro of industrial organization. The new operation was usually some company's old operation, spirited somewhere else with a lot of bad faith and hocus-pocus. The main purpose of these chains was not industrial (seeking out value in the earth's far corners) but political (getting across the border to someplace, anyplace, where the obligations to workers that American companies had accumulated since the New Deal could be repudiated).

Sneaking a manufacturing operation out the door one stage of production at a time aroused less disruption, suspicion, and controversy than moving it lock, stock, and barrel. Avoiding controversy was of the essence. The voting public's permission was required to emancipate American capital owners from the American workforce. It was granted in principle in the battle over the North American Free Trade Agreement (NAFTA) in 1993.

Now the United States was operating in a larger, global economy. At a time when international competition was bidding down the price of industrial handwork, corporations retooled in order to capture the global economy's ever-more-lucrative brainwork: the design, the marketing, the public relations. The problem was, and remains, that only a small fraction of people in any society is equipped to do brainwork. Big though the New Economy may have looked to American executives, professors, and philanthropists, American workers experienced it as smaller than the old one. They were in a catch-22: Until they consented to the outsourcing of their jobs, they were called pampered obstructionists, and berated; once their jobs had left and their consent was no longer needed, they were called nostalgic losers, and forgotten.

Bill Clinton capitalized on the resulting unease. He argued that the sensible course was to set off on the great adventure of globalization, but to make sure that those who lost out from the transition were compensated.

It looked like a wise compromise. This position became a model, rhetorically, at least, for revivifying moribund social-democratic parties everywhere. Imitators of Clinton were elected in all the major industrial countries of the West: Wim Kok in the Netherlands in 1994, Tony Blair in the United Kingdom and Lionel Jospin in France in 1997, Gerhard Schröder in Germany in 1998. But there was a problem: It was never clear *how* these left-behind workers were supposed to be protected, especially since globalization was accompanied everywhere by a hollowing out of welfare programs and an atrophy of trade unionism. Helping the less well off no longer meant helping them find jobs. It meant helping them borrow money.

Until the 1980s, the U.S. financial system was heavily regulated. Banks could not lend across state lines. Nor could small banks speculate in stocks. The system drove financiers and financial experts crazy. Americans had to pay more for loans and earned less on their savings deposits than they might otherwise have done. It is shortsighted, however, to call the old system of "unit banking" inefficient. In theory, individual banks were liable to shocks, since they could not spread credit risk across regions, classes, and industries. In practice, banks failed rarely or never.

In light of experience, we can say that, even if families paid slightly higher interest rates when they tried to borrow, the old system gave them a more than equivalent return in stability. It captured bankers and their assets for local communities, keeping money and credit in the area during downturns, when it might have fled elsewhere. Franklin Roosevelt's Banking Act of 1933 (also known as Glass-Steagall) codified that system, insuring deposits and capping interest rates. But these caps could hold only so long as the government kept inflation in check. When Lyndon Johnson launched his two-front war on segregation and North Vietnam, inflation rose, and the middle class began to demand more interest income from its saved money. To get that additional income, banks would seek out new markets and take on more risks.

By the end of the 1970s, the United States was operating under two new and dangerous conditions: First, a middle-class constituency had arisen for more financial risk-taking. Institutions at the edge of the banking system were permitted to cater to it. Starting in 1980, the country's savings-and-loan companies, basically mortgage and car-loan makers, were deregulated, with dismal results. A third of them went bankrupt between 1989 and 1995. Second, the public rebelled against paying for the social programs of the 1960s, on which interracial comity had come to depend.

Those two discontents merged in the coalition that elected Ronald Reagan. They would remain closely bound for almost three decades after Reagan left office. Bill Clinton deregulated private-sector borrowing, creating an even more illusory picture of prosperity. George W. Bush and Barack Obama incurred debts that no politician in Reagan's time had dreamed of. Those debts would be paid by a third party: the children and grandchildren of the Baby Boomers. By the time of the presidential election in November 2016, the national debt stood at just under $20 trillion and the government's unfunded liabilities were at least five times that.

Banking, as it had traditionally been understood, could not accommodate that pace of debt creation. At the end of the twentieth century, the banking system was deregulated at its very heart. On November 12, 1999, Clinton signed legislation repealing Glass-Steagall. "The era of big government is over," he had said in his 1996 State of the Union address. But that was not true. What was over was the way big government had heretofore been financed. The United States transformed itself from a welfare state that operated through taxes and transfer payments to one that operated through regulations and credit markets.

The largest of these markets was for the mortgages on Americans' homes. The real estate market is heavily supported by government. Big tax breaks—from deductions for mortgage interest to homeowners' exemptions from capital gains tax—subsidize home owning over renting. And "government-sponsored enterprises" (GSEs) purchase, guarantee, and securitize home loans, issuing trillions in debt to do so. They create a deep secondary market in mortgages, making possible that socially transformative product—the 30-year mortgage at a low and preferably fixed rate—on which rests the way of life of the American middle class.

Let us look at these GSEs. The Federal National Mortgage Association (Fannie Mae) was launched as a government bureau with the New Deal of the 1930s. It became a company in 1968, when Lyndon Johnson, desperate to bring his war budget closer to balance, privatized it. Most investors understood that privatization as a fiction, meant only to take the government's housing debts off-balance-sheet, but its consequences were real enough.

The office now became a corruption-sowing hybrid. It was public in the sense that it carried an implicit guarantee of government support—which the government bailout it received in September 2008 would make perfectly explicit. But it was private in the sense that its government-connected executives earned salaries that, by the turn of the century, ran into the tens of millions. In 1968, Congress also calved off part of Fannie Mae to form the Government National Mortgage Association (Ginnie Mae). Two years later it established the Federal Home Loan Mortgage Corporation (Freddie Mac), in order to give the other GSEs "competition."

Politicized lending and the finance crisis

On October 28, 1992, at the end of an election campaign shadowed by the outbreak in Los Angeles that spring of the deadliest race riots in a quarter-century, President George H. W. Bush signed a Housing and Community Development Act. It inaugurated the process we have seen at many junctures in this book: the sudden irruption of civil rights law and diversity promotion into an area from which it had been mostly absent, in this case mortgage finance. The GSEs would now have "mission goals" of supplying "affordable housing," particularly in "underserved areas"—the government's euphemism for ethnic-minority neighborhoods.

That meant lowering underwriting standards. GSEs would now be able to "establish a down payment requirement for mortgagors of 5 percent or less" and "approve borrowers who have a credit history of delinquencies" as long as the borrower could show that his credit had been reasonably good for twelve months. There would be a "prudential regulator" to ensure that the loans did not violate sound lending practice, but he would be located at the Department of Housing and Urban Development—that is, he would not regulate lending so much as promote it.

The economist Viral Acharya and three of his colleagues at the New York University business school saw the first President Bush's reckless housing plan as a "Rubicon" on the way to the financial crisis that, in the following century, would nearly destroy the world economy under the presidency of Bush's even more reckless son. Suddenly the government had room to deal in dangerous mortgages—ones with suspect borrowers and high loan-to-value ratios.

Bill Clinton, elected in 1992, made this mission his own. Starting in the summer of 1994, he crusaded against the dearth of private housing credit in poor, black, urban neighborhoods. He used the term "redlining," which described the practice, illegal for decades and subjected to intense federal scrutiny since the Fair Housing Act of 1968, of systematically denying credit to black neighborhoods. The word would have meant little to Clinton's white supporters, but it was part of the basic vocabulary of the civil rights movement. It imparted to blacks the incendiary accusation that the lower rates of mortgage lending to black people were due not to their poverty but to a conspiracy of racist bankers.

There was no evidence of redlining. Clinton's allegation rested on a study from the Boston office of the Federal Reserve, the shortcomings of which were laid out almost immediately on the front page of the *New York Times* business section. Once the effects of poverty were adequately modeled and two outlying banks put aside, there was no discrimination to be found. There was inequality, certainly, but inequality was not the same thing as discrimination.

Except that, increasingly, in the minds of civil rights enforcers, it was. Remember Alan David Freeman's distinction from chapter 2 between perpetrators' and victims' perspectives on discrimination. Sometime between the passage of Lyndon Johnson's civil rights laws and the long Bush-Clinton march through the country's financial institutions, the victims' perspective had won. Now any inequality was an injustice, and one did not need a clear account of what had caused it to demand redress from the system.

President Clinton enlisted and empowered community organizers, using the Community Reinvestment Act, a nearly forgotten piece of legislation from 1977 that gave community groups a way to stymie banks by accusing them of discrimination. The groups threatened to halt the approval of a string of envisioned bank mergers unless largesse was steered their way. President Clinton brokered deals. In the quarter-century after 1992, $850 billion in loans was steered through these community groups. The banks took the precaution of showering gifts and grants on the community groups directly, too. After 1993, the Association of Community Organizations for Reform Now (ACORN), which would later attract controversy for its role in electing Barack Obama president, received $9.5 million from JPMorgan Chase, $8.1 million from Citibank, and $7.4 million from HSBC.

By the time Clinton left office, the Department of Housing and Urban Development (HUD) required that low-income loans make up 50 percent of the GSEs' portfolio. Republicans never objected. As long as the "payment" was in the form of a risk distributed across society, with no dollar sign in front of it, then it must be free. Jack Kemp campaigned for vice president in 1996 calling for "a new civil rights agenda based upon expanding access to credit and capital." As part of its agenda of "compassionate conservatism," George W. Bush's administration in the new century raised the GSEs' quota for low-income loans to 56 percent. That brought an astonishing deterioration in the quality of housing assets. By 2007, high-risk mortgages (as distinct from low-income ones) made up 22 percent of the GSEs' portfolio, up tenfold from a decade before. The University of Chicago economists Atif Mian and Amir Sufi discovered that, between 2002 and 2005, "income and mortgage credit growth [were] negatively correlated." The less likely you were to pay off a mortgage, the more likely you were to get one.

The GSEs' underwriting standards became those of the whole industry. By 2006, 46 percent of new homeowners were making no down payment at all on their houses, and banks had trillions of dollars in loans on their books that would never have been made, absent government pressure. No well-informed accountant thought these loans could survive an economic downturn, and they did not. The politicization of poor people's mortgages in a single country brought the world to the brink of economic disaster.

Everything the Clinton and both Bush administrations *thought* they were doing in domestic policy pales next to the financial crash of September 2008—the most dramatic and sudden market loss in Western history, not excepting that of the Great Depression. It destroyed trillions of dollars in economic value and stalled tens of millions of careers.

Although the crisis arose out of American politics and American banking customs, virtually all of the most incisive diagnoses of the problem were done by those uninhibited by American political taboos—foreigners, in a word. Simon Johnson, an English-born former IMF economist, likened it to a late-twentieth-century emerging markets crisis of the sort he had seen in Ukraine, Russia, Thailand, Indonesia, and South Korea, with their crony capitalism and their corrupt, politically allocated credit.

Raghuram Rajan, born in Bhopal and trained at MIT at the same time as Simon Johnson, had warned central bankers before the crisis that many American financial innovations meant to minimize risk, such as derivatives and swaps, were in fact amplifying it. (After the crisis Rajan would become governor of the Bank of India.) With extraordinary social sensitivity, Rajan linked the financial crisis to the gradual rise of American inequality. Since 1992, the U.S. economy had recovered slowly from recessions. All its recoveries were "jobless recoveries"; after the 2001 recession, it took 38 months for the economy to return to full employment. And, Rajan warned, "the United States is singularly unprepared for jobless recoveries." It has no big transfer programs. Under such circumstances, any recession with the slightest perceptible effect on the public will end political careers by the score.

The result was reckless government extension of credit under both Democratic and Republican leadership. As a remedy for downturns, expanding credit has two practical advantages over government spending. First, it does not bother political conservatives as much. Second, as Rajan put it, "Easy credit has large, positive, immediate, and widely distributed benefits, whereas the costs all lie in the future. It has a pay-off structure that is precisely the one desired by politicians, which is why so many countries have succumbed to its lure."

Rajan said something sensitive about the human side of mortgage lending, too. Sometime in the past generation, the old-fashioned method of vetting mortgage applicants—through face-to-face interviewing and rigorous investigation of applicants' character and community standing—had given way to an anonymous, bureaucratic, arm's-length process that could be carried out online or over the phone, but could easily be abused. "The judgment calls historically made by loan officers were, in fact, extremely important to the overall credit assessment," Rajan wrote. ". . . It really does matter if the borrower is rude, shifty, and slovenly in the loan interview."

The change in procedures was not just a matter of bankers' cutting corners. To inquire too closely into borrowers' creditworthiness would leave bankers in danger of falling afoul of anti-discrimination laws, particularly after Clinton's redlining initiative. It is easy to call George W. Bush a fool for raising the quota for Fannie Mae's low-income lending from 50 to 56 percent. But is there any doubt that he would have been called a racist had he sought to lower it? The Indian-born Rajan never enunciated the unavoidable conclusion, but walked much closer to it than any American-born academic would have dared: The "off-balance-sheet liabilities" of the finance crisis were largely those of the civil rights revolution.

As Woodstock had marked the entrance of the Baby Boom generation onto the American public scene, the crash of 2008 marked its spectacular exit, along with the archetypal political type of their era: the "Happy Warrior." Reagan, Clinton, the Bushes—they avoided confrontation when they could. Their Baby Boom supporters did not view politics as a "zero-sum game." If a cynic is one who, as Oscar Wilde said, knows the price of everything and the value of nothing, the Boomers were the opposite. They knew the value of everything and the price of nothing. But that could not last.

The debt crisis was a sign that the United States was nearing the limits of its ingenuity in finding new ways to borrow money. Without extra money, the country could no longer afford to pay for both a pre– and a post–Great Society social order. When we speak of "polarization" today, what we mean is the conflict between those two social orders, newly reactivated under conditions of curtailed resources.

Anti-racism, women's rights, sexual liberation, world hegemony, government through technology—none of these was free. All would have to be paid for, which meant that they would be fought over. Some people, the public rightly began to suspect, would have to surrender what they considered their rights and submit to a political order designed for others' benefit. A long-running and deceptively natural-seeming period of "both . . . and" was being replaced by the more usual human condition of "either . . . or." That is the drama that would enter its final stage with the presidential election of 2016.

Civil rights as a ruling-class cause

Barack Obama was the president the finance crisis called forth. Its timing, in September 2008, favored his electoral fortunes. Had the crash

come two months later, after the general election, the economic ignorance of Obama's Republican opponent, Arizona senator John McCain,
might have bothered voters less on Election Day. That is to say nothing of his running mate, Alaska governor Sarah Palin, who, measured
against the gravity of the emergency, became a figure of ridicule. On
the other hand, had the crash come a few months earlier, before the
primaries, Obama's own thin résumé might have bothered voters more.

McCain's strength was his heroism as a Navy pilot and prisoner
of war in Vietnam. Obama's was his opposition to the losing war that
George W. Bush had chosen to fight in Iraq. Almost all nationally prominent Democrats had bet that backing the war would seem the more
patriotic option. Now that Bush had added the near-destruction of the
world economy to his trophy case alongside his two lost wars, any Republican nominee would probably have been sunk. Since Democrats
were still the party of bureaucratic expertise and bold government action, Obama was well positioned to address the finance crisis. But because his political career had been built at the intersection of billionaire
finance and community-based race activism, the very place where the
crisis had occurred, he was also well positioned to symbolize it.

Obama was a black candidate with a difference. He had been
raised in Hawaii, his father a Kenyan scholarship student he never really knew and his Kansan mother an activist scholar of international
development. By his own account he was an "eighth or ninth cousin"
of Confederate president Jefferson Davis. On a state visit to Ireland,
Obama visited his Irish cousins in County Offaly. African half siblings
turned up all over the world in the course of Obama's campaign and
presidency, not all of them previously known to Obama himself, and
many of them quite accomplished: Auma the scholar at Heidelberg;
Abongo the estranged right-winger; Mark the Jewish concert pianist
in Shenzhen, China; George the mechanic in Nairobi. But Obama had
no black American cousins. He was the descendant of American slave
owners but not of American slaves.

He was not even descended from the same people as most

American blacks. The vastness and diversity of Africa, so loudly insisted on in other contexts, is something people ignored when they spoke of Obama's ancestry. When Obama and his wife visited the eighteenth-century House of Slaves in the onetime slave port of Gorée in Senegal in 2013, she was presumably standing near her ancestral homeland, but he was not. Gorée, in fact, is closer to New York (3,820 miles away) than to Nairobi (3,865 miles away), the Kenyan capital from which his father had emigrated. Until he went to college, Obama had had less direct contact with black American culture than almost any of his white Senate colleagues. His yearning toward blackness, his training himself in American black ethnicity as if it were a foreign language, is the subject of his poignant and gracefully written autobiography and of David Remnick's sensitive study *The Bridge*. But this story owes more to postmodern university narratives of chosen identity than to anything inherited from the racial confrontations and injustices of the segregated South.

Maybe race relations were already deteriorating when Obama became the country's first black president, but there was no outward sign. The idea of having a black president had seemed realistic for at least a decade. The mere rumor of a presidential run by the black general Colin Powell, months before the 1996 New Hampshire Republican primaries, had put him ahead in the polls there. It was a bridge that Americans seemed eager to cross. But the exhilaration of it, widespread in the immediate aftermath of Obama's election in 2008, quickly evaporated.

An episode near Harvard Square in the first months of his presidency seemed to freeze the way many white Americans had come to think about Obama and race. On July 16, 2009, police got a cell phone call from a grand neighborhood in Cambridge. It came from a young female speaking on behalf of "an elderly woman" who had seen two men enter a house by breaking a screen. They had been carrying suitcases. The caller gave no information as to their race. When pressed by the dispatcher, she said one of them "looked kind of Hispanic, but I'm not really sure."

It was Henry Louis Gates, Jr., the celebrity professor of African-American studies at Harvard and a friend of the new president. He was returning from filming a television special in China and did not have his key. His airport taxi driver had helped him break into his own house. It should have been an easy matter to resolve. But according to the police report, when officer James Crowley asked Gates if he would step outside his house, he replied, "No, I will not." The officer explained that he was investigating a break-in. Gates said, "Why, because I'm a black man in America?" When Crowley's partner, Carlos Figueroa, arrived, Gates was warning Crowley, "You don't know who you're messing with." Gates made a call in which he said, "Get the chief," and "What's the chief's name?" and complained that he was in the hands of a racist police officer. "Ya," he added to Crowley, according to the police account, "I'll speak with your Mama outside." The cop described his behavior as "tumultuous" and arrested him.

Although Gates was soon released, President Obama weighed in:

> I don't know, not having been there and not seeing all the facts, what role race played in that, but I think it's fair to say, number one, any of us would be pretty angry; number two, that the Cambridge Police acted stupidly in arresting somebody when there was already proof that they were in their own home; and number three, what I think we know separately and apart from this incident, that there is a long history in this country of African-Americans and Latinos being stopped by law enforcement disproportionately. That's just a fact.

In the two decades since Al Campanis had been ruined over a few ill-chosen words, every TV watcher had learned to recognize the mise en scène: Crowley was being set up to have his life destroyed. The Cambridge police could read the signs, too. They held a press conference to express their resentment and insisted that Obama apologize for calling them stupid. "The president used the right adjective," said the president of the Cambridge Police Superior Officers' Association, "but directed it to the wrong party."

Now it was Obama who was in an awkward position. Gates had been arrested for disorderly conduct, not for breaking and entering as the president had implied, and there had been many witnesses at the end of it. What Americans saw was not racism but something equally familiar: a president defending a powerful crony from the law. Within 48 hours, Obama had appeared in person at a White House press briefing to acknowledge, without apologizing for, his role in "ratcheting up" the controversy. He now saw the incident as "an overreaction" on both sides. He invited Gates and the officer to the White House to talk things over over a beer. He mispronounced Crowley's name every time he used it.

That seemed to resolve the issue to everyone's satisfaction. Crowley had a spotless record on race relations, as the president himself acknowledged; he actually happened to be a diversity trainer in the police department. He also claimed to back the president "110 percent." He even made Gates a gift of the handcuffs he had been arrested in. But what would have happened to Crowley, wholly blameless in this case, if his record had been anything less than spotless, or his politics at odds with the president's?

Professor Gates had been right all along. He was indeed too powerful to mess with. His histrionics had nearly undone Crowley. But once power had done its work, Gates showed no sign of understanding that he had been accorded the special treatment due a powerful man. He donated those handcuffs to the National Museum of African American History and Culture, as if he had been some kind of downtrodden civil rights victim rather than a Harvard bigwig on whose behalf the president of the United States had intervened.

At the level of constitutional abstraction, it had always been true that civil rights laws created two classes of citizens. Now it seemed to be true as a matter of lived experience. Every tool of civil rights rhetoric had been used by the White House not to challenge privilege but to protect it.

Obama served two terms without ever managing to consolidate a broad white base. His white backers were rich and powerful but not numerous. He got 43 percent of the white vote in 2008, a better-than-average showing by the standards of his party, but that support eroded. Obama was the first president since Kennedy for whom the days after his inauguration were the high point of his popularity. His steady decline from then until the last year of his term masked a divergence. Non-whites came to like him more and more, whites less and less. Running for re-election in 2012, he got only 39 percent of the white vote, and by late 2014, even white voters 18 to 29 years old, his strongest age group, were giving him only 34 percent approval in the polls. In the middle of his term, only 8 percent of whites said they trusted the government "always or most of the time."

Obama's presidency extinguished an important illusion on which the consensus for civil rights laws had rested: the illusion that its more intrusive tools would be temporary. There would be no need for affirmative action, Americans trusted, once we were all standing on Martin Luther King's mountaintop. In the then most recent Supreme Court examination of affirmative action, *Grutter v. Bollinger* (2003), the University of Michigan Law School had assured the court that it "would like nothing better than to find a race-neutral admissions formula" and would get rid of affirmative action as soon as it did. That assurance was taken seriously. Justice Sandra Day O'Connor wrote in her opinion: "We expect that twenty-five years from now the use of racial preferences will no longer be necessary to further the interest approved today."

So now we were done, right? Once the country had placed the mightiest army ever assembled, along with its nuclear codes, at the disposal of the son of a wayward African scholarship student, surely its people could declare mission accomplished. They could pass out of the tutelary democracy they had inhabited since 1964 and assume their full republican liberties once more. That was an implicit promise of Obama's candidacy. At the 2004 Democratic National Convention, he had said, "There's not a black America and white America and Latino America and Asian America; there's the United States of America."

It was a shock, then, when Obama governed in such a race-conscious way. Apparently there was much, much more still to be done, for almost all of Obama's policy making was tied up in race and identity. After the Army medic and self-taught Muslim fanatic Nidal Hasan killed 13 people at Fort Hood in Obama's first year in office, Army chief of staff Gen. George W. Casey, Jr., said, "Our diversity, not only in our Army, but in our country, is a strength. And as horrific as this tragedy was, if our diversity becomes a casualty, I think that's worse." For Casey, to be accused of racism was literally a fate worse than death. The following summer, Gen. Charles F. Bolden, Jr., the chief administrator of NASA, told Al Jazeera during a trip to the Middle East about the president's wishes for the agency. "Perhaps foremost," Bolden said, "he wanted me to find a way to reach out to the Muslim world . . . to help them feel good about their historic contribution to science, math and engineering."

If the more intrusive tools of civil rights were not a temporary set of measures, as Justice O'Connor assumed, but a permanent regime, then everything appeared in a different light. Then working-class white people were not engaged in any heroic enterprise of welcoming their black neighbors. They were being ousted, rather, on someone else's say-so, from their niche in American life. They were not saints but suckers. Although Obama was the opposite of an incendiary politician, this interpretation of things, as it sank in, had an alarming effect on the public, especially when it was coupled with similar impressions they were forming about the economy.

Google and Amazon as governments in embryo

During the Obama administration, the country passed a milestone: It moved closer to the time when the futuristic cartoon *The Jetsons* was set (2062 A.D.) than to the time it was made (1962). Where people had thought they were heading during the Kennedy administration could be summed up in the word "space." Where they were actually heading required a new word: "cyberspace," coined by the novelist William Gibson only in 1984. Americans would enter cyberspace with the development of the internet a decade after that. It was in some ways an improvement on the old dream and in others a scaled-down replacement fobbed off on a public easily diverted by novelty.

To those brought up in the second half of the twentieth century, in the wake of Hiroshima and Auschwitz, such a scaling-down seemed a boon. "Either we must allow the human race to exterminate itself, or we must forgo certain liberties," wrote Bertrand Russell in 1952. Limits on the scope of human action that had once looked tyrannical began to look prudent. The same could be said of limits on the scope of human inquiry, given that mankind's most advanced technologies were the largest source of danger. Intellectual ideals that had been taken for granted for two centuries—a "questing intelligence," an "open mind," a "spirit of inquiry"—seemed menacing. If humanity was going to have big weapons, it was going to need small people.

The internet fulfilled a social yearning—you could tell that from the rise of the journeyman disc jockey and sportscaster Rush Limbaugh. As the Reagan years ended, Limbaugh took nationwide a talk show he had developed in Kansas City and Sacramento. It was aimed at conservatives in whom hope sprang eternal. Soon reaching 14 million daily fans, it was the most listened-to radio broadcast since before the television age. Not since the populist priest Charles Coughlin was banned from the airwaves in 1939 had there been anything like it. In hundreds of cities across the country, Limbaugh's most ardent listeners would spend their lunch hours in barrooms and diners that carried the show. "Rush rooms" were harbingers of internet-age sociability. It was not enough to follow politics in your community—now the politics you followed *were* your community.

Already in the 1970s, as noted earlier, *Our Bodies, Ourselves* had been an exercise in anti-authoritarian "disintermediation." Women whose doctors wouldn't give them the whole truth could assemble it from bits and pieces available somewhere in the wider world. By the 1990s, few professions were as walled off from their clienteles as gynecology had been two decades before. But all professions were on watch. The Reaganite hostility toward government agencies—the belief that they were full of time-servers, featherbedders, rent-seekers—fed into a wider cynicism toward retailers, agents, and middlemen of all kinds. Who needed a shopkeeper to mark up the product? Who needed a journalist to interpret the fact? Internet businesses were favored, and even subsidized, in ways that would remove middlemen from every walk of life, most conspicuously from retail.

Now that people interacted with almost everything through a computer, their tiniest velleities could be tabulated. As Google, Facebook, and Amazon served customers, they were also harvesting and correlating information on them. Around 2010, this process came to be called Big Data. It was, at first, an entertaining curiosity. Walmart discovered through its algorithms that, when storms are coming, people buy more strawberry Pop-Tarts. Target could identify pregnant women from their tendency to buy unscented lotion in the third month of a pregnancy and then mineral supplements a few weeks thereafter.

Marketers and advertisers now felt they held in their hands the same kind of esoteric, all-explaining truth that Alfred Kinsey's *Sexual Behavior in the Human Male* had provided enthusiasts of sex in the late 1940s—a truth that is indifferent to what you say your morals or opinions are. Because the internet was measurable, it was authoritative. It defined morals around what behaviors really are, not vice versa. Any aspiration to see things from a perspective beyond that of day-to-day reality came to seem pointless and risible. Western religion in all its expressions was undermined. As radical Islam spread through both terror and *dawah* at the start of the new century, it was atheism, not any traditional confession, to which Western opinion leaders rallied. They could do no other, as Islamists themselves seemed long to have understood. *God Is Not Great: How Religion Poisons Everything*, a broadside by the political journalist Christopher Hitchens, topped the *New York Times* bestseller list.

Less well understood was that the internet approach to data, and to reality, undermined *all* types of thinking aimed at understanding systems from the outside—not just religion but also science, political ideology, and deductive reasoning. Big Data worked by correlation, not by logic. As the Oxford technology expert Viktor Mayer-Schönberger put it, "Society will need to shed some of its obsession for causality in exchange for simple correlations: not knowing *why* but only *what*." Big Data was a reassertion by powerful corporations of a right that had been stripped from other Americans: the right to stereotype. If you're the sort of person who does *x*, you're the sort of person who'll like *y*.

The information-gathering capacities of the new internet firms brought them into both collusion and competition with government. Google claimed to predict the onset of flu season better than the Centers for Disease Control. SWIFT, the Brussels-based financial telecommunications company, could generate precise measures of total economic activity in a society by using the data from the bank transfers it handled. When pundits sought new ways to harass Russia, they often suggested denying its banks access to SWIFT's services. Google and SWIFT were private companies—yet their regulatory and public information roles made them look like governments in embryo.

Of course government itself could use the new ability to amass, store, index, and easily retrieve data on private citizens. No sooner had big government been "discredited" than the computer revolution tipped the balance of power back in its favor, much as the introduction of artillery in the fifteenth century, by permitting the reduction of upstart noblemen's castles, had restored certain lost prerogatives of kings. With the help of technology, Reaganite capitalism undid the democratic achievements of Reaganite politics. The problem was not the expansion of government until it crowded out the private sector—it was the expansion of the private sector until it became a kind of government.

Eliot Spitzer, Edward Snowden, and surveillance

The internet, for a while, empowered people as consumers, but it left them more vulnerable as citizens. The ambitious New York attorney general Eliot Spitzer was a pioneer of information-age government, waging a selective investigatory crusade against those who did business in the state. He rooted out abuses in the investment banking world, where the regulatory regime had not caught up to the conflicts of interest unleashed by the Clinton administration's bank deregulation. In their communication with investors, for instance, research analysts at Merrill Lynch and Salomon Smith Barney routinely overrated the stock of companies to which they hoped to sell investment banking services. Spitzer also pursued a variety of progressive causes associated with the civil rights revolution. He fought crisis pregnancy centers, often connected to the Catholic church, that sought to dissuade women from getting abortions. He opposed "stop and frisk" policing in black neighborhoods. He tried to provide driver's licenses to all illegal immigrants. A lot of people thought he represented the future of the national Democratic party.

Spitzer was presumptuous. The New York attorney general's office had never been the enforcer of first resort for the finance industry—the Securities and Exchange Commission and the National Association of Securities Dealers had done that. But, like the bankers he went after, Spitzer took advantage of the ambiguity about what's legal and what's not that always arises when a society moves from one technological platform to another.

There were a lot of emails lying around in companies' private servers and those of internet service providers. The simplest way to treat them was as private and personal. Most users of the internet in its first decade assumed that the rules of privacy from the old pre-internet world would "map" commonsensically onto the new one. A gentleman didn't read others' emails, any more than his grandfather would have read people's letters. The Fourth Amendment, which protects against illegal searches and seizures, would operate in cyberspace by some kind of analogy.

But there was another way of looking at things: In sending emails, which passed through the private hands of various data processors and wound up stored on a supercomputer in some sparsely inhabited state, the sender had given custody of them to other private parties and had thereby forfeited his legal right to privacy. Without ever laying out a formal theory, Spitzer proceeded as if the whole of a company's correspondence ought to be open to him. In 2002, he issued a subpoena to Merrill Lynch's internet group for all emails on all subjects.

It was sometimes hard to tell whether Spitzer was motivated by public-spiritedness or by ambition. Much of the ambiguity was cleared up after he was elected governor in 2006 and assigned state police to keep his main political rival, the Senate majority leader, under surveillance. It took an accident to trip him up. Two years later, a wire transfer he had made to pay for a session with a prostitute at the Mayflower Hotel in Washington, D.C., drew the attention of financial investigators under the Bank Secrecy Act, which was just then being aggressively used to fight terrorism. Politically, Spitzer lived by the sword and died by it.

Cyberspace not only held private repositories of data that the state could subpoena and examine. It also offered undreamed-of avenues for government to set up its own surveillance. In the early summer of 2013, Edward Snowden, a young infrastructure analyst with experience at both the National Security Agency and the Central Intelligence Agency, fled to Hong Kong and then to Russia after revealing to the *Guardian* and other newspapers the extent of the U.S. government's spying programs. Snowden was a contractor with an impressive intellect, great initiative, and top-level security clearances. Politically he was hard to pigeonhole. A hero to the *Guardian's* left-wing readers, he had nonetheless supported the libertarian Republican Ron Paul in the previous year's election and spoke in similarly idealistic tones of the Constitution. "I do not want to live in a world where everything I do and say is recorded," he said.

Snowden revealed considerable detail about U.S. spycraft in the ongoing war against Islamist radicalism. The NSA used a technique called "method interdiction," intercepting ordinary digital data packages on their way to a user and infecting them with software that could trace the recipient's every online move and execute malicious operations. It tapped the phones of foreign leaders. It spied on the internet pornography–viewing habits of Muslim radicals in hopes of compromising them. It took over public and private servers. Accidents happened. The agencies "bricked"—knocked out—the internet across Syria using these tricks.

That the government ran such programs around the world was not altogether surprising. What made the story more serious was the revelation of how widely the spy agencies had cast their net domestically and how closely they worked with Silicon Valley. A program called Prism gave the NSA access to information from Microsoft, Google, Yahoo!, Facebook, YouTube, Skype, AOL, and Apple. The companies' role in sharing it was never fully clear, but Verizon, for example, was ordered to share with the NSA the records of all American phone calls, domestic and international.

Either the United States was monitoring its citizens through a twentieth-century-style secret police operation run as a public-private partnership (the sort of thing Ron Paul's libertarian followers worried about), or it was singling out a fifth column of mostly immigrant Muslim radicals (the sort of thing the American Civil Liberties Union worried about). Those who knew the most about internet security often took the most consequential precautions against being tapped. Mark Zuckerberg taped over his laptop's webcam. Apparently it was no longer out of the question that the government might put its own citizens under routine surveillance. What once would have required unconstitutional legislation and the hiring of tens of thousands of agents could now be carried out with the flip of a switch or the cooperation of one of the larger high-tech companies.

The culture of internet moguls

The New Economy was bound up in government from the get-go. Much turn-of-the-century "entrepreneurship" involved lobbying and lawyering to corner markets in emerging classes of intellectual property, and by the second decade of the century, high-tech companies were lobbying more aggressively than banks. But for a decade or so, the great internet fortunes required relatively little political bullying to amass. The spirit of the age sufficed.

As noted, Amazon was able to destroy the country's traditional bookstores and chains, thanks to an extraordinary tax subsidy, conferred by both judicial shortsightedness and congressional design. A 1992 Supreme Court decision had given states the right to tax only companies that had a "physical presence" there. The justices did not envision that a retailer using emerging technologies might grow into a half-trillion-dollar company by cannibalizing local stores while having a physical presence almost nowhere. The 1998 Internet Tax Freedom Act, mentioned earlier, banned taxes for internet access and email "postage," as well as special levies at any level for online shopping. It foreclosed the possibility that brick-and-mortar stores might compete on an equal footing, and ensured their eventual demise.

By 2011, when California's new governor, Jerry Brown, broached the idea of making the tax burden more equitable, it was already too late for Amazon's competitors. Amazon was still collecting sales tax in only five states. Its pricing advantage over physical bookstores in California was 7.5 percent. Amazon nonetheless threatened to evade any imputation of "physical presence" by severing ties with its thousands of California-based "affiliates," websites to which it paid a commission for "click-through" purchases.

Then Amazon made good on the threat. It moved to close facilities in Arkansas, Connecticut, Illinois, and Texas when plans to tax e-commerce were debated. Clearly it was favored tax treatment (and the financing and pricing advantages that went along with it), rather than any technological innovation, that most distinguished Amazon from its rivals. Amazon agreed to pay taxes to California the following year, and other states soon managed to tax it. Half a decade later, a normal sales tax regime was in place for Amazon in 45 states.

By that time, though, Amazon had acquired other advantages that rendered it undislodgeable. Taking in more than half the American money spent online, it had no retail rivals in the free world. Its decade-and-a-half-long tax subsidy, coupled with quiescent anti-trust enforcement, had allowed it to amass a trove of customer data that no competitor could match. A quarter-century after the internet began to reach a broad public, the shopping districts of many small cities, where middlemen of all kinds once gathered, had either disappeared or turned into bizarre, semi-abandoned places in which a couple of espresso bars and automatic teller machines stood amid long rows of empty store-fronts, their plate-glass windows X-ed up with masking tape.

The marketing campaigns of the internet giants were sweet narratives of liberation. Their inner workings were bossy, shifty, and ruthless. At Amazon, a *New York Times* exposé revealed, you could "earn a virtual reward proclaiming, 'I'm Peculiar'—the company's proud phrase for overturning workplace conventions." What "conventions"? Wearing a tie? Those had been overturned years ago. "Peculiarity," it turned out, was Amazon's word for conformity. There were annual "cullings" that one former Amazon human resources director called "purposeful Darwinism," and employees were encouraged to be "vocally self-critical." They were also encouraged to snitch on one another through the use of an "Anonymous Feedback Tool."

In August 2014, Christian Rudder, president of the online dating service OkCupid, announced in a blog post that the site had, as an "experiment," given certain pairs false information about their compatibility. Two months before, Facebook had been exposed as doing something similar: omitting emotionally positive messages from certain users' news feeds. "We noticed recently that people didn't like it when Facebook 'experimented' with their news feed," Rudder posted.

"Even the FTC is getting involved. But guess what, everybody: if you use the internet, you're the subject of hundreds of experiments at any given time, on every site. That's how websites work."

Moguls didn't usually admit as much. The country's newest billionaires and their sidekicks, almost all of them under forty, behaved as if there were something enlightened, altruistic, patriotic, and even heroic about knocking down things that other people had spent lives, and sometimes generations, building up. To call a businessman "disruptive" became a compliment in the 2010s, just as it had been a compliment to call one "aggressive" in the 1980s. The saps who visited websites bore the cost of these experiments, and corporations pocketed the profitable information their experiments generated.

Internet bosses often sought to absolve themselves of responsibility for this inequity by presenting it as a free-market transaction. But that was not true. The internet was no longer something one could take or leave. The problem was not that a new public square had been created but that the old public square had been destroyed. The bookstore where you could go if you didn't like shopping at Amazon was *no longer there*. The social gatherings for high school girls bored with Facebook, or for high school boys who didn't feel like strapping on headphones and shooting people in virtual reality games, *no longer happened*.

Online dating, of the sort that OkCupid profited from, was becoming one of society's bedrock institutions. According to the National Academy of Sciences, more than a third of Americans who married between 2005 and 2012 had met online. As for the two thirds of people who didn't meet their spouses online, they were yesterday's people. They may have been a majority, but their type was doomed to disappear. They therefore mattered less. This was a new phenomenon in American democracy: the illegitimate majority that, because it was on the wrong side of history, could justly be thwarted, constrained, or ignored.

The rules of life used to be set according to the jostling interests of individuals and groups. Now they would be set by the algorithms tech entrepreneurs wrote into their internet applications. The law professor

Lawrence Lessig had warned of this development in *Code and Other Laws of Cyberspace* (1999). The book had received good reviews, but the profundity of the change described by Lessig wasn't fully understood. Until the turn of the century, one could still assume there was a limit to how far such code could diverge from inherited laws and customs—because it would have to win the trust of internet users.

It turns out it didn't have to. The high-tech firms had a kind of power not envisioned in Ayn Rand's theories of capitalism from the 1980s or in traditional models of market regulation. These firms were not new entrants to market systems but new market systems. They were networks. As the computer scientist Robert Metcalfe had shown, a network's value increases exponentially with its growth. Over time, the most attractive thing about a network may be simply that a large number of people have already chosen it. When a network reaches critical mass, competition becomes pointless. Yes, some other company might design a "better" network, but that wouldn't necessarily make it a competitor. "As the network power of a standard grows," the legal theorist David Singh Grewal wrote in *Network Power* (2009), "the intrinsic reasons why it should be adopted become less important relative to the extrinsic benefits of coordination that the standard can provide." Google soon commanded 88 percent of online search traffic in the United States, and 90 percent in Europe and the United Kingdom. Facebook, if you include its subsidiaries WhatsApp and Instagram, was responsible for 77 percent of mobile social media.

Citizens had a "choice" whether or not to join the new networks cropping up, but it was actually a choice only for people middle-aged and older, who already had an economic or social status earned offline. For the youngest generation—those born in the last two decades of the twentieth century—opting out of the web meant opting out of society altogether. They were called "digital natives," but native-born status appeared not to offer the perquisites that it had in the old analog world of national citizenships.

By many traditional measures of well-being this first internet generation was worse off. By 2016, about a third of people aged 18 to 34 were still living with their parents, more than lived with a spouse or other partner—the first time in American history that had happened. The internet was exacting an enormous price for social missteps at a stage in life when young people traditionally try on new personalities. A chubby French-Canadian adolescent lost track of the fantasy video-tape he had made of himself acting out an episode from *Star Wars* in a school rec room. It turned up, though. It was posted on the internet and viewed 900 million times.

The affinity between high tech and civil rights

"The college campus rather than the factory chimney is likely to be the distinctive feature of the megalopolis," Peter Drucker predicted in 1968, "the college student rather than the 'proletarian' its central political fact." He proved right. The two elite projects that caused the most institutional upheaval at the start of the twenty-first century—diversity and digitization—were hatched, headquartered, and run in universities. There was an affinity between them. Computers looked like the solution to many problems of intolerance and inequity. The algorithms they ran on were neutral and dispassionate. They couldn't be taught to hate like the flag-waving men who drove eighteen-wheelers or the paranoid housewives who sat on school boards in Kansas.

It was dismaying when, a couple of decades into the internet age, the cyber world of tomorrow started to resemble the bigoted world of yesterday. Google showed its ads for high-paying jobs to men more often than to women. Arrest-related ads popped up when people searched for common black surnames or historically black fraternities.

A software program for gauging convicts' likeliness to reoffend proved especially scandalous. Developed by computer statisticians at a company called Northpointe in Colorado and used in Broward County, Florida, and elsewhere, the Correctional Offender Management Profiling for Alternative Sanctions (COMPAS) software used algorithms to decide whether to release, parole, or continue to lock up a given prisoner.

There were serious constitutional problems with using private software packages that way. Tech companies resist divulging the algorithms that account for much of their products' value. Google's are top-secret, and so were Northpointe's. A convict could thus be denied an explicit explanation of the grounds on which he received harsher or more lenient treatment. But in this case the complaint involved not Northpointe's property rights or its transparency but its results. The COMPAS algorithm tended to assess black inmates as more likely to reoffend than whites.

Problem was, they were. Any accurate system gauging the probabilities of reoffending would have shown a similar imbalance. But neutrality was no defense. A *Guardian* report described the working of the COMPAS software as "stunning," "frightening," and "nefarious."

It is worth again recalling Alan David Freeman's distinction between the "perpetrator" perspective on civil rights (which seeks only to eliminate bias, and will leave things alone when bias cannot be proved) and the "victim" perspective (which assumes bias, and seeks to eliminate the inequality associated with it). The perpetrator way is punctilious and slow-moving; the victim way dramatic and disruptive. For half a century the victim perspective had been imposed by courts, backed with the threat of criminal and civil penalties. Eventually people lost the ability to tell the difference between inequality and racial discrimination. In almost all of the media coverage of the COMPAS controversy, the two terms were used as synonyms. Indeed, it was evidence of bad faith to assert that an inequality might ever result from something *other* than discrimination.

Though the contrast between the two perspectives was not new, computers put it into starker relief. It had always been hard to rule out conscious prejudice when an innkeeper or personnel manager claimed he "didn't like the look" of a minority customer or applicant. But you could rule it out with Northpointe's software—the program didn't even know the race of the inmates being considered. The computer did, however, look at 137 variables, ranging from poverty, employment, and previous criminal record to subtler questions about attitude and personal beliefs. Clearly, some of these variables, and maybe a lot of them, were correlated with race.

To obtain a less "biased" result—i.e., a result that better accorded with post–Civil Rights Act policy goals—one would need to "unknow" facts that were present in the data set. There were precedents for this in the real world: Certain college admissions committees allowed candidates to forgo submitting College Board test scores, whether because doing so would give closely watched colleges more discretion or because it would drive up their students' average scores. Experts cited in the *New Republic* suggested a different remedy for COMPAS: "diversifying the range of inputs for AI systems, especially those related to marginalized groups—photos of men doing the dishes, say, or of two women getting married." "Diversifying the range of inputs" was a euphemism for providing the past with alternative facts. There was a real-world precedent for this, too: By 2016, in all but a handful of states, people who had undergone sex-change surgeries could request that authorities alter the sexual designation on their birth certificates.

Reformers were caught in an ethical and logical dilemma. On one hand, the past was unfair. "With data inevitably drawn from the past," a British science writer lamented, "the algorithm's logic is imbued with the biases, flaws and injustices that come with it." On the other hand, the past is where the data of science are to be found—that's what makes science scientific.

It was demoralizing. Diversity was the ethical credo, just as high tech was the business credo, of an elite that prided itself on its technocratic rationality. Ethics and business were presented as two faces of the same coin. When the high-tech consultant Dave Goldberg, 47, died suddenly in the spring of 2015, the *New York Times* reported that "even strangers were shocked at his death, both because of his relatively young age and because they knew of him as the living, breathing, car-pooling center of a new philosophy of two-career marriage"—as if feminism allowed one to overcome not just sexism but also mortality.

Diversity advanced primarily at top universities, at the moment when hundreds of entrepreneurs were using the financial and computer algorithms developed there to build billion-dollar fortunes. In time it would be emulated at less prestigious universities.

The professors who presided over Harvard's undergraduate houses used to be called "house masters." In 2016, the masters voted unanimously to change their title to "faculty dean," with some citing the connection of the word "master" to slavery. Bizarre: Harvard was not just the most elite educational institution in the world. It had also managed to confer a majority of spots in its undergraduate student body on non-whites and had reduced its intake of white Christian males from close to 100 percent in the early twentieth century to only about 10 percent or so in the early twenty-first. Yet here the university was, worried that those paying $63,025 a year to stroll across Harvard Yard discussing the lyrics of Edmund Waller and the oils of Corot, to scull on the Charles and attend openings at the Hasty Pudding, to eat cucumber sandwiches and sip amontillado at what used to be called "master's sherries"—here Harvard was, worried that these kids would be unable to distinguish their house master from a slave-driving antebellum overseer.

By 2016, "diversity" was a desideratum for media companies that wanted to show themselves on the cutting edge of business. Cheddar, a live-streaming financial news channel founded by a former employee of BuzzFeed and aimed at younger viewers, ran a story and video explaining how a "Luxury Fashion Line Empowers Women" while "employing formerly incarcerated women" and "supporting an amazing, amazing crowd-funding campaign . . . that helps people carbon-offset," according to a co-founder, the actress Alysia Reiner. The Silicon Valley–based online magazine *Ozy*, funded by Steve Jobs's widow, Laurene, and the German media conglomerate Springer, showcased a similar mix of entrepreneurship and civil rights. "Jackie Robinson, Business Pioneer" was a not-atypical story. The word "diversity" had become a marker of money, class, and power.

The rise of philanthropy

An extraordinary inequality, unmatched since the nineteenth century, had begun to prise apart the American social structure after the 1970s. The share of wealth held by the top 1 percent of American households, which reached its lowest level in recorded history in 1978 (23 percent), had nearly doubled (to 42 percent) by 2013, a generation later.

Americans were remarkably *un*-cynical about the wealth of the wealthy, even after the financial crash of 2008. In 2010 the investor Warren Buffett won praise for backing President Obama's suggestion of a 30 percent minimum income tax for those making over a million dollars a year, a guideline that Obama tried to endear to the American public by attaching Buffett's name to it. Buffett admitted he paid a rate of only 17.4 percent (about $6 million) on his income of $40 million a year. It took the supply-side economist Arthur Laffer to point out—correctly—that in 2010 Buffett's net worth had actually risen not by $40 million but by $10 *billion*, a figure that was 250 times as large as the one Buffett cited. And, because it was in the form of unrealized capital gains, it was almost completely sheltered from income tax. Buffett's effective tax rate was not 17.4 percent but 6 one-hundredths of 1 percent. He was proposing to raise it to 12 one-hundredths of 1 percent. The so-called Buffett rule was a means not of tapping Buffett's wealth but of sheltering it.

Yet Buffett himself regularly showed up on lists of the country's most admired men. The country had taken Ayn Rand's Reagan-era dream to heart, submitting to "inspirational" business leadership. It was a historian of the New Deal, James MacGregor Burns, whose 1978 study *Leadership* had resuscitated the idea, dear to the steel magnate Andrew Carnegie, that there existed some identifiable human quality of "leadership"—a part-moral, part-intellectual endowment shared by all the great leaders of men. The titans of capitalism had proved in the marketplace their capacity to move vast sums and organize vast enterprises. "There must be great scope," Carnegie wrote, "for the exercise of special ability in the merchant and in the manufacturer who has to conduct affairs upon a great scale." Control over the machinery of political power was only a fitting reward for such men.

Now here they were again, albeit in slightly different shapes. The fungible excellence that entitled one to rule could today be revealed not just on the stock market or factory floor but also on the big screen or the soundstage. Why shouldn't Bono harangue the public on development aid or Angelina Jolie on family policy? Leadership was leadership. Rich people should be powerful people. And vice versa, politicians chimed in. "If the American people give you the honor of serving them," former president Bill Clinton told the Brazilian advertising company Grupo ABC in 2012, "you should keep doing it after you leave office." Grupo ABC paid him $450,000 for his services.

Much of the influence that the very richest sought to exercise was in the form of charitable gifts. It was thus assumed the rich were "earning" their power by providing something useful. Unlike other peoples, Americans could deduct the money they give to charity from their taxable income. Donors could exclude up to half their adjusted gross income, and could carry this deduction forward for five years. A dedicated political agitator earning $10 million a year could thus deduct $25 million in taxable income over that period.

Over time, the law evolved so that "charitable gifts" were understood to include not just buying soup for the homeless but also "educating" the public about such contentious political issues as abortion, education, health policy, or gun control. Philanthropy, the Princeton historian Olivier Zunz wrote, is "a capitalist venture in social betterment, not an act of kindness as understood in Christianity."

Most of those who donated on a large scale were political agitators of one kind or another. Foundations, vast empires of advocacy organized along philanthropic lines, could be tightly controlled by rich people to influence politics. Eliot Spitzer's father used part of his half-billion-dollar fortune to set up the Bernard and Anne Spitzer Charitable Trust, which gave $140,000 to the National Abortion Rights Action League and other groups that backed his son in the New York governor's election of 2006. Mark Zuckerberg's $100 million gift of Facebook stock to Newark's public schools drew a promise of matching contributions from Democratic mayor Cory Booker and Republican governor Chris Christie, though it was hotly disputed whether Booker (as opposed to the school board) even had the authority to run the schools. Until a court intervened, Booker refused to release information relating to his deal with Zuckerberg, saying it fell outside the framework of his official duties.

These foundations were not only large—they were also subsidized by taxpayers. Where taxes are progressive and high, deductions are regressive and incentives perverse. The rich not only had the money to build bigger institutions but also paid for those institutions in more deeply discounted dollars. It was *cheaper* for them to amass charitable power than it was for the average citizen. "We all pay, in lost tax revenue, for foundations," wrote the Stanford political scientist Rob Reich, "and, by extension, for giving public expression to the preferences of rich people." Reich estimated the value of this subsidy at $54 billion.

The danger that such incentives would draw the rich into a political role incompatible with democracy had long been understood. The Massachusetts chief justice Horace Gray addressed it squarely in the middle of the nineteenth century in *Jackson v. Phillips*, arguing that trusts aimed at changing laws are something other than charities. Gray held that a charity could fight slavery—"a bondage which [Massachusetts] law regards as contrary to natural right, humanity, justice, and sound policy." But fighting for female suffrage involved changing the constitution. Those who did so were therefore not engaged in charity and not "entitled to peculiar favor, protection, and perpetuation from the ministers of those laws which they are designed to modify or subvert."

But there is always a lot of money behind the contrary opinion.

Over time the charitable deduction transformed Carnegie's philosophy into Washington's law. The "compassionate conservative" of his time, the engineer Herbert Hoover, turned his success at using charities to feed much of Europe during World War I into his calling card for the presidency. Bringing philanthropic organizations into government became his signature reform. His successor, Franklin Delano Roosevelt, in building his New Deal, wanted no part of foundations. Harry Hopkins, a top advisor to FDR who was himself a veteran of the foundation world, warned the president that private interests backed charitable organizations mostly as a means of running them, and could take his programs over.

The Kennedy and Johnson administrations invited philanthropists back. The Ford Foundation, established to allow the family members of Henry Ford to keep control of their automobile company in the face of the inheritance tax that went into effect in 1936, became a pillar of the civil rights movement. Its officers did community organizing and set up the inner-city community action agencies that were command centers of the War on Poverty. "In effect," wrote the political scientist and later senator Daniel Patrick Moynihan, "the Public Affairs Program of the Ford Foundation invented a new level of American government."

The most effective giving leveraged private fortunes into government power, and the most effective government power leaned more and more on private fortunes. "Farsighted philanthropists," wrote former Clinton aide Matt Miller, "all come to realize that advocacy—i.e., efforts to shape how public resources are utilized—offers the best possible bang for the charitable buck." What Harry Hopkins had seen as the biggest danger of philanthropy, the domination of democratic institutions by energetic and moneyed elites, Miller now saw as its promise. Despairing of the country's "two-party tyranny," he even called, midway through the Obama administration, for a "patriotic billionaire" to make a run for president as a way of shaking things up.

Carrying out various progressive functions would, for a half-century after the civil rights revolution, do much to raise the morale of the rich. David Rockefeller, George Soros, Ted Turner, Bill Gates, Michael Bloomberg, Oprah Winfrey, and other extremely wealthy people met as an informal group reportedly known to its members as "the Good Club." Their foundations, initiatives, schools, and institutions were responsible for much of the governance of society. In the vocabulary of the nonprofit sector, the word "governance," with its overtones of flexible technocratic planning, had replaced "government," with its overtones of slow-moving institutional accountability. By 2008, "governance" was being used 30 times as often as it had been half a century before. Governance was more lucrative than government, and offered an army's worth of leadership roles for meritocratic stars. Diversity mandates, set-aside requirements, and affirmative action criteria— they saddled corporate executives, nonprofit administrators, and university deans with big responsibilities. But they also assigned them a governing role that was much more a perquisite than a hindrance.

It would not have surprised Harry Hopkins that America's elites rallied to the agenda of race and gender equality, and used the institutions it brought as a way of legitimating their own wealth. An elite is a minority, too. The Dutch East India Company, the British Raj, the *szlachta*, the Holy See—these elite minorities were different from historically marginalized ones, such as American blacks, immigrants, or gays. But both kinds of minority, elite ones and marginalized ones, live under threat from democratic majorities, and benefit in the same way from laws passed to constrain majority power. Public political discussion has been slow to draw a connection between the "good" stymieing of democratic majorities by the civil rights legislation of the 1960s and the "bad" stymieing that followed in its wake.

Obama: governing without government

Whether or not Barack Obama was well disposed to oligarchy, he was operating in a society in which rich people had more and more sway over government and politicking. He used and emulated the power of philanthropy. His education reform Race to the Top did not straight-forwardly fund state education departments. It made available billions of dollars in federally budgeted prize money to reward the states that were quickest to adopt the "Common Core," a curricular philosophy that Bill Gates had used his foundation and its $40 billion endowment to push.

The educator Diane Ravitch complained that education policy, once the part of American government most answerable to grassroots democracy, was now being made, top-down, by three powerful fam-ilies: the Gateses of Washington State, the Waltons of Arkansas, and the Broads of Los Angeles. They were abetted by gifts from the owners of Dell, Netflix, and the Gap, and by an array of foundations driven sometimes by political ambition, sometimes by political prudence: billionaire New York mayor Michael Bloomberg's family foundation; the Laura and John Arnold Foundation, built on the hedge fund for-tune of Enron's sharpest young energy trader, which now also backed the journalistic collective ProPublica in its crusade against assessing prisoner risk through algorithms; Jonathan Sackler of Purdue Pharma, which had made billions from sales of the omnipresent opioid Oxy-Contin; and the DeVos family of Michigan, founders of the cosmetics and health conglomerate Amway.

One was reminded of the *catorce familias* who ruled El Salvador during the Cold War or of the system of "cacique democracy" that the historian Benedict Anderson described in the Philippines, except that these latter-day philanthropic worthies spoke in the idiom of high tech. The distinction between politicians and "innovators" blurred. Real political decisions were now being made by businessmen who owed their fortunes (or thought they did) to mottoes like "First, break all the rules."

Foundations certainly found it easier to get things done. Where governments faced accountability, a billionaire could say that what he did with his money was none of anyone's business. Why should a lion of philanthropy, giving away his money to promote a project that was self-evidently virtuous—say, black empowerment—have less leave to "break the rules" than he had had in his youth, when he was merely peddling internet gadgetry for profit? In 2011, with money from his own foundation and George Soros's Open Society Foundations, Bloomberg launched a Young Men's Initiative aimed at mentoring and advancing black and Latino men. Was this a sop that a shrewd urban politician was lobbing at an important voting bloc? Or was it the personal initiative of a nice guy who just happened to be mayor and that only a churl would cast a suspicious eye at?

President Obama sought to scale Bloomberg's program for non-white boys up to national level, renaming it "My Brother's Keeper." Friendly banks subject to government regulation (such as American Express) and foundations linked to military contractors (such as the Northrop Grumman Foundation) funded the program for the last two Obama years.

The program was shrouded in a vagueness that was never dispelled—about whether it was designed to exclude whites, about whether it was a government program at all. It was trumpeted in White House press releases as part of a race-specific presidential agenda: "President Obama is taking action to launch *My Brother's Keeper*—a new initiative to help every boy and young man of color who is willing to do the hard work to get ahead." But the White House issued a disclaimer, too: "The My Brother's Keeper Initiative logo may not be used in any matter that could give rise to the appearance that the U.S. Government owns, operates, or is affiliated with any nongovernmental entity or its programs, products or services."

The administration used its ingenuity to fund programs without recourse to congressional appropriations. Between 2012 and 2014, U.S. financial enforcement agencies collected $139 billion in fines from the banks they regulated—an amount larger than the entire federal budget in the early years of the Vietnam War. That fines could serve as a form of taxation was a principle familiar to anyone who had ever driven through a small-town police speed trap, and in 1998 a consortium of state attorneys general had, through the courts, confiscated as damages a quarter-trillion dollars of tobacco companies' assets in the so-called Master Settlement Agreement. It seemed an aberration at the time, but in 2013, JPMorgan Chase alone paid $20 billion in fines. Since that bank was Obama's most important early campaign backer, and since not a single major executive, there or elsewhere, was ever jailed for what, to judge from the size of the fines, would have been the largest financial crimes in history, it is natural to wonder whether this fining arrangement was disciplinary or collusive.

President Obama's policies were sometimes popular, sometimes not—but he often spoke as if the normal give-and-take of society's democratic institutions were an obstacle to governing rightly. He mused aloud about bypassing Congress on controversial matters, especially guns, and then did so. He ruled by executive order, delaying by fiat the implementation of his signature Affordable Care Act. The Consumer Financial Protection Bureau that he established in 2010 drew its funding from the semi-independent Federal Reserve, not from Congress. Obama appointed the CFPB's first director, Richard Cordray, through a recess appointment, bypassing Congress in that way, too. He sought to regularize the status of millions of illegal immigrants using his war-making authority, a move for which his defenders claimed the Emancipation Proclamation as a precedent.

Intellectuals and pundits egged him on. They recommended lines of policy that would only recently have been thought autocratic. In 2011, when a Republican-dominated Congress showed itself reluctant to add to the country's debt, then $16 trillion, *New York Times* columnist Joe Nocera cited Section 4 of the Fourteenth Amendment, which included language meant to prohibit the Southern states readmitted to the Union after the Civil War from repudiating debts the rump Union had incurred when the South was outside of it. Nocera claimed the language in Section 4 authorized the president to "unilaterally raise the debt ceiling." Although Obama resisted this batty construal, there was an impatience with democracy in the air.

Nudge and behavioral economics

The fallibility of human decision-making had lately preoccupied social scientists. They were out to show that *Homo economicus*, the reliably rational calculator of his own advantage who inhabits the works of Adam Smith and Alfred Marshall, did not exist. In 2002 the Israeli psychologist Daniel Kahneman of Princeton had won the Nobel Prize in economics for work done with his late compatriot Amos Tversky of Stanford. Their work in so-called behavioral economics described people's tendency to mis-predict and mis-assess. Human reason, it turns out, can cut its way through problems only if the choices are laid out in the proper way. When you ask people what the product of the first eight integers is, much depends on whether you express the multiplication in the form

$$1 \times 2 \times 3 \times 4 \times 5 \times 6 \times 7 \times 8$$

or in the form

$$8 \times 7 \times 6 \times 5 \times 4 \times 3 \times 2 \times 1$$

Given five seconds to make an estimate, the average person thinks the product of the first string is 512 and of the second 2,250. Neither guess comes close. The actual answer for each string is 40,320. What was troubling about such failures is that they were not due to wishful thinking or superstition or corruption—problems correctible by education and indoctrination. They were flaws in the way the normal human mind normally works. "Bias" was the word Kahneman and Tversky often used for these flaws. For a generation, every imputation of bias in public life had required the ransacking of institutions and the shredding of reputations. Now the word "bias," which had once carried overtones of bigotry and evil, had come to mean something like "human nature."

During the presidential campaign of 2008, two of Barack Obama's friends and advisors from the University of Chicago collaborated on a book called *Nudge*, which used behavioral economics to justify an activist state. The law professor Cass Sunstein would become the senior advisor on regulation to the Obama White House. The economist Richard Thaler, an early collaborator of Kahneman, would take up a similar role as head of the Behavioural Insights Team for Britain's Conservative prime minister David Cameron.

Thaler and Sunstein laid out the baleful consequences of poorly designed choosing systems and suggested ways to fix them. Schoolchildren carrying their trays through lunch lines don't usually mull over which dessert they prefer; they often grab the first thing their eyes alight on. So why not put at eye level apples and pears rather than Cheetos and Funyuns? Corporate employees want to save for retirement but, when young, underestimate how much they will need. So why not require that the default option for workers be a "Save More Tomorrow" plan, which would cause their deductions to escalate automatically as the years passed?

The authors called such measures "choice architecture" or "libertarian paternalism." No one would be ordering anybody around. Authorities would just firmly steer subjects to a choice that was obviously superior. You didn't *have* to contribute to your retirement, the way you did with Social Security. Rather than fine or jail you for not conforming, the government would resort to other, more intimate tools, starting with inconvenience. Still, there was something obnoxious and humiliating about this approach that was hard to put one's finger on.

Nudge challenged the "harm principle" that John Stuart Mill had laid out in his book *On Liberty* (1859). Mill held, basically, that the state ought to intervene in people's lives only if there is a risk of their harming others. One of Mill's reasons for not intervening is that people tend to be the best judges of what is good for them. Sunstein disagreed: What is good for them, he wrote elsewhere, is "largely an empirical question."

But Sunstein was leaving out the first and most important step. What is good for people, at least for free people, depends on their priorities. The question becomes empirical only once a priority has been set. The important political matter is who gets to set it. Thaler and Sunstein were disguising the arrogant project of setting priorities as a modest and commonsensical project of measuring outcomes.

The strongest case for letting people make choices without the interference of the state rests not on their competence as choosers but on their dignity as persons. Ordinary people's reasoning might give mediocre results in picking a cafeteria lunch or managing a retirement plan. Why wouldn't it? The human mind evolved its rational abilities in order to address challenges across a wide variety of life situations—not structured games involving time-discounting, devised by actuaries.

Behavioral economists seemed unaware that there were benefits to this non-specialized human way of reasoning, and even in some contexts to the skewed sense of reality it produced. If people often plan in ways that are unduly optimistic, including by saving too little for retirement, that is because the voice running in any person's head must not only assess reality but also motivate him to get out of bed in the morning.

The *Nudge* philosophy was an exercise in so-called Socratic ignorance. In Plato's *Apology*, Socrates is told by his friend Chaerephon that the Delphic oracle considers him the wisest of men. So Socrates visits a statesman known for his wisdom. It is not clear why he makes this visit—whether to test his own intellectual mettle, seek counsel, or fish for compliments—but Socrates comes away unimpressed:

> So I left him, saying to myself as I went away: Well, although I do not suppose that either of us knows anything really beautiful and good, I am better off than he is,—for he knows nothing, and thinks that he knows; I neither know nor think that I know. In this latter particular, then, I seem to have slightly the advantage of him.

Socrates's claim to know nothing is, to use a twenty-first-century term, a humblebrag. It may demean Socrates in the normal hierarchy built around questions of who's smarter than whom. But it simultaneously establishes a more important hierarchy, a meta-hierarchy, in which Socrates arrogates to himself a role as supreme judge over what wisdom is. Once that role is granted, Socrates's intelligence is not just better than the politician's—it transcends it. *Nudge* was making similar claims.

If there's no *Homo economicus*, there's no *Homo democraticus*. In a lot of languages the word for "vote" is the same as the word for "voice" (голос, Stimme, voix). Democracy is the system in which the voice of the people is sovereign and beyond appeal. *Nudge* puts conditions on that sovereignty. In this sense its principles are those of civil rights law, in which the voice of the people is sovereign, *once it has been cleared of the suspicion of bias*. If people are blocked by bias from understanding the "true" nature of human relations, authorities have the license, even the obligation, to overrule them. Civil rights thus does not temper popular sovereignty, it replaces it. What we call political correctness is the natural outcome of civil rights, which makes fighting bias a condition for the legitimacy of the state. Once bias is held to be part of the "unconscious," of human nature, there are no areas of human life in which the state's vigilance is not called for.

But wait: If people's calculations are always under suspicion of bias, then what places the calculation of "activists"—of politicians and professors, behavioral economists and diversity counselors—in the Socratic position, above suspicion? Aren't their minds fallible, too? Why do *they* get to be the "choice architects," while others merely inhabit the structures of their design? This is a bit of a mystery. Just as the sky deck of the Shard gives the best view of London because it is the only high place from which one cannot see the Shard, the biases of those intervening against bias are invisible. As long as no one questioned the claim of activists to be fighting bias, the burden of proof on society's "choice architects" was virtually zilch.

For the improvements in government efficiency that Thaler and Sunstein sought, no cost in damaged traditions and institutions was too high:

We agree that long-standing traditions may be quite sensible, but we do not believe that traditionalists have a good objection to libertarian paternalism. Social practices, and the laws that reflect them, often persist not because they are wise but because Humans, often suffering from self-control problems, are simply following other Humans. Inertia, procrastination, and imitation often drive our behavior.

The authors were ready to enforce conformity to their own new institutions but deaf to others' claims for conformity to older ones. Marriage, for instance.

From gay rights to gay marriage

When *New Republic* editor Andrew Sullivan first publicly suggested it in 1989, the idea that gay people might want to marry one another sounded preposterous, and not just because it contradicted certain treasured stereotypes. Marriage was an institution of sexual regulation. Gay rights was advancing pari passu with the radical feminist cause of delegitimizing such institutions and the traditional idea of masculinity that they served. In some lights, the two causes, feminism and gay rights, had come to seem one.

After decades of deploring the "objectification" of female bodies in advertising and popular culture, feminists had made little headway. But their focus on equality helped open the culture up to an analogous exploitation of male bodies, however ironically it may have been intended at the beginning. The first male strippers started performing in 1979 at a club called Chippendales off the Santa Monica Freeway. Although the performances were advertised as a "Male Exotic Dance Night for Ladies Only," men sued to be admitted. To promote its new line of underpants in 1982, Calvin Klein rented a billboard above a JVC record-and-stereo store in Times Square to display a five-story-high photo of the amateur pole vaulter Tom Hintnaus standing, tanned and glistening in the sunlight, in clingy white briefs. By the middle of the decade, the Soloflex exercise machine company, with its "twenty-four traditional iron pumping exercises," was running a series of magazine ads that featured not the machinery but the finished product: a hard-bodied, V-shaped man in jeans, naked from the waist up, his hip cocked like a stripper's, removing a wife-beater undershirt stretched taut between his arms and obscuring his face like a mask.

To non-gays, gay liberation appeared to be about sex and how much of it society was willing to tolerate—or embrace. It meant putting up with a certain amount of "gayness" in public, sometimes of an earnest erotic kind, like those ads; sometimes of a slapstick kind, like the political street performances of Sister Boom Boom and other San Francisco–based drag troupes.

Gay activists would have seen this sexual focus as at best a partial truth. Like civil rights marchers and feminists before them, they were demanding, whether they realized it or not, not just tolerance but a conferral of dignity. Without dignity, integration would only be an opportunity to insult the out-group at closer quarters. Civil rights was always this way: dignity was an integral and non-negotiable part of what was demanded, and a government interested in civil rights must secure it, no matter what the cost in rights to those who would deny it.

Delivering this dignity to gays was more complicated and disruptive than it was for other groups. Homosexuality was not just an identity but a conduct—a conduct, moreover, that was a crime in much of the country and a source of potential dishonor in all of it. Until the elimination of the draft in the 1970s, homosexuals were, like everyone else, answerable to the armed forces, yet they were not welcome there—at least not as homosexuals. The military summoned men out of their anonymity and, if they revealed their sexual inclinations, left them with a lifelong stigma in the form of a "blue ticket" administrative discharge. The post-war gay subculture in the Eisenhower and Kennedy years was a photographic negative of the military-industrial virtues and vices. Well into the twenty-first century, gay rights was bound up with conditions in the military in a way that may have looked arbitrary to others. It did not look that way to gays. In order to provide gays with their public dignity, authorities were going to have to alter, delegitimize, and eliminate a lot of institutions in which people had made large moral investments.

Freedom of association is the master freedom—it is the freedom without which political freedom cannot be effectively exercised. But in seeking the freedom to associate with one another, gays faced a problem other minorities did not: identifying one another in the first place. That is why the earliest stirrings of gay liberation were demands for what the historian Lillian Faderman called "slivers of space": coffee shops, clubhouses, and dance clubs in which they could communicate in peace, free of police harassment.

There was a small-scale riot at Cooper's Donuts in Los Angeles in 1959. There was a clash with police over the leafleting of Dewey's coffee shop in Philadelphia in 1965. The uprising outside the mafia-run West Village dance club the Stonewall Inn in 1969 is striking for the specter it raised of hundreds of men overpowering an urban police department, and it has passed into mythology because it was around the corner from the offices of the *Village Voice*, whose young reporters gave a minute-by-minute account of it. But by the time it happened, gays had been seeking ways to connect with one another for years. A desperate felt need to identify political allies would eventually lead in the 1990s to the ruthless practice of "outing" those who had kept their sexuality secret.

Gays sought sanctuary not just in buildings but in institutions. It was a long time before it occurred to anyone that marriage might be one of them. In 1973, when the Homosexual Rights Committee of the Southern California Branch of the American Civil Liberties Union (ACLU) made a list of six long-term priorities, marriage was not on it. In 1983, gay leaders had an opportunity to grill Democratic presidential candidates Walter Mondale and John Glenn about issues they cared about. They didn't mention marriage. In 1991, when the

National Gay and Lesbian Task Force asked its membership to rank civil rights issues in order of importance, marriage did not even make an appearance. As Paula Ettelbrick, the legal director of Lambda Legal, put it in 1989, "Being queer isn't setting up house and seeking state approval for doing so."

As the AIDS virus spread through the gay population after the early 1980s, though, the absence of state approval came to seem Kafkaesque. The *special* damage visited on gays at the height of the AIDS era—i.e., the damage that differed from the grief that death brings to everybody, and that AIDS brought to others who suffered from it—came from probate law and medical regulations designed for heterosexuals. Men died in hospitals, denied the company of their lovers of several decades; couples were thrown into penury because American-style health benefits, designed to protect spouses, did not convey to partners; parents and siblings successfully challenged the last wills of men who had bequeathed their life's savings to otherwise destitute boyfriends (who themselves needed expensive experimental drugs); and so on. The broad public's reaction was not one of pity. In 1985, a majority of Americans polled (51 percent, according to the *Los Angeles Times*) favored quarantining those suffering from AIDS.

And yet, as that happened, AIDS was stripping away many of the habits that had separated gays from the American mainstream. AIDS brought an end to almost all of the institutions on which a promiscuous "gay lifestyle" had been built in the 1970s, starting with New York's sex clubs and San Francisco's "bathhouses." By revealing closeted gays to one another, albeit in the cruelest way possible, AIDS turned the "gay community"—once a slogan—into a real community, cohesive and with a capacity for political action.

When gays began to sue over visitation and other matters, they discovered that judges looked more indulgently on their demands than the general public did. That changed everything. Gays who sought marriage turned their focus to the courts—to civil rights law. In 1993, a Hawaiian court opined that limiting marriage to men and women was a bias. Although three quarters of the state's voters disagreed, the state's Supreme Court backed up the lower court in 1996. Hawaiians voted in a landslide (69 to 28 percent) two years later for a constitutional definition of marriage as a solely heterosexual institution. Judges elsewhere were undaunted. In 1999, Vermont's Supreme Court ordered the legislature to come up with a plan to give gays marriage rights. Hence the first "civil unions" bill in 2000.

Bowing to public demand, Bill Clinton signed the Defense of Marriage Act in 1996. In the event some state started marrying gays, judges in other states would now be on solid ground in refusing them the "full faith and credit" that would otherwise be their constitutional due. Well into the twenty-first century, there was not a single state in the union where voters viewed gay marriage favorably. Before 2012, when Maine, Maryland, and Minnesota approved gay marriage ballot initiatives, it had been repudiated in referendum after referendum, 31 in all, despite the vastly superior economic resources and lobbying networks that pro–gay marriage forces drew on.

They drew on other advantages, too. Though homosexuality does not produce children, homosexuals sometimes do. Administrators and judges had grown more inclined to permit full parental rights to homosexuals who had previously been married. Soon they permitted gay men and women to adopt their partners' natural children. Eventually they allowed gay couples to adopt children outright. Families formed this way wound up being nine tenths of the law. Gays' fates were now obviously bound to the destiny of families and communities in a way they had never been before.

Cases were now arising in which the main question before the court concerned whether it were better that a gay couple raising a child be married or unmarried. In one of them, *Hillary Goodridge & Others v. Department of Public Health* (2003), seven Massachusetts couples sued the commonwealth for the right to marry. Four of the couples had children, whether adopted or through a previous marriage.

Judge Margaret Marshall of the Massachusetts Supreme Judicial

Court announced that there was no rational basis for denying gay people the fruits of marriage. There was sleight of hand involved: Marshall reasoned *from*, not *to*, a redefinition of marriage, taking it not as a foundation of society *anterior to* and *recognized by* government but as a welfare institution *established by* government, like a dog park or a VA hospital, which carried a "cornucopia of substantial benefits." The more important anthropological question of what marriage was could thus be replaced by a different question, that of equal access to state favors, claimed less on gays' individual behalf than on behalf of the families they had formed.

That approach reversed the burden of proof on all marriage questions that came before courts. Barely a decade later, as a landmark gay marriage case approached the Supreme Court in 2015, the activist and law professor David Cole could speak of "discrimination on the basis of sexual orientation, such as the same-sex marriage bans at issue in *Obergefell.*" *Bans?* It was one thing to say that an antiquated definition of marriage needed to change with the times, quite another to say that an *intent* to harm gays (for in order to have a "ban," there must be an intent) was one of the reasons marriage had arisen in the first place. Until that point it had been as reasonable to speak of a ban on gays marrying as it would have been to speak of a "ban" on men breast-feeding. "One must identify a reason for preserving traditional marriage," Cole continued, "and a theory for why recognizing same-sex marriage will undermine that interest."

Marshall's redefinition of the conflict came with an exorbitant promissory note. On a sentimental level, the challenge first posed by Massachusetts congressman Barney Frank in the mid-1990s—when he asked "how two people loving each other somehow threatens heterosexual marriage"—had always been a devastating argument for gay marriage, unanswerable, especially inside a loving family that had a gay person in it. After *Goodridge*, it was clear that gay marriage did carry a threat, because, as we have said, it overturned the understanding that marriage was something antecedent to government. On that antecedence rested the inviolability of marriages and families, the convention that what they did, how they built their little micro-community of love, was none of the government's business.

Overturning this understanding did not immediately damage any heterosexual marriages. But it diminished and threatened marriage as an institution.

Windsor: the convergence of elites

The lawsuits out of which gay marriage law was built were almost never launched by couples who had just decided they were fed up and stormed into City Hall. They were carefully designed—one could say scripted—by tax-exempt foundations, public interest law firms, and Manhattan and Washington corporate lawyers working pro bono. Because public opinion was unsympathetic toward gays and suspicious of their fidelity, plaintiffs were recruited for high standards of bourgeois comportment. To sway a judge and charm the public, plaintiff couples ought to be exemplary, the sort of people one would want for one's own sons, or one's own grandmothers. They had to avoid public displays of affection and talking about sex.

It was presumably with reference to the stage management of such cases that the talk-show host Rachel Maddow applauded *United States v. Windsor*, a case aimed at undermining part of Clinton's Defense of Marriage Act (DOMA), for its "tactical brilliance." Gone were the misgivings about barratry raised half a century before by Herbert Wechsler and Harry Kalven, who had spoken of the NAACP's litigation strategy as "an almost military assault on the Constitution."

Were courts still really operating as courts when private parties could write the script the courts would follow? The NAACP's legal culture had triumphed to such an extent that this question could no longer be asked in polite company. The sense must have persisted, nonetheless, that no solidly grounded constitutional right should require "tactical brilliance" to assert.

There was never a more attractive plaintiff than Edith Windsor. Good-humored, emotionally balanced, debonair, she had fallen in love in the 1960s with a woman named Thea Spyer and had never fallen out. They had long wished to marry, and had expressed that wish. For decades Windsor had cared for Spyer, who had developed multiple sclerosis and was a quadriplegic by the time the two married in Ontario in 2007. Under the Defense of Marriage Act, the federal government would not recognize their marriage. So when Spyer died two years later at the age of 77, her property could not be passed on tax-free, saddling the 79-year-old Windsor with a federal estate tax bill of $363,000.

If you looked at marriage the way the *Goodridge* case had, as a government program that is either fair or unfair, this was the sort of clear-cut injustice that could doom DOMA as unconstitutional. As Windsor's lawyer put it, "If Thea had been 'Theo,' Edie would never have had to pay a penny of estate tax."

There was another way to look at it. Only estates in the richest micro-fraction generate estate taxes. In 2009, 5,700 estates in the entire country, roughly the top fifth of 1 percent, were liable for it. In addition to their liquid assets, the pair had an apartment in Manhattan and a house in the Hamptons, on the eastern tip of Long Island. From that angle their tax problem was not that they were gay people but that they were rich people. Activists keen to overturn DOMA were divided on whether this was the right case to do it with.

The gay rights movement, as it began to focus on marriage, was an odd mix of political idioms. While it used a rhetoric of exclusion traditionally deployed by downtrodden ethnic minorities, gay marriage was also the single cause that most united the richest and best-connected people on the planet. It united them politically more than either tax rates or financial regulation did. The Human Rights Campaign, which lobbied for gay rights legislation and backed gay rights litigation, was bankrolled by Amazon, American Airlines, Apple, Citibank, Coca-Cola, Dell, Goldman Sachs, Google, Hershey, Hyatt, IBM,

Intel, Lexus, Macy's, MasterCard, Microsoft, Morgan Stanley, Nationwide, Nike, Northrop Grumman, Orbitz ("Visit GayOrbitz.com"), Pepsi, Pfizer, Pottery Barn, Prudential, Shell, Starbucks, Target, Tylenol, UPS, Whirlpool, and Williams-Sonoma—to give only a selective list of its very largest contributors. It had moved its staff of 150 into the old headquarters of B'nai B'rith in the heart of Washington, D.C., midway between Dupont Circle and the White House. In a neighborhood where any major lobbying firm might consider it a status symbol to rent a floor, the Human Rights Campaign owned an entire nine-story, two-wing building.

The investors George Soros and Michael Bloomberg, tech billionaires Bill Gates and Jeff Bezos, entertainers David Geffen and Brad Pitt, Republican financiers Paul Singer and Seth Klarman—all backed gay marriage with millions in donations. Support for gay marriage in Silicon Valley was almost unanimous. Google's employees gave 96 percent of their campaign contributions, and Apple's 94 percent, to oppose California's anti–gay marriage Proposition 8. There were no equivalents on the other side. When it was discovered in 2014 that Mozilla chief executive officer Brendan Eich, the designer of the web browser Firefox, had given $1,000 to *support* Prop 8 six years before, a storm of outrage forced his resignation.

There was a similar pattern for celebrities and elites who volunteered their time and services: They were all on the pro–gay marriage side. Literally all. Reuters discovered in 2014 that of the country's 200 largest law firms, 30 were representing lawsuits against state Defense of Marriage acts. Not one was defending these laws. The gay rights activist and litigator Roberta Kaplan worked pro bono on behalf of Edith Windsor—a coup, because it permitted Windsor to tap the vast paralegal and social resources of Kaplan's firm, Paul, Weiss.

Kaplan's heavily subsidized, expertly staffed machine of constitutional revision was fully armed to do battle against . . . nothing. Midway through the case, the Obama Justice Department informed Kaplan that it would not be defending its law. In the case that eventually became

Hollingsworth v. Perry, California attorney general Jerry Brown opted
not to defend his state's marriage law, either. When the veteran Republican Supreme Court advocate Paul Clement agreed to defend the law
on behalf of a congressional advisory group, pro–gay marriage activists
pressured the corporate clients of his law firm, Atlanta-based King &
Spalding, which not only did not support him—it cut him loose.

Pipe dream though gay marriage had seemed at the turn of the
century, unstable though its support appeared in opinion polls, it was
now next to impossible to find a member of the so-called One Percent
who had anything bad or even skeptical to say about it. There was an
interlocking of directorates in journalism, the foundation world, the
legal profession, and the bench. Kaplan wrote that NPR legal correspondent Nina Totenberg had helped her pick out her outfit before
her oral arguments in *Windsor*, that Ariel Levy, covering the case for
the *New Yorker*, wept tears of joy when the decision was handed down,
that oral arguments for the *Obergefell* case in 2015 "felt like old home
week for LGBT civil rights advocates at the Supreme Court," with
Gavin Newsom, the San Francisco mayor who had illegally issued
marriage licenses in 2004, and Margaret Marshall, the Massachusetts
judge who had penned the *Goodridge* decision, sitting side by side. An
understanding of such dynamics is surely what led Kaplan to dismiss
colleagues' worries that Edith Windsor might be too rich or too privileged to serve as a plaintiff in a high-profile rights case. "Edie did not
live differently in relationship to many of the judges and the justices
who might hear her case," she later wrote, "and frankly, those were the
only people we needed to persuade."

Nationwide public opposition had never been a reason to give up.
The reforms of the 1960s had created mechanisms for forcing social
change even against the democratically expressed wishes of the electorate. As Rosa Luxemburg had written of the Russian Revolution,
"The real dialectic of revolution stands the parliamentary cliché on its
head: The road leads not through majorities to revolutionary tactics,
but through revolutionary tactics to majorities."

The gay marriage argument followed that road. A public boiling with rage at gay marriage in the 1990s, with the antis outnumbering the pros by a factor of two, three, or four, seemed to change its mind. In the aftermath of the landmark *Obergefell* decision of 2015, Gallup's poll question showed a solid majority of 58 percent favorable.

Certainly, the question was worded in such a way as to disengage Americans' moral sentiments about the reform. It *assumed* the legality of gay marriage rather than inquiring about it, in such a way as to add to the "pro" column those who disapproved on principle of breaking the law. ("Do you think marriages between same-sex couples should or should not be recognized by the law as valid, with the same rights as traditional marriages?") Still it measured *something*. Americans had been told what to think by judges, bureaucrats, and journalists, and, rather than rebel against official presumption, most had seemed to conform to it, after a little embittered grumbling. They included a good number of conservative Republicans. Either their opinions had been lightly worn, or American democracy was undergoing an epochal shift.

Bill Clinton said, not long after the turn of the century: "If you look back on the sixties and on balance, you think there was more good than harm, you're probably a Democrat. If you think there was more harm than good, you're probably a Republican." As a Democrat, Clinton was speaking primarily of minorities who could vindicate their rights against the majorities that had ignored them. But they were not the only ones for whom the intervening years had done more good than harm. The new "capitalist" elite encouraged by Reagan had not overthrown the old statist elite he wrongly thought he was fighting; it had merged with it, multiplying the power of both. The Democrats were the party of these people, too. In the 2008 presidential election, voters in 19 of the 20 richest zip codes in the country gave the bulk of their campaign contributions to Barack Obama, most of them by landslide margins.

By the time Obama left office, the country's top ten political donors were putting $323 million a year into the political system, and most of them were Democrats. It was common to complain about the influence of the Kansan Koch brothers on Republican politics, but David Koch barely scraped onto the top ten list, accounting for less than a tenth of the contributions ($6.2 million) that the San Francisco hedge fund manager and environmentalist Democrat Tom Steyer ($74.3 million) did. Democrats accounted for most of the names in the top hundred contributors, too.

At the same time, the internet was stripping the media industry of both geographical and ideological diversity, as the writers Jack Shafer and Tucker Doherty explained. In 1990, 455,000 people had worked in journalism as reporters, clerks, ad salesmen, designers, and the like, according to the Bureau of Labor Statistics. A quarter-century later, there were only 173,900 such jobs—and they were different.

Media jobs in the old days had been spread nationwide and linked to the political cultures of their diverse readerships. "The Sioux Falls *Argus Leader* is stuck in South Dakota just as the owners of hydroelectric plants in the Rockies are stuck where they are," Shafer and Doherty pointed out. But three quarters (73 percent) of twenty-first-century internet media jobs were either in the northeast corridor, on the West Coast, or in Chicago. Those places were rich and overwhelmingly Democratic: 90 percent of people working in the reconfigured news industry lived in a county that Democrats would win in the 2016 presidential election. Only rarely now did people at the top of society meet people who disagreed with them.

Obergefell: triumph of the de facto constitution

Supporters of gay marriage often viewed those who disagreed with them as corrupt and vicious. For Kaplan, DOMA was simply an "odious law." Morally speaking, this was not an open-ended debate but the orderly and inevitable procession toward an already known civil rights "truth," the only question being whether justices and activists, working together, should occasionally slow the pace of reform in order to avoid provoking a democratic "backlash." In his midstream history of the gay marriage movement, Harvard law professor Michael Klarman (brother of the financier Seth) wrote, "A Supreme Court ruling in favor of gay marriage in 2012 or 2013 would also split the country down the middle. Yet, given how quickly public opinion is evolving in favor of gay marriage, within a decade or two such a decision would probably also become iconic."

The unanimity of the One Percent meant that the main controversies surrounding gay marriage could be swatted away "blithely," as the late Massachusetts justice Martha Sosman had seen early on, warning in her eloquent dissent in *Goodridge* that "this proffered change affects . . . a load-bearing wall of our social structure." That was still true when Anthony Kennedy's decision in *Obergefell v. Hodges* (2015) made gay marriage the law of the land. Antonin Scalia's dissent focused a bit on the inconsistencies in Kennedy's reasoning: Whereas in *Windsor* Kennedy had invalidated the Defense of Marriage Act on the grounds that "the Federal Government, through our history, has deferred to state-law policy decisions with respect to domestic relations," in *Obergefell* he had imposed a federal standard of marriage on all the states.

But that was a decidedly minor aspect of Scalia's dissent. More significant was his attack on the decision as undemocratic. Here, for the first time in a systematic way, emerged the critique that an elite had hijacked the language of civil rights and used it to alter the country in its essence. "A system of government that makes the People subordinate to a committee of nine unelected lawyers," Scalia wrote, "does not deserve to be called a democracy." He called the decision an upper-class "putsch," noting that every single member of the Supreme Court had gone to either Harvard Law School or Yale Law School, and concluded:

> The strikingly unrepresentative character of the body voting on today's social upheaval would be irrelevant if they were functioning as *judges*, answering the legal question whether the American

people had ever ratified a constitutional provision that was under-stood to proscribe the traditional definition of marriage. But of course the Justices in today's majority are not voting on that basis; *they say they are not.*

In this he was right. While asserting that gay marriage was gain-ing in popularity, Kennedy explicitly repudiated certain conceptions of democracy that had until recently been sacrosanct. "It is of no mo-ment whether advocates of same-sex marriage now enjoy or lack mo-mentum in the democratic process," he wrote. Unless someone was expecting the Court to apologize for *Brown v. Board of Education*, this thwarting of majority rule in the name of civil rights was what the Supreme Court was *for*. Kennedy used the language of an affirmative action case, *Schuette v. BAMN* [By Any Means Necessary] (2014), to assert "the right of the individual not to be injured by the unlawful exercise of governmental power."

That is, in order to pre-empt Scalia's argument that the decision was anti-democratic, Kennedy was constrained to say that the marital laws under which a dozen generations of Americans had met, wed, and multiplied had been illegitimate all along—an "unlawful exercise of governmental power." Again, for Kennedy and those who thought like him, the Civil Rights Act of 1964 had not enhanced the Constitution as it had once been understood but had replaced it. This was turning into a constitutional problem of the profoundest kind.

Barack Obama was the first president to understand civil rights law this way, as a de facto constitution by which the de jure constitution could be bypassed, and to lead the country on that new constitutional basis. His second inaugural address in 2012, an explicitly Constitution-focused address in which he repeated "We the People . . . ," honored "Seneca Falls and Selma and Stonewall" (i.e., women's rights, civil rights, and gay rights) as the great constitutional achievements of modern times, and extra-parliamentary protest and Supreme Court jurisprudence as the high roads that led there.

No one would ever call *Brown v. Board of Education* an achievement of Dwight Eisenhower, or say that *Roe v. Wade* was a blot on Richard Nixon's otherwise skillful handling of domestic policy; the spheres of executive action and constitutional review were held to be operationally separate. But the gay marriage cases under Obama (*Hollingsworth, Windsor*, and *Obergefell*) were quite different. Obama was not merely a witness to but a field marshal of the litigative strategy that culminated in the Supreme Court's removal of the country's marriage laws from democratic scrutiny. As he told *Rolling Stone* editor Jann Wenner near the end of his term, he had been pursuing this strategy for years, even as he campaigned as a champion of traditional marriage:

> WENNER: You got up there and said legalize same-sex marriage, and you pushed it right over the edge . . .
>
> OBAMA: Well, you know, no. . . . If you will recall, what happened was, first, very systematically, I changed laws around hospital visitation for people who were same-sex partners. I then assigned the Pentagon to do a study on getting rid of "don't ask, don't tell," which then got the buy-in of the Joint Chiefs of Staff, and we were then able to [repeal] "don't ask, don't tell." We then filed a brief on Proposition 8 out in California. And then, after a lot of groundwork was laid, then I took a position.

Clearly, there had never been a moment in his political career when Obama did not believe in gay marriage. Lillian Faderman had asked him directly about it during a Florida stop on his 2006 book tour. "How could *I* be against gay marriage?" he replied, adding ". . . though if I were running the movement, I wouldn't start with gay marriage." And when he began running for president a year later, he didn't. He professed himself a believer that marriage was a thing for a man and a woman.

Obama was not "evolving." He was dissembling. He was able to communicate his support for gay marriage to gays, while communicating the opposite to the rest of the country. Establishment gay rights groups never offered more than the mildest pro forma criticisms of the president's public position opposing gay marriage, but private citizens who expressed exactly the same position were often keelhauled. In the summer of 2009, Miss California, Carrie Prejean, told a Miss America judge she thought marriage should be between a man and a woman and got called a "dumb bitch" for it on the judge's website. The president's views on a pressing public controversy passed without remark, while the identical views of a powerless college-age girl were subject to misogynistic calumny. That standard of accountability would have made no sense unless there had been some *real* political system operating behind the scenes, while the fake one was being rattled around as a distraction in front of the public.

What was operating behind the scenes was, once more, civil rights. As enacted in 1964, civil rights had meant a partial repeal of the First Amendment. It had withdrawn the right to freedom of association long implicit in the freedom of assembly. But now, when authorities and judges hit difficulties or resistance in advancing civil rights, they were tempted to insist on ever-larger derogations of First Amendment rights, perhaps believing themselves to be working in the "spirit" of civil rights. Civil rights meant affirmative action. Civil rights meant political correctness. And in the wake of court-ordered gay marriage, it quickly became apparent that civil rights would mean court-ordered *approval* of gay marriage.

The years after *Obergefell* were taken up with arguments that would have shocked a First Amendment lawyer of 1964—arguments over, for example, whether a baker could be compelled to bake cakes for gay weddings. In 2015 and 2016, various states were informed that it was incumbent on them to allow transgender students to use the high school bathroom they identified as matching their gender. When North Carolina legislated against that principle, it fell afoul of the Obama Justice Department's civil rights division, which threatened to sanction the state's economy, as if North Carolina were some belligerent rogue state in the former Third World. Corporations and celebrities rallied behind the administration's threat: Walmart, PayPal, Deutsche Bank, Bruce Springsteen.

According to the progressive understanding, which in the early twenty-first century became the official understanding, American history was "the story of the extension of constitutional rights and protections to people once ignored or excluded." The vote, for instance, which in colonial times had been limited to property-owning males, became the right of all adult males. Then women. Then blacks. This was the route followed by the dissident tendency within the American constitutional tradition that culminated in civil rights.

But now civil rights was no dissident tendency. It *was* the American constitutional tradition—the whole of it, if President Obama's second inaugural address was to be believed. And now civil rights, like other constitutional traditions before it, was fated to see its protections, its prerogatives, and its logic claimed by people once excluded from it. Civil rights had been devised for blacks. But its remedies proved useful to a widening circle of groups that, at the time of its passage, had not seemed similarly ill treated: First immigrants. Then women. Then gays. Then, in the *Hobby Lobby* case that came before the Supreme Court in 2014, Christians.

A terrible irony of civil rights, obvious from the very outset but never, ever spoken of, was making itself manifest as the 2016 election approached. The civil rights approach to politics meant using lawsuits, shaming, and street power to overrule democratic politics. It encouraged—no, it required—groups of similarly situated people to organize against the wider society to defend their interests. Now it became clear that the members of *any* group that felt itself despised and degraded could defend its interests this way. Even whites.

8

Losers

*The rise of the Tea Party—The decline of white America—Race
as the entirety of culture—"Nigger" and "white supremacy"—
Margaret Seltzer and Rachel Dolezal—Manliness and crime—The
Ferguson uprising—Black Lives Matter—The Yale uprising—
"Who we are as Americans"*

The Tea Party movement emerged in Barack Obama's first
month in office. The Americans who belonged to it had come
to believe that they had been hoodwinked out of their country.
They never came to an explicit consensus on how or by whom. Sometimes their complaints concerned health care, sometimes states' rights,
sometimes political correctness. This was not, however, a reason to dismiss them.

Republicans had until then been a complacent party for the complacent middle classes, happily ignorant of the new institutions being built
up for the benefit of the classes above and below. They were unlikely to
have a well-thought-out policy on, say, internet password protection,
single-sex bathrooms, dioxin abatement, or bike trails. Optimistic or
idiotic, they had been that way for decades. Although the Democrats
were the party of information technology and finance, although Democrats dominated the faculties and even the student bodies of almost
all elite universities, Republicans still thought of themselves as the
party of the well born and the well bred, which they had remained into
the 1960s. Even when, under Newt Gingrich in the 1990s, they broke

with Reaganite sunniness and began waging a "culture war," with warnings about American decline, they retained the naïve expectation that winning arguments would allow them to win elections, and winning elections would allow them to change the country. They were a whole party of Happy Warriors. Now that changed.

The rise of the Tea Party

A sparsely watched Thursday-morning tirade by CNBC business journalist Rick Santelli in 2009 gave the Tea Party its name. Santelli complained that the Obama administration was subsidizing "losers' mortgages" and called, in a Chicago twang, from the floor of the Chicago Mercantile Exchange, for a "Chicago Tea Party." In those early days it was common to snicker at the Tea Party for misunderstanding, and applying inconsistently, the Reaganite message of small government. President Obama drew laughs when he quoted a letter in which an old lady had admonished him, "I don't want government-run health care. I don't want socialized medicine, and don't touch my Medicare."

But the Tea Party was never an outgrowth of Reaganomics or of any other practical preoccupation of the Reagan-era Republican party. Even the business-focused Santelli eventually saw this. "The tea party image that was in my mind that day," he explained five years later, "is more a philosophy."

It was a pessimistic philosophy, rooted in Patrick Buchanan's Republican and Ross Perot's third-party campaigns of 1992, both of them dissents from Reaganism. Buchanan's supporter and sometime advisor, the late columnist Sam Francis, had seen back then that even as they celebrated their ascendancy, conservatives were losing ground. A long, unwarranted celebration was, in a sense, what all of modern conservatism was. "The Old Right, composed mainly of the organized conservative resistance formed in the mid-1950s and centered around *National Review*, failed to understand that the revolution had already occurred," Francis wrote. "Those who continued to adhere to Old Right doctrines were no longer in a position to 'conserve' much of anything." This was perhaps too pessimistic a description of *National Review*. Its founder and editor, William F. Buckley, Jr., after all, had launched his career with a book called *God and Man at Yale* (1951), which forthrightly addressed the overthrow of certain Western traditions and asked what could be preserved and what rebuilt.

But Tea Party followers (the movement would never acquire leaders) took Francis's view to heart. Since Buckley's time, another revolution had occurred, and conservatives had been on the losing side of that one, too. Their complaints were similar to those beginning to emerge from European conservatives. In July 2014, Hungarian premier Viktor Orbán lamented the results of the human rights–based liberal democracy that the United States had been spreading ever since the Cold War ended. Under communism in the late 1980s, Orbán had been a fearless defender of what he thought were Anglo-American ideas of liberty, but now he saw that they were subject to a terrible paradox. "The liberal organisation of society," he said, "is based on the idea that we have the right to do anything that does not infringe on the freedom of the other party." That was the basis on which Hungary had been reconstructed in the two decades after the end of the Cold War. And now Orbán sensed a terrible problem at its core:

> Although this is an extremely attractive idea, it is unclear who is going to decide the limits beyond which someone is infringing on our freedom. And since this is not automatically given, somebody must decide it. And since we have not appointed anybody to decide it, what we experienced continuously in everyday life was that the strongest decided. What we continuously experienced was that the weak were trampled over. Conflicts on the acceptance of mutual freedom are not decided according to some abstract principle of justice, but what happens instead is that the stronger party is always right.

However mildly and sensibly put, it was a bleak vision. Orbán's detractors described his speech as a call for "illiberal democracy"—a fair enough description, since Orbán himself had used the adjective. But more central was his diagnosis that the West's democracies had already turned illiberal themselves, and the problem had begun with American-style doctrines about rights. At some point in the half-century leading up to 2014, the United States had ceased to be a classic, open-ended democratic republic. It had taken on features of a "managed democracy" along European lines.

In the fall of that year, Kentucky Senate candidate Rand Paul fashioned himself into the mainstream politician most in sync with the Tea Party's views. "I have a message," he said on the night of his nomination, "a message from the Tea Party." Progressives believed they knew exactly where Paul was going with that message. First the Louisville *Courier-Journal*, then National Public Radio, then Rachel Maddow of MSNBC questioned him aggressively about the Civil Rights Act of 1964. Paul professed to "abhor racism" and to approve of nine tenths of the articles in the act but to be uncomfortable with its revocation of business owners' rights to do business with whomever they saw fit. "Does the owner of the restaurant own his restaurant? Or does the government own his restaurant? These are important philosophical debates, but not a very practical discussion."

It certainly wasn't practical. As constitutional orders went, civil rights was well and securely anchored. It had won the loyalty of those it was intended to empower. Blacks voted almost unanimously for the party of civil rights, giving Democrats 90, 88, 95, and 93 percent of their votes in presidential elections after 2000. The civil rights regime could also claim the overwhelming loyalty of other minorities, those non-white, non-male, and non-heterosexual groups to which it had been extended. It reserved a special role for the country's moneyed leadership class, too, providing a haven from unruly democracy that members of that class always seek. Finally, civil rights, more than any American political movement since Prohibition, rested on a conception of *evil*. It had a moralistic, even a religious, component that was a powerful weapon for building esprit de corps among insiders and intimidating and shaming outsiders. Its promoters saw their foes as evil incarnate.

The day before Santelli's rant, attorney general Eric Holder also professed himself fed up. "Though this nation has proudly thought of itself as an ethnic melting pot," he lamented at an African-American History Month celebration, "in things racial we have always been and continue to be, in too many ways, essentially a nation of cowards."

It was an odd time to say so. The White House, both houses of Congress, and the federal judiciary from coast to coast and at all levels, were in the hands of Democrats, who had never in their history been more united and voluble on civil rights matters. The silence was elsewhere. Americans who were not activists in this way had learned to duck and dissemble. Even the most conservative politicians in the Republican party, as noted earlier, had acquired the self-protective habit of praising civil rights while lamenting the way it at some unspecified point had been "hijacked." "Prudence" was probably a better word than "cowardice" for such behavior. Whatever you called it, though, it was not an obstacle to Holder's vision of civil rights but a precondition of it. Partly because of that prudence, partly because the Tea Party had no organization or leadership and wrote no manifestos, the spirit of the new movement was hard to discern.

Perhaps the emergence of the Tea Party movement mere weeks after the inauguration of the country's first black president could be explained without reference to race. The 2008 campaign, after all, had coincided with the worst financial collapse in three generations, and the country was entitled to an accounting. But by the end of Obama's term, race divided the parties more than anything else. Democrats, by 84 to 12 percent, thought racism was a bigger problem than political correctness. Republicans, by 80 to 17 percent, thought political correctness was a bigger problem than racism.

This polarization around civil rights resembled the polarization around slavery that emerged into public view only with the vote on the Wilmot Proviso in 1846. Similar questions of affiliation and identity were emerging. Republicans held the allegiance of the vast majority of white people. Their party united almost the entirety of both the pro–New Deal and the anti–New Deal coalitions of fifty years before. The Democrats were the party of those whose concerns had never been in the forefront of American political life until the 1960s—blacks, gays, and women (as women)—and of tens of millions of immigrants and their offspring, who back then had not been in the country at all. The culture of civil rights was what American politics had come to be about, even if Americans had trouble talking about it.

Starting with the passage of the Civil Rights Act in 1964, whites were "racialized" in a way they never fully understood. They were the people whom American politics was *not* about. They were excluded—at least as claimants—under civil rights law. As civil rights spread to cover groups other than blacks, the term "people of color" marked whites off as the only people so excluded, and legitimized that exclusion. In this sense the United States had re-created the problem that it had passed the Civil Rights Act to resolve: It had two classes of citizens.

Hannah Arendt had pointed out in the 1950s that, since states were the means through which modern people acceded to all of their rights and dignity, to be stripped of citizenship and rendered "stateless" was an assault on a person's humanity. Stateless people were "forced outside the pale of the law," suspect in the eyes of the authorities even when doing harmless things, and at the mercy of those who did have access to state power. Similarly, when race rather than citizenship becomes the structure through which people accede to their rights, one *must* have a race, willy-nilly. And under the law, whites were "raceless."

That was the civil rights project's great Achilles' heel. It eventually drove a critical mass of whites to conceive of themselves as a race, whether they wished to or not. The process through which most white Americans came to understand the dynamic of the system was not fast, but it was inexorable. It took fifty years, years that saw a steep decline in their social status and a degradation of their way of life.

The decline of white America

In 2010, the fifteen most common surnames in the country were Smith, Johnson, Williams, Brown, Jones, Garcia, Miller, Davis, Rodriguez, Martinez, Hernandez, Lopez, Gonzales, Wilson, and Anderson. There had been no Hispanic names on the list in the 1990 census. The six that suddenly appeared bumped out Moore, Taylor, Thomas, Jackson, White, and Harris. The country now had more Nguyens than Bakers or Turners or Coopers or Cooks, and more Patels than Powells. Wong, Wang, and Yang outranked Davidson, Pearson, and Benson.

The roughly 40 million foreign-born living in the country, along with their many descendants, had brought about a massive ethnic transformation. Optimists, like the social scientist Ben Wattenberg, saw in these arrivals the birth of the First Universal Nation, to cite the title of his 1991 book. Peter Brimelow, an editor at *National Review*, published a book the following year that treated the idea of a universal nation as an oxymoron. All nations were special. A nation too cavalier about who fit in and who didn't was losing sight of what *made* it special, and would not be a nation much longer. An Alien Nation, to cite the title of Brimelow's book, was a more likely outcome.

Most historical experience would lead one to fear that the pessimists were correct. Yet the United States, faced with a comparable wave of mass migration between 1880 and 1920, had confounded similar predictions. "In fifteen of the largest cities of the United States," the historian Arthur M. Schlesinger had warned in 1921,

> the foreign immigrants and their children outnumber the native whites; and by the same token alien racial elements are in the majority in thirteen of the states of the Union....
> Whatever of history may be made in the future in these parts

of the country will not be the result primarily of an "Anglo-Saxon" heritage but will be the product of the interaction of these more recent racial elements upon each other and their joint reaction to the American scene.

Schlesinger's numbers were correct, but his intuition was wrong. By the 1960s, all of those "alien racial elements" had somehow been transformed into members of a "90 percent white" majority—a majority so homogeneous, moreover, that the country would seem stultifying in its monotony to the immigrants' own offspring. Something—whether luck, statesmanship, or divine providence—had allowed Americans to change ethnically while somehow remaining the same people.

Of course, that did not make it prudent to stake the nation's survival on the likelihood that its luck would hold a second time. The last migration had been a lot less racially "alien" than it appeared to Schlesinger. It had brought Europeans, and only Europeans, to a society that was of 98 percent European descent. Yes, 98 percent, for it is often forgotten or ignored that all of the country's "diversity," as we would now call it, was then concentrated in the South and West, areas that the great immigration passed by.

The immigration wave at the turn of the twenty-first century was different. Although the government's use of a linguistic term ("Hispanic") as a proxy for a racial one clouded matters, the migration really did change the country racially. What would happen if this wave resembled not the migration of Europeans to the American northeast a century before but the conspicuously less successful northward migration of Southern blacks that followed?

And the new migrants came at a less propitious time. They were not a fillip to an advancing population but the replacement of a shriveling one. The country's traditional population had no dynamism whatsoever. More than half (53 percent) of the country's 3,100 counties had declining white populations at the start of the century, and the population of white children was falling in 46 of the country's 50 states. It fell by 12 percent in Vermont in just a decade. By the election of 2016, the white population was declining in the nation as a whole. Metropolitan New York and metropolitan Los Angeles had each lost a million white people since 1990.

Then, after decades in which life expectancy had risen steadily in most Western countries, in 2014 it began falling year-on-year in the United States. The statistics masked a continuing rise in life expectancy for all non-white groups and a sharp drop for whites, whose life expectancies had lagged behind those of Asians and Hispanics to start with. Increases in white mortality were concentrated among those aged 25 to 54, the period that used to be called the "prime of life." The 2015 study by the Princeton University economists Anne Case and Angus Deaton that first brought these trends to public attention noted, too, that whites were regressing in their ability to carry out ordinary daily tasks. White people were in more pain, less able to work, less competent, and less able to face other people than they had been a generation before.

Case and Deaton offered an explanation: The increase in white mortality was "largely accounted for by increasing death rates from drug and alcohol poisonings, suicide, and chronic liver diseases and cirrhosis." After 1996, the legalization and mass marketing of new forms of pharmaceutical opioids, notably Purdue Pharma's OxyContin, had led to the most destructive epidemic of addiction in the country's history. Opioid addicts who could not (or could no longer) afford the pills turned to shooting heroin. Drug dealers began substituting for heroin a cheap Chinese synthetic, fentanyl—powerful, hard to dose correctly, and deadly. In 2016, 63,600 people died of overdoses. This was not a slum problem. It hit hardest the whites living in what fifty years before would have been called the "wholesome" suburbs and countryside.

Given that the country's leaders had spent fifty years crying wolf about one drug epidemic or another, the twenty-first-century one must be put in perspective. At the end of the Vietnam War, the return of heroin-addicted soldiers from the combat zones coincided with a scourge of drug pushing in America's housing projects, bringing the rate of overdose deaths to 1.5 per 100,000. Neil Young released his falsetto folk dirge "The Needle and the Damage Done" in 1972, Curtis Mayfield his soul ballad "Freddie's Dead" in 1973, Steely Dan its hypnotic piano song "Charlie Freak" in 1974. It was not just a crisis but a cultural event and a moral outrage. There was a sense that middle-class Americans were ignoring the problem and denying the humanity of those living in the "ghetto."

During the epidemic of concentrated, smokable "crack" cocaine in the 1980s, George H. W. Bush addressed the nation about the prevalence of drugs. To say that that crisis, too, produced some memorable songs would be to commit a gross understatement. It give birth to an entire new world-spanning genre: "gangsta" rap, which would echo through the banlieues of Paris and the dusty villages of West Africa; turn Tupac Shakur and Biggie Smalls into symbols of the inner city's violence but also its romance, wisdom, and swagger; and vie with rock 'n' roll for a while before rap (more generally understood) supplanted rock as the music of American youth of all races. The crack epidemic was at least as serious a problem as the 1970s heroin spike, with a death-by-overdose rate reaching almost 2 per 100,000.

By the time of the 2016 election, which it did much to decide, the opioid epidemic that had begun with OxyContin was killing not 1.5 or 2 but 20 Americans per 100,000. In New Hampshire, Ohio, and Pennsylvania it was killing almost 40 per 100,000, and in West Virginia it was killing 50. Yet until the Republican candidate began to mention it, the airwaves were nearly silent about it. So were the newspapers. Case and Deaton noted that there had been only "limited comment" in scientific circles about rising white mortality more generally.

This was a health emergency of maximum gravity, comparable to the outbreak of AIDS in the early 1980s. The tepid response had to do with how drugs were tied up with race and class. Since to be alarmed about heroin was to be alarmed on behalf of poor white people, Americans were hesitant—perhaps "frightened" would be a better word—to be seen to take account of it. Unlike blacks in the decades after the Vietnam War, twenty-first-century suburban and rural whites were not protagonists of the nation's official moral narrative. Indeed, they barely figured in it.

And certain familiar tools developed to deal with drugs back when drugs had been a black problem had been discredited. The so-called War on Drugs had begun in September 1986, when Nancy Reagan urged youths to "just say no" to them. Stepped-up federal and state drug laws brought a vast increase in the American prison population, to the point where the United States, with 4 percent of the world's population, was by the end of the following decade housing a quarter of the world's prison inmates. The War on Drugs also provided a convenient, non-racial pretext for the militarized policing of black neighborhoods, drastically reducing inner-city crime and ironically doing more to promote racial integration than any other policy since the 1960s.

As the new century dawned, however, many of the pre–Baby Boom voters who had favored a hard line were dying, and the incarceration rate peaked. By 2012, when Colorado legalized marijuana, the oldsters had been replaced by a generation that looked at the drug experimentation of the 1960s as rather cool. Spurred by Michelle Alexander's tract *The New Jim Crow* (2010), Obama accelerated the movement away from mass incarceration that had begun as George W. Bush came to office in 2001.

Drugs were only a proximate cause of white decline. Now poor rural whites were being discussed as a deep social "problem" the way urban blacks had been until a generation before. There were, as always, essentially two philosophies about problem populations: Blame the people, or blame the circumstances under which society compelled them to live. Conservative commentators found themselves in an especially awkward position. When it had been black people suffering from drug addiction, they had for the most part recommended an iron-fist policy. Now, it seemed, they could choose between administering the same measures to whites (which looked heartless) and trying to find a milder way (which looked racist). Most chose heartless. Kevin Williamson of *National Review* admonished readers interested in the plight of such white areas as upstate New York, eastern Kentucky, and west Texas to "take an honest look at the welfare dependency, the drug and alcohol addiction, the family anarchy—which is to say, the whelping of human children with all the respect and wisdom of a stray dog."

In his influential book *Coming Apart* (2012), the sociologist Charles Murray attributed the failings of poor whites to family structure, just as the young White House aide Daniel Patrick Moynihan had done in his 1965 report *The Negro Family*. But there was a difference. At Howard University in 1965, when Lyndon Johnson gave his presidential endorsement to affirmative action, he noted his aide Moynihan's theories of the black family, but added, "For this, most of all, white America must accept responsibility. It flows from centuries of oppression and persecution of the Negro man. It flows from the long years of degradation and discrimination, which have attacked his dignity and assaulted his ability to produce for the family." If shattered family structure were self-evidently blamable on someone else's "oppression and persecution," on "degradation and discrimination," then who was now oppressing poor white people and attacking their dignity?

The economy, perhaps. Lakshman Achuthan of the Economic Cycle Research Institute noted that almost 9 million jobs had been created between the previous economic peak, in November 2007, and the closing months of 2016, a period roughly coincident with the Obama administration. Unpacking those numbers showed that non-whites had gained almost 10 million jobs over those years, while whites had lost 700,000. That had not necessarily been anyone's plan. Whites lived disproportionately in small towns and rural areas at a time when growth was clustering in cities. They made up 78 percent of the rural population but only 56 percent in the major urban areas.

Until the 1970s, the countryside was considered the home of the country's virtues. Robert Pirsig marveled at the "hereness and nowness" of people along the back roads, and Aleksandr Solzhenitsyn, warning Harvard graduates about decadence and unbelief in June 1978, nonetheless felt his optimism swell as he imagined the countryside. "Gradually another America began unfolding before my eyes," he wrote, "one that was small-town and robust, the heartland, the America I had envisioned as I was writing my speech, and to which my speech was addressed." Perhaps the places Solzhenitsyn and Pirsig were admiring in the 1970s actually represented the America of the 1950s. They were places that the reforms of the 1960s simply hadn't yet reached. Now there were no such places. That older America had been well and truly wiped out. In 1975, rural America had meant banjos, bait shops, and cornbread. By the election of 2016, it meant SNAP cards, internet pornography, and OxyContin.

Cities and suburbs, by contrast, prosperous or not, tended to be under the control of the various minorities and well-educated groups whom *Los Angeles Times* journalist Ron Brownstein often described as a "coalition of the ascendant." Their interests inevitably diverged from those of a people going down the tubes. Whites were aging, hedonistic, and barren. The newest Americans were young, diligent, and fecund. Sixteen percent of whites were over 65, versus 7 percent of minorities. Their ideas about where society's resources ought to go, and who deserved to tap them, diverged. Whites wanted cheap meds, lavish pensions, and a labor market in which young people would push wheelchairs and fix meals for next to nothing; immigrants wanted new schools for their children, government-funded day care, and a so-called living wage.

Race as the entirety of culture

A Tomorrow-Belongs-to-Me tone crept into many descriptions of American demographic change. The torch had been passed to a new generation of Americans, who had a message to convey to their elders. The message was: Die. "We often talk openly," said CNN's commentator LZ Granderson in 2014, about the different generational views when it comes to same-sex marriages and how we cavalierly say, as the older generation die off, so does that hatred and perspective die off in our country as well. And it needs to be said, the same thing about race. When it comes to certain aspects of talking about people of different races, certain ideas and perspectives, it's time to die off. I'm not saying people need to die off, but those attitudes need to die off.

The lines between white racism, white failure, and mere whiteness blurred. "With white people heading toward minority status and becoming a lower percentage of the voting public every cycle," wrote Gary Younge of Britain's *Guardian*, "the message necessarily gets cruder—particularly with the presence of a black president." The commentator Fareed Zakaria compared America's working-class whites to Russians after the Soviet collapse: "They were central to America's economy, its society, indeed its very identity," he wrote. "They are not anymore." Paraphrasing a Princeton sociologist to the effect that white people were just complaining because they had been spoiled, he then contrasted them unfavorably with poor blacks and immigrants, who "do not assume that the system is set up for them."

But why shouldn't the citizens of a republic assume that the system is set up for them? The Gettysburg Address said it was set up for them. White politicians began to convey that they weren't oblivious to being spoken of this way. A truculent tone unheard in mainstream political oratory since the 1960s crept back in. When Maine governor Paul LePage tried to explain to a mid-winter town hall meeting in Bridgton who the drug dealers were who were profiting from the opioid crisis that was killing the region's young people, he said:

These are guys with the name D-Money, Smoothie, Shifty—these types of guys. They come from Connecticut and New York, they come up here, they sell their heroin, then they go back home. Incidentally, half the time they impregnate a young white girl before they leave, which is a real sad thing because then we have another issue that we've got to deal with down the road.

LePage's talk was striking not just for the opinions in it but also for the unbullied nonchalance with which he delivered it. It was an offense against a new formality that required that race never be alluded to except in leaden officialese. "At Prudential, we strongly believe that talent comes in every color, gender, origin, religion, sexual orientation, and physical capability imaginable," ran a typical twenty-first-century oath of allegiance. "For this reason, we actively seek out employees, vendors, and business associates from a deep and diverse pool." At a time when any corporate human resources department could be hauled into a courtroom for professing any other belief, the sincerity of such pronouncements was open to question.

A gift that civil rights promised non-blacks was to make the wearying subject of race disappear. *Everyone* was invited to "emancipate yourselves from mental slavery," as Bob Marley sang at the end of his short life, drawing on a formula that the black nationalist Marcus Garvey had used in a speech in Nova Scotia in the 1930s. After a (very) few years of self-denial, Americans would be able to speak openly to one another. Somehow they got instead an America where people were kept on their Ps and Qs about race and gender as never before. Far from suppressing the Southern obsession with race and "blood," civil rights conveyed it to every nook and cranny of the country. The entire culture—all journalism, all art, all books—was suffused with it.

A couple of weeks after LePage's remarks on drug dealers and a short hour's drive away, the hosts of a tequila party at Bowdoin College handed out miniature sombreros, which campus activists deemed an act of cultural appropriation demeaning to Mexicans. "Cultural appropriation," an imprecisely defined concept that had only recently come into vogue, was a sort of racial or ethnic plagiarism. It somehow involved an imperial power's theft and exploitation of a subordinate society's cultural practices. Two students were placed on probation for the offense, and there was a move to oust two members of the student government who had attended the party. Uninvolved undergraduates interviewed by a *Washington Post* reporter sent to cover the controversy asked that their names not be used in the article.

Just why cultural appropriation was bad was never made clear. Wasn't it simply what all people had always done with successful cultural styles and products?

They were doing it now, in fact. Much contemporary culture consisted of reinterpreting and, where necessary, bowdlerizing the history and culture of the half-millennium from the Renaissance to the fall of communism to make its achievements more congruent with the twenty-first-century ideology of diversity. In 2015, *Star Wars VII: The Force Awakens* laundered the plot of the original 1977 *Star Wars* film into a more multiracial cast, and in 2016 the 1984 comedy *Ghostbusters* was remade with all-female agents. The BBC announced a more multicultural remake of Kenneth Clark and David Attenborough's classic *Civilisation* series from the late 1960s. (The new one was to be called *Civilisations*.)

At one point in 2015, the *Washington Post* called the black incendiary Ta-Nehisi Coates the country's "foremost public intellectual"— and it was probably right, since race was getting to be the sum total of what the country's intellectual life was about. There were columnists in the *Post* and the *New York Times* who had the job of sounding off about race morning after morning, not because their readerships had swollen with marginal crackpots but for the benefit of the new establishment, from deputy assistant secretaries in Cleveland Park in the District of Columbia to the trust fund hipsters of Williamsburg, Brooklyn.

One now got the impression that racism and sexism must be hiding everywhere. Rooting them out enlisted the zeal of citizens in a way that resembled the hard-line anti-communism of the 1950s, but on a far larger scale. Now as then, the rarity of actual unmaskings was taken as evidence of the adversary's guile. Unlike communism, which involved an actual organization with a membership list, racism had a flexible definition. Anyone might be accused of it. The social scientist Andrew Hacker cited as evidence of rank-and-file Republicans' racism their agreement with the statement "If blacks would only try harder they could be just as well off as whites." But of course *disagreeing* with that statement would have been even stronger evidence of racism.

The burden of proof on those with racial grievances was lighter than air. Farai Chideya, a Harvard-educated television and radio pundit, wrote in the *Guardian* in 2015:

> My grandmother died 12 years ago this week from colon cancer, at what some people might call the ripe old age of 82. I know the truth: due to lack of adequate medical care, she died too young. I also believe that race was a key factor. That I can only infer, though with plenty of evidence black lives are cut short through inadequate healthcare.
>
> Reading Ta-Nehisi Coates's lauded new book, *Between the World and Me*, and the many responses to it, I am cheered, in a grim fashion, by the rise in attention to physical and economic violence against black Americans. Part of that physical violence comes at the hands of the medical establishment.

This goes beyond lamenting the human condition or lamenting inequality. Chideya implied that the doctors who treated her grandmother committed "physical violence" against her—and stated unambiguously that doctors wreak physical violence on black people as a matter of course.

Nathan Glazer had foreseen such misunderstandings in the mid-1970s, when certain radical civil rights policy makers had assumed that "any deviation from statistical parity could, and should, be interpreted as owing to unconstitutional discrimination." All difference, all inequality, was becoming actionable. But now there need not even be difference or inequality at all. Racism was becoming an official narrative in newspapers, on television, and on the internet. Those who encountered that narrative took it to heart.

The overestimation of black people's part in contemporary society was extraordinary. About 12 percent of the country was black at the turn of the century, according to the U.S. Census. But the average American believed 33 percent of Americans were black, a Gallup poll found. A sixth of Americans believed it was a *majority* black country. The closest to accurate were those who held postgraduate degrees, and even they guessed that the black population was double its actual size. Why wouldn't they? Most people don't spend their days boning up on demographic statistics or counting people by race. If America were only one-eighth black, then the obsessive way politicians and journalists spoke about race made no sense.

The same was true of the way politicians and journalists spoke about gays. In the second decade of the century, Americans, on average, came to believe that the country was between 23 and 25 percent gay, bisexual, or transgender—about 1 in 4. Again, given the doggedness with which the president and the courts took up the cause of gay marriage, and the eagerness with which newspapers and television reported on every step of their progress, why should they have believed otherwise? Who would have guessed that gays, bisexuals, and transgender people together made up 3.8 percent of the population, closer to 1 in 25? Americans had a distorted view of social reality. Their language evolved to reflect it.

"Nigger" and "white supremacy"

Before a performance at the Stockholm Konserthus in the autumn of 1976, the rock singer and poet Patti Smith was asked by a Swedish radio journalist what freedom meant to her. She replied:

> Freedom is inside of me. It means that I'm not hung up with, like, anyone's idea of how I should be, you know? I'm outside of society.

I'm an artist. Rock 'n' roll is my art. I'm a nigger of the universe. And I'm free because I can leap up and scream. I can put my fist up in the air. I don't give a shit, you know? I'm not afraid of death. I'm not afraid of anything except for . . . fear itself.

In almost any year of American history, the word "nigger" in Smith's answer would have shocked listeners. Forty years before she spoke, it would not, to put it mildly, have been the likeliest word to crop up in any discussion of American freedom. Forty years *after* Smith's interview, people couldn't bring themselves to utter the word in any context, and prohibitions against saying "the N-word," as it came to be called, were applied with deadly earnest. In 2015, when the president of the United States himself used the word in the course of an interview meant to rally the country after a racially motivated massacre in a South Carolina church, Fox News and MSNBC bleeped it out. It was a theocratic proscription. No colonial Calvinist or antinomian had ever submitted to his Third Commandment with a more perfect obedience.

Smith spoke in a brief historical window when things appeared to be changing. "Nigger" seemed on the verge of becoming one of those semi-archaic words, like "glebe" or "farrier" or "topgallant," that retain their dictionary meaning but have lost their living cultural context, and with it the lion's share of their emotional impact. Slurs are special cases, but they, too, undergo such changes. Modern Latin-Americans, with their own legacy of slavery and oppression to live down, nonetheless manage to call one another *negrito* or *cholo* or *chino* without coming to blows. In the made-for-TV movie *Brian's Song* (1971), about the friendship between Chicago Bears running back Gale Sayers and his doomed white teammate, roommate, and friend Brian Piccolo, Piccolo tries to call Sayers a nigger, but cannot do so with any conviction, and Sayers laughs at him.

There nonetheless remained a dangerous ambiguity in such words, and in newer transvalued insults such as "queer." American Civil Liberties Union president Nadine Strossen wrote, during the brief,

Let-a-Hundred-Flowers-Bloom period of national soul-searching about free speech and political correctness in the early 1990s, "While these terms may actually connote endearment when used among group members, it still is generally not 'permissible'—i.e., appropriately sensitive and respectful—for non-group members to use them." Strossen was right in her general point, but wrong to suggest that "permissible" somehow meant "sensitive." No—permissible meant permissible.

In the old days, the word "nigger" had demarcated empowered people from disempowered along racial lines. As interracial power became less oppressive, the word seemed destined to become less offensive. It might even become a symbol of liberation and fellowship. It clearly was such a symbol for Patti Smith, who was speaking at the very zenith of civil rights optimism. For her, "nigger" was a badge of creativity, defiance, and courage. It was a glorious word.

But there was a problem. The borderline between empowerment and powerlessness was also the borderline between innocence and guilt. The essayist Shelby Steele saw in whites' easy appropriation of the word not a new openness but a self-interested forgetting. He accused, for instance, wealthy feminists who referred to "woman as nigger" of "attaching themselves to the moral authority and hard-earned legitimacy of the black struggle." Steele was unwilling to let white people devalue that moral authority, whatever intentions they might profess.

This led to a paradox: The word was needed by civil rights activists as a marker of white attitudes at a time when whites had not used it in its original sense in a long time. Now "nigger" was used more often *by* than *of* blacks, not to describe their own thoughts but to impute evil intentions to white people. When arguments erupted at Stanford during the 1986–87 academic year over whether "Western Culture" should be removed from the campus curriculum, the president of the university's Black Student Union wrote in the *Stanford Daily* of two men who had defended the traditional curriculum in the paper's pages, "These individuals are sending me, women and all people of color a message that says loud and clear: 'Niggers go home.'" In an essay aimed at explaining the results of the 2016 election Ta-Nehisi Coates described it as, in part, a reaction to "an entire nigger presidency with nigger health care, nigger climate accords, and nigger justice reform." The word, which had once frightened black people, was now used primarily to frighten white people.

Under the alternate spelling "nigga"—which music executives may have hoped would shelter them from prosecutions for indecency—the word became a shibboleth of "gangsta" rap. A song wasn't gangsta unless it had that word in it, and it usually appeared in the context of violence. In the autumn of 2015, driving along a highway listening to Hip Hop Nation on Sirius XM, you could hear YG doing "Twist My Fingaz":

> *You shoulda seen how a nigga pulled up in the ride*
> *Got two motherfuckers want to fight me outside*

followed by Future singing "Real Sisters":

> *Players turn to friends with that Godzilla*
> *Sell that heroin in the trap I'm a dog nigga*

continuing on to Hit Boy's "Stay Up":

> *She used to niggas tellin lies and pullin schemes on her*
> *They don't never want to put a mothafucking ring on her.*

The development of two separate language codes, one for whites and one for blacks, was ominous. The rules of American public decorum now resembled medieval strictures that permitted only noblemen to carry weapons or ride horses, or laws that forbade certain classes of citizens to address others by a certain name.

The expression "white supremacy" underwent a similarly paradoxical boom: The less it existed, the more it was invoked. By the turn of the century it was being used more frequently than it ever had been in

American history. The epithet "white supremacist" was being used five times as often as it had been in its previous heyday—which was not, incidentally, during the Jim Crow era but at the end of the 1960s.

If one surveyed the years since the first settlers arrived in the seventeenth century, the early twenty-first century would seem an unlikely time to worry about white people getting above themselves. Weeks after the 2016 election, Sally Boynton Brown, running for the chair of the Democratic National Committee, discussed the moral standing of whites at a candidates' forum: "My job is to listen and be a voice," she said, "and my job is to shut other white people down when they want to interrupt." Here Boynton Brown herself was interrupted, by applause.

Margaret Seltzer and Rachel Dolezal

Naturally people want to be counted among the heroes, not the villains, of their country's story. If they cannot feel that way, something is wrong. The most poignant piece of evidence for the plaintiffs in *Brown v. Board of Education* had been a so-called doll study done by the child psychologist Kenneth Clark. It found that 63 percent of black children, offered a choice, would rather play with a white doll than a black one. Whatever that meant (and it was open to interpretation), most people could agree that those children and their parents deserved more consideration and support.

Half a century later, there was a similar puzzle involving self-esteem. Somewhere in the beat of Motown, soul, disco, and hip-hop, the liberating machismo (at a time when it was off-limits to white men) of various taunting wide receivers, the grace of Magic Johnson and LeBron James, and the didacticism of after-school specials and MLK Day commemorations, not to mention the threats of official punishment and social ostracism . . . somewhere in all of that, it seemed that many whites (though, again, this was open to interpretation) had acquired a burning regret that they were not black.

In 2008, an unusual literary scandal broke. It involved Margaret Jones, the author of *Love and Consequences*, the memoir of a half–American Indian girl adopted into a caring but star-crossed black family in gang-infested Los Angeles. The *New York Times*'s Michiko Kakutani had praised Jones's "novelist's eye for the psychological detail." Novelist's eye was right: "Margaret Jones" was the invented identity of a 33-year-old, white, middle-class suburbanite named Margaret Seltzer, the product of private Episcopal schools and various creative writing programs. She had made the whole thing up.

The reaction was pitiless. "Taking risks" may be something literary critics profess to admire, but apparently they admire it only so long as the risks aren't real. Now Seltzer/Jones's book was reassessed—not as a clever literary hoax or even as a cry for help but as a wicked blasphemy. The nice things people had said about its literary craft were forgotten. Riverside Press pulped the whole print run. Seltzer had done something terrible: Belonging to a racial minority conferred moral authority that no one must be allowed to counterfeit or compromise.

Once we understand that, we can hazard a guess at why Seltzer decided to write as a minority gang member in the first place. She was doing the same thing that immigrants had done a century before when they changed their names from Svensson to Swanson or from Bellini to Bell. She was bartering away a bit of her identity in exchange for moral authority and belonging. She was concealing, as best she could, her membership in a low-prestige ethnic group in order that she might participate in the national conversation on a firmer footing.

Seven years later the scandal would find an explicitly political echo. The president of the Spokane chapter of the National Association for the Advancement of Colored People, the bronze-skinned, kinky-haired race radical Rachel Dolezal, was revealed by her fundamentalist Christian parents to be white—Czech, German, Swedish. There ought to have been no scandal in that alone—the NAACP had been founded as an organization meant to bring blacks and whites together.

Dolezal's fault was to have said she was black, an imposture for which she was both disciplined and publicly shamed. She lost her job teaching Africana studies at Eastern Washington University. The *Daily Mail* repeatedly called her the "Infamous Race Faker." *Vanity Fair*, barely a year after lecturing its readers that it was a "misconception" to think that the Olympic decathlon winner Bruce Jenner would have to have surgery on his genitalia in order to call himself a genuine trans-gender woman, accused Dolezal of "Refusing to Apologize for Lying About Being Black."

Lying? Dolezal was 37. Everyone her age had been taught that lying is one thing and demanding a say in the construction of one's own identity quite another. When interviewed, she didn't deny any of the facts. She just recited a lot of slogans about the right to follow your dreams and choose who you really are, in the tone of one who assumed everyone else would eventually "get" what she was talking about. "You know, race didn't create racism," Dolezal told NBC's *Today* show. "Racism creates race." *Everyone* said that. It was racist to say otherwise. In choosing to be black, Dolezal was following society's most cherished anti-racist slogans to their logical anti-racist conclusion.

And if anyone had the right to make such a choice, it would seem to be she. Dolezal had four black siblings, adopted by her parents when she was in her teens, by which time she had grown fascinated by black people from reading *National Geographic*. She had married a black man and had had black children. She was widely read in black literature and had the degrees to prove it. She fought for black causes. Her black students loved her. She would eventually change her name to Nkechi Amare Diallo.

You would think that wanting to be black rather than white would be an insult to whites and flattery to blacks. But that was not the case. "Apoplectic" was too mild a word to describe the reactions of the black establishment. Columnist Charles M. Blow of the *New York Times* could barely catch his breath. "This," he wrote, "is about privilege, deceitful performance and a tortured attempt to avoid truth and confession by co-opting the language of struggle, infusing labyrinthine logic with the authority of the academy, and coat-tailing very real struggles of transgender people and transracial adoptees to defend one's deception."

Certainly Dolezal hadn't told the truth about everything. She had claimed to have been the victim of multiple hate crimes, involving nooses, swastikas, whips, and kidnapping threats. But that was not what she was being publicly shamed for. She was being shamed for trying to pass. "She's making these claims without any biological basis," the USC law professor Camille Gear Rich told the *Los Angeles Times*. In so doing she had somehow stolen something from blacks. Preferential treatment under affirmative action rules could conceivably have been part of it: Dolezal had applied for jobs as a black person. But that was not it, either. One Facebook commentator was close to the mark: "It's no different from someone claiming to be a war veteran and joining the VFW, when they never served a day in their life." The country's diversity-oriented intellectuals were doing what they had so often faulted intellectuals of the past for doing: They were "policing the boundaries" of the racial classifications on which their privileges rested.

Martin Luther King's description of those black people under Jim Crow "who, as a result of long years of oppression, are so drained of self-respect and a sense of 'somebodiness' that they have adjusted to segregation" seemed to describe certain whites' adjustment to the post-1960s regime of race relations. This "somebodiness" was something they had somehow been robbed of. Dolezal was seeking to reacquire it through an imposture.

In the prevailing culture, whiteness was a lower spiritual state, associated with moral unfitness and shame, and it was hereditary. Whiteness was a "bloody heirloom," as Coates wrote. Even if they sincerely believed there was no such thing as inherited race, white people seemed also to believe they were at risk of inheriting racism, and scrambled to separate not just themselves but their families, their bloodlines, from any taint of it. In an elegant memoir about what he had learned from playing and watching football, the literary scholar Mark Edmundson wrote of his father, with whom he spent Sunday afternoons in the 1960s watching the New York Giants, and of his father's particular affection for Jim Brown, a great black running back for the Cleveland Browns. "No racist word ever passed his lips," Edmundson wrote, "at least in my hearing or my brother's. He was the only white man I knew well that I could say this about. My father looked at Jim Brown as a fellow human being."

Among the media enterprises of Harvard professor Henry Louis Gates was a PBS television series called *Finding Your Roots*, which investigated the ancestries of various celebrities. (The BBC had an equivalent, *Who Do You Think You Are?*) When the actor Ben Affleck discovered during research for the show in 2014 that he was descended from a slave owner, he lobbied Gates to omit discussion of it. Gates obliged. But Gates had been emailing descriptions to a friend at Sony of the pressure Affleck had brought, and those emails were revealed to the public months later when Sony's servers were hacked.

It turns out to be a difficult and unnatural thing to replace a system of prejudice with a system of real equality and respect. It's a lot to ask of people. As Friedrich Nietzsche understood, it is far easier, for both former perpetrators and former victims alike, simply to *transvalue* the prejudices—so you wind up with the old world turned upside down.

Manliness and crime

Throughout the period in the 1990s when gangsta rap was supplanting rock in the headphones of white 15-year-olds, it consoled a lot of conservative social commentators to dismiss black urban culture as criminal, even pathological. Such condescension was getting the wrong end of the stick. As the Harvard philosopher Harvey C. Mansfield explained, black culture had remained mostly immune to the purging of manly virtues that white culture had undergone in the age of feminism. That was a plus. You might be right to call gangsta rap crass, but you would be shortsighted to ignore that its Beowulfian braggadocio had once been a hallmark of the "high" European culture that other Americans were heedlessly throwing out. America's white upper middle class was producing so many "tough-minded" computer scientists and so few English majors that it had lost sight of some simple lessons that ten minutes spent with "The War-Song of Dinas Vawr" will teach you: Under certain circumstances, women prefer, and men follow, the kind of men who burn cities.

In 1992, after the acquittal of four Los Angeles police officers whose beating of black fugitive Rodney King had been captured on video, black and immigrant youths ransacked much of South Central Los Angeles, leaving 63 dead and thousands injured. The riots' climax came when a gang of young men were videotaped from a traffic helicopter hauling the hapless white truck driver Reginald Denny out of his cab, crushing his skull with a concrete block, and doing a celebratory dance in front of the camera.

It was a deadlier riot than any that had taken place in the civil rights era, and it presented troubling new features. It was the work of lumpen blacks bolstered in some cases by other non-whites. The riots took place at a time when, a generation after King's marches, blacks seemed to be fleeing from, not rallying to, the broader American culture. Traditionally blacks had watched the same TV shows as other Americans, but in the autumn after the Rodney King riots not one of the top ten shows for the country at large (*Roseanne, 60 Minutes, Murphy Brown, Coach, Home Improvement*, etc.) was on the top ten list for blacks (*The Fresh Prince of Bel Air, Roc, In Living Color, Martin, Blossom*, etc.). Whites and blacks were diverging culturally.

And they were diverging in how they saw the law. The Rodney King riots were the first act of domestic unrest that influential observers described not as a *riot* but as a *rebellion*. One man's hoodlum was another man's freedom fighter. For most whites, until black crime fell, blacks would not have the standing to complain about equal justice. For most blacks, until there was equality in all walks of American life, whites would not have the standing to call all black misbehavior "crime."

The murder trial of O. J. Simpson in 1995 hardened this division. Simpson, in his youth the greatest running back in the history of American football, in middle age a beloved movie star and television personality, had been accused of stabbing to death his white ex-wife Nicole Brown Simpson and her friend Ron Goldman, and had fled arrest. The evidence against Simpson—blood at the scene, blood in his car, blood in his house, the prints of his rare Bruno Magli shoes, and seemingly incontrovertible DNA testing—pointed to an open-and-shut case. But Simpson's lawyers turned it into a way for a largely minority jury to send a message. As Simpson's lead defense lawyer, Johnnie Cochran, told his partners in a private discussion:

> I know it's our job to get Simpson off, but I think our legacy should be to show this country that the cops will do just about anything. They will lie because they believe that the end justifies the means. . . . If Goldman gets up there and says, "Simpson butchered my son," fuck him. He's not on the fucking jury and I won't take that shit. My heart goes out to him, but he's simply wrong. The client is presumed innocent. That's the bulwark of our system.

Though Cochran most often railed against "our system," here he praised it. He had reason to. Cochran had more rights in the trial—both statutorily and informally—than his prosecutorial counterparts: The Simpson defense could appeal the verdict if, for instance, it found the state was purging the jury of blacks (under the 1978 case *People v. Wheeler*). That the prosecution had no such recourse allowed the defense to purge the jury of whites.

Simpson was acquitted. Roughly three quarters of whites thought he was guilty, and roughly three quarters of blacks thought he was innocent. "Ten years from now," the journalist Jeffrey Toobin said, "the importance of this case for race relations will be all people remember about it." That was partly true. By the twenty-first century, the crime rate was falling across all races, and a majority of blacks accepted that

Simpson had committed the murders. But the division over the legitimacy of the criminal justice system remained.

It was complicated by the advance of technology. What had been a spectacular coincidence at the time of the Rodney King beatings—the presence of cameras at an arrest—was now the norm. After the start of the century, a dozen or so encounters between police and black youths turned into national scandals over allegations of police brutality, some resulting in convictions of police, some in exonerations.

A judicious analyst would have borne in mind that the country now had over 300 million people, and, firearms being legal, more than a third of them had guns in their homes. Diversity, whatever its other effects, pushed together people of diverse folkways. Tens of millions of people living in the United States were new to the country's laws. Under the circumstances, the country was policed well, and with an impressive fairness.

It had become hard to say that publicly, though. A disproportionate number of the most serious offenses continued to be committed by blacks. In 2009, blacks, who made up 13 percent of the population, accounted for almost half the arrests (49.2 percent) for murder and more than half (55.5 percent) for robberies. The traditional explanation was that blacks commit about half of those crimes. But, applied to racial disparities, traditional explanations were coming into disrepute. Alan David Freeman's "victims' perspective" had triumphed here, too, and with it the idea that any disparity was the sign of an injustice. Like water poured into the corner of a tilted ice-cube tray, this idea had gradually tumbled into one compartment of American life after another, starting with public facilities and moving on through hiring to education.

Barack Obama's second term happened to coincide with the moment in history when the victim's perspective became the semi-official way of looking at crime and violence. Now the disproportionate incidence of black arrests was taken, in some quarters, as prima facie evidence of white racism.

The Ferguson uprising

On August 9, 2014, 18-year-old Michael Brown was shot dead by policeman Darren Wilson after a confrontation in a housing project in Ferguson, Missouri, a fast-changing but relatively well integrated town in St. Louis County. The incident sparked three waves of riots, the first one lasting two weeks, the second one coming three months later when a grand jury chose not to indict Wilson. There was additional unrest on the first anniversary of the shooting.

The controversy was, in hindsight, unwarranted. According to an investigation into Wilson's conduct by the civil rights division of the Obama administration's Justice Department, the 289-pound Brown, high on THC and accompanied by his friend Dorian Johnson, had stolen several boxes of cigarillos from an Indian-owned variety store, manhandling the diminutive owner when he protested. The incident was captured on video. When Wilson, making his rounds in a squad car, encountered the pair a few moments later, Brown moved to the driver's window, blocking Wilson's exit, punched him in the face, reached into the car, and got a hand on Wilson's gun. Wilson fired a shot into Brown's hand. He pursued Brown when he ran and shot Brown only when Brown turned and charged him.

The Justice Department's novel-length report, full of lab work, cell phone records, and dozens of interviews, showed that there was no case for indicting Wilson for any kind of police misconduct. Brown's DNA was found on Wilson's collar, shirt, and pants. Gunpowder soot was found on Brown's hand, and evidence of change in the skin from heat discharge was "consistent with Brown's hand being on the barrel of the gun." On detail after detail, in multiple interrogations, Wilson's account matched that of the material evidence.

A mythological account spread nonetheless. Brown, it was said, had been raising his hands to surrender. He had been saying "Hands up, don't shoot!" Most, perhaps all, of these stories had their beginnings in tales that Brown's accomplice Johnson (known as Witness 101 in the civil rights investigation) had told in the aftermath of the shootings. Johnson claimed that Wilson had shot Brown in the back and then killed him with a volley of shots as he stood with his hands up, pleading that he was unarmed.

There were no credible witnesses to Brown's saying "Don't shoot." There were no bullet holes in Brown's back. But the alternative account had begun circulating while Brown's body still lay in the street, and it soon became dangerous to contradict it. Brown died at noon. By 12:14 p.m., crowds were shouting that someone needed to "kill these motherfuckers." At 12:45 and again at 1:17, there was gunfire. At 1:55 and 2:11, police heard the sound of automatic weapons. Chants of "Kill the police" arose. Police were reinforced by the Highway Safety Unit at 2:38 and the Tactical Operations Unit at 2:44. The second great grievance, besides the allegation that the police had murdered Brown in cold blood, was that they had disrespected his body by leaving it in the middle of the street for four hours. That was likely due to security concerns provoked by the chants, threats, and shooting, the Obama administration's civil rights investigation found.

The violence and looting that exploded in Ferguson that night would last two weeks and preoccupy the media for months. In November, days after the grand jury's decision not to indict Wilson and the riots that followed, black players on the St. Louis Rams took the field for a Sunday-night football game with their arms raised in a hands-up-don't-shoot pose. Ta-Nehisi Coates raged in a short book that would become a number-one bestseller about the difficulty of telling his son why "the killer of Mike Brown would go unpunished." The country's official culture was now squarely on the side of the protests, even if any neutral reading of the evidence showed that Brown's killer, Wilson, should have gone unpunished.

Black Lives Matter

Alongside the legend of Ferguson—not the incident itself but the legend, as Dorian Johnson first laid it out—was born the Black Lives Matter movement. The weakness of the movement's argument that justice miscarried in this or that case is not a reason to dismiss it. On the contrary, it is a sign that the era was pregnant with such movements, which are often driven as much by aspirations and opportunities as by grievances.

Three black women who described themselves as "queer" had launched the hashtag #BlackLivesMatter in 2013 after the acquittal of a Florida neighborhood watch captain, George Zimmerman, who had claimed self-defense after fatally shooting a young black man, Trayvon Martin. Their posts were the equivalent of Rick Santelli's 2009 "rant," which introduced the concept of a Tea Party before there was one. Indeed, Black Lives Matter could be considered a youthful, mostly minority counterpart to the aging, mostly white Tea Party. The Tea Party had launched an insurrection against Barack Obama and what it held him to represent, and now Black Lives Matter was entering that fray on the other side.

Infuriated inner-city residents, idealistic college students, hip-hop musicians, billionaire managers of foundations, criminals and prison inmates, athletes—Black Lives Matter brought together these establishment and anti-establishment elements in an extraordinary ferment. It had support inside the Obama White House, and it had elements of support in the most radical parts of the American left. Black Lives Matter backers used the concept of staying "woke" (drawn from Erykah Badu's 2008 song "Master Teacher") to describe their initiation into esoteric ideological truth, in the same way enthusiasts of the rising "alt right" would use the concept of being "red-pilled" (drawn from the dystopic 1999 film *The Matrix*).

The historian Todd Gitlin, a 1960s protester who had written a classic account of his own era's rebellions, saw in Black Lives Matter a movement of young people who were civic-minded in the way his con-temporaries had been. They had a constructive agenda for reforming law enforcement: an end to the "broken windows" philosophy of po-licing, which had seen many city kids jailed for minor offenses; reform of the bail system; and the introduction of dashboard cameras and other technology to put the police on watch. That did not make the Black Lives Matter movement irresponsible, Gitlin insisted. "Contrary to what white racists and police like to say, the spirit of 'Black Lives Matter' does not mean '*Only* Black Lives Matter,'" he wrote. ". . . It's the third term in a syllogism that goes like this: 1. All lives matter. 2. Black lives are lives. 3. Black lives matter."

That is what a 1960s radical wished Black Lives Matter to mean, to the point that he was willing to tar as racist anyone who disagreed with him. Problem was, the leaders of Black Lives Matter addressed Gitlin's syllogism explicitly and repudiated it outright. All three candidates for the following year's Democratic presidential nomination tried to make peace among their fractious constituents by uttering a version of the all-lives-matter syllogism, and all were forced to apologize for doing so. One of them, the former Maryland governor Martin O'Malley, attend-ing a Netroots Nation conference in Arizona, was booed for saying "All lives matter." Days later, Joseph Curtatone, the mayor of Somerville, Massachusetts, flew the Black Lives Matter banner and spent several days sparring with local police, who wanted him to hoist an "All Lives Matter" banner instead.

The very name Black Lives Matter, once it changed from a hashtag to a political movement, implied that there was a group of people in American society who did not believe in the right to life of a significant part of the population. It was an incendiary accusation: Who did Black Lives Matter believe these people were, indifferent to others' lives, who had supposedly sprung up at a moment when the races had never been more equal or mixed? If they were in government, Black Lives Matter looked like a party of revolution, for how legitimate can a government be that does not care if its citizens live or die? If those people were outside government, Black Lives Matter looked like something more threatening still: a party of race war.

Every time someone was shot dead by police under difficult-to-piece-together circumstances, a daily occurrence in a vast and well-armed country, there were tensions. In the last days of 2014, an unstable Baltimore man named Ismaaiyl Brinsley drove to Brooklyn and murdered two police. Two officers were shot outside the Ferguson, Missouri, police station in March 2015. When Freddie Gray, another young man from Baltimore with a long rap sheet, died of a spinal injury in police custody a month later, there were nights of wild rioting.

The following summer, in the middle of presidential election season, two armed black men were shot and killed by police on consecutive days. On July 5, in Baton Rouge, Louisiana, Alton Sterling, a street vendor of music CDs, was wrestled to the ground while resisting two policemen and shot dead. A day later Philando Castile was shot dead at a traffic stop in Falcon Heights, Minnesota, by a policeman who (video released a year later seemed to show) panicked when Castile calmly told him he was carrying a weapon. The videos available at the time were ambiguous, but sufficient to bring a full mobilization of Black Lives Matter.

Protests on July 7, the day after the Castile killing, ended in insurrectionary confusion. At the edges of the Black Lives Matter march in Dallas, Micah Xavier Johnson, a well-trained and heavily armed black veteran of the Afghan war, shot 14 policemen, killing five. Soon thereafter, a politically excitable St. Louis black man named Gavin Long stole a car and drove it to Baton Rouge, where, on July 17, between the B-Quik convenience store and the Hair Crown Beauty Supply on Airline Highway, he shot six police officers, killing three.

The rage of young blacks against the police was turning into something bigger than a protest. "You can't stop the revolution," they chanted in Chicago. Black Lives Matter activists announced they would continue their marches even after the killings of policemen in Dallas. "It's not a setback at all," one said. "That's showing the people of this country that black people are getting to a boiling point."

But why were they getting to a boiling point *now*? It was improbable that police departments would be turning into nests of white vigilantism at a juncture when all the urban ones had been integrated, when blacks were (measured by population percentages) over-represented in some of them, including that of Washington, D.C., and when police officers of all races were being more closely surveilled. Dallas had a black police chief. Baton Rouge had a black mayor. Baltimore had a black mayor, a black public prosecutor, and a black police chief, and three of the six officers tried in the Freddie Gray case were black.

And the president was black. "Part of the reason this time will be different," Obama said during the Ferguson controversy, "is because the president of the United States is deeply invested in making sure this time is different." Eric Holder visited Mike Brown's family in St. Louis. "I spoke to them not just as Attorney General but as a father," he said.

Black Lives Matter had some of the traits of an official protest movement. The White House would serve as an activist clearinghouse for social movements, including edgy, confrontational, identitarian ones. Black Lives Matter was building bridges to a variety of other groups—but they were almost exclusively the communities that made up the Democratic party's electoral and fundraising base. Democrats were three times as likely (51 percent) as Republicans (17 percent) to support its goals. The Movement for Black Lives (M4BL) called for an "end to the war on Black trans, queer and gender nonconforming people." Travis Gosa, an Africana studies professor at Cornell and the author of *Remixing Change: Hip Hop and Obama*, likened it to the Silicon Valley philosophy of disruptive innovation and called the movement "digital." There was a place in Black Lives Matter for the Democratic donor class, too. Across the country you could see rainbow flags flying alongside Black Lives Matter posters in rich and academic neighborhoods—and only in those neighborhoods. The antithesis between "the regime" and "the street" was fading.

Every radical movement is a rebirth of sorts, because political establishments are built on doctrines, and changing doctrines requires as much unlearning as learning. Radicals reconnect with wisdom that the existing regime, in order to prevail, has had to discard or suppress. Black Lives Matter reconnected to certain realities of the 1960s civil rights movement that had been buried under official celebrations of the movement as pacifistic, harmonious, and Christian. Ta-Nehisi Coates insisted on his own atheism, and Travis Gosa stressed that Black Lives Matter was "atheist or at least non-denominational." Black Lives Matter arose amid a revival of the black power or even (in Coates's case) the Black Panther tendency.

As Jeanne Theoharis, the biographer of Rosa Parks, showed, this history was a bigger part of the 1960s civil rights movement than twenty-first-century Americans of any race were comfortable acknowledging. Theoharis chastised Atlanta mayor Kasim Reed for saying, amid the 2016 protests, "Dr. King would never take [over] a freeway." What did Mayor Reed think the Selma march was? "These framings," Theoharis wrote, "misrepresent the movements that BLM activists are building across the country and the history of the civil rights movement." That was true. The editors of the *Philadelphia Inquirer* headlined an article by Harvard Law School professor Randall Kennedy "Black Lives Matter, the Next Stage of the Civil Rights Movement."

If Black Lives Matter was civil rights, then the country had a problem. Because, as we have noted, civil rights had become a de facto constitution. The various extensions that black and white progressives had successfully fought to attach to civil rights—above all affirmative action and political correctness—had ceased to be temporary expedients. They were essential parts of this new constitutional structure, meant to shore it up where it was impotent or self-contradictory, in the way that Chief Justice John Marshall's invention of judicial review in *Marbury v. Madison* (1801) had been a shoring-up of the first constitution.

Without these innovations, the civil rights system was illogical and unstable. If you didn't like affirmative action and political correctness, you didn't like civil rights. For their part, politicians who claimed civil rights as a governing ideal grew uneasy when they saw a movement as truculent and implacable as Black Lives Matter speaking in its name. They called it "identity politics," as if it were an aberration. It was not. It was a culmination.

The Yale uprising

Noting the prevalence of college kids in the ranks of Black Lives Matter, the cultural critic Roger Kimball, who had studied at Bennington College and Yale, looked at the movement as a problem that could be got rid of by eliminating affirmative action. "Henceforth," Kimball proposed,

> admission to college will be granted on the basis of merit, not skin color, "ethnic background," or sexual deformation. Furthermore, grades and honors and advancement will be determined by color-blind examination invigilated by independent external examiners. I promise you that, were these simple expedients imposed, the "black lives matter" nonsense would evaporate within a term.

It was a reasonable suggestion in its context, but its context was an American culture that had been overthrown a generation before.

Kimball partook of a great, almost unanimous misunderstanding about the reforms of the 1960s. White Americans wanted to believe that the new constitution tended toward race-neutrality and toward freedom, just as the old one had. To the contrary, as those who administered it understood almost immediately, it tended toward race-consciousness and government direction. But the ideal of color-blindness was tenacious. So stirring were its resonances with the rhetoric of Abraham Lincoln and Martin Luther King, so necessary had it been to public acceptance of civil rights in the first place, that it became a sort of official fiction.

In the exhilaration of the 1960s, every expression of anti-traditionalism, every destruction of a tradition, had given reformers the feeling that they were rationalizing, validating, and thus perhaps even *enhancing* the power of tradition. That is what cardinals at Vatican II thought of clerical authority, what readers of *The Feminine Mystique* thought of male sexuality, and what civil rights activists thought of elite white institutions of higher education. The *New Yorker* writer George W. S. Trow told a revealing story about a racial confrontation in a university classroom back then, when white students thrilled to hear a black classmate describe a Dutch painter as "belonging" to them but not to him:

> They acknowledged that they were at one with Rembrandt. They acknowledged their dominance. They offered to discuss, at any length, their inherited power to oppress. It was thought at the time that reactions of this type had to do with "white guilt" or "white masochism." No. No. It was white *euphoria*. Many, many white children of that day felt the power of their inheritance for the first time in the act of rejecting it, and they insisted on rejecting it and rejecting it and rejecting it, so that they might continue to feel the power of that connection. Had the young black man asked, "Who is this man to you?" the pleasure they felt would have vanished in embarrassment and resentment.

The story is almost biblical in its capacity to cast everything, the whole development of the past half-century, in a different light. The reformers, it turns out, had not been heroes to their valets, swinging open the castle gates to a grateful mass of the excluded. They had been as blind and vain in throwing their traditions away as their forefathers had been in defending them.

There was a dust-up at Halloween in 2015 that saw two Yale faculty advisors, the sociology and medicine professor Nicholas Christakis and his developmental psychologist wife, Erika, hounded from campus. The couple had an idealistic conception of academic freedom. While at Harvard, they had defended black students who had belittled members of the university's exclusive "finals clubs." When Nicholas

Christakis became master and Erika associate master of the Silliman residential college at Yale, they continued in a similar spirit.

The Yale faculty had sent out a scolding communiqué of the sort that was common at the time. It admonished students to wear appropriate Halloween costumes and avoid offense to minorities. Erika Christakis, in a "Dear Sillimanders" letter, remarked that Halloween, because it had traditionally been a day of subversion, was also "an occasion for adults to exert their control." She urged students to stand on their own two feet and use their own judgment. She wrote about having owned a sari when she lived in Bangladesh and added that she saw nothing wrong with "a blonde-haired child's wanting to be Mulan for a day." That began a week of confrontations with minority students, most of them black, who claimed the Christakises were promoting cultural appropriation and failing to provide a "home" for students of color.

On several occasions, each of the Christakises was surrounded by angry crowds. In one instance, filmed on a cell phone camera and circulated widely on the internet, a black undergraduate woman emerged from a crowd to tell Nicholas Christakis that his wife's email had been inappropriate, given their positions as master and associate master. Christakis said he believed the duty of a university administrator was to create a space in which ideas could thrive. As for the idea that his wife's "Dear Sillimander" letter had been inappropriate, he said, "No, I don't agree with that." It brought a howl of rage from the young woman:

> Then why the fuck did you accept the position? Who the fuck hired you? You should step down! If that is what you think about being a master you should step down! It is *not* about creating an intellectual space! It is *not*! Do you understand that? It's about creating a home here. You are not doing that!

In all of these encounters, mobs snapped fingers, taunted Christakis with hoots, shouted at him to "Be quiet!" and told him that it was "not your turn." His demeanor was meek, even sycophantic. The

Christakises announced that they were registered Democrats, as if that would help. The protesters demanded advance warning of when Erika Christakis planned to be in the dining hall so they would not have to look at her. One undergraduate seemed to object less that Nicholas Christakis was recommending freedom of speech than that he was befouling her field of vision:

> I am sick looking at you. I am disgusted arguing with you. You are not listening. You are disgusting. I don't think you understand that. . . . Now I want your job to be taken from you. I don't want you to have this job. I am disgusted knowing that you work at Yale University where I will get my degree, where I will look back and think, I used to argue with you.

The student got her wish. Yale and other outposts of the American credentialocracy now belonged to her and to "activists" like her. The Christakises canceled their spring courses, and resigned their Silliman positions shortly thereafter. Next Yale, which described itself as "an alliance of Yale students of color and our allies," had demanded the Christakises' resignation, the installation of a bias-reporting system, the renaming of three of Yale's colleges after non-whites, more non-white psychologists, the institution of "racial competence and respect training," and millions for ethnic studies programs. Yale met most of their demands and added $50 million to hire professors "who would enrich diversity." Brown University, after a similar uprising, earmarked $100 million to create a "more just and inclusive campus."

LZ Granderson's remark about the old generation's dying off was rude. That did not make it wrong. The physicist Max Planck once wrote, "A new scientific truth does not triumph by convincing its opponents and making them see the light, but rather because its opponents eventually die, and a new generation grows up that is familiar with it." Even radical movements that have appeared to fail often go on wreaking institutional change slowly and quietly. When armed black students took over Willard Straight Hall at Cornell in 1969, the university's president, James Perkins, tried to negotiate a deal under which they would face no sanctions. The university's conservative board, trustees, and donors, along with much of its faculty, rose in rebellion, forcing Perkins's resignation. But over the decades, things changed. By the new century, one of the Cornell occupiers, Tom Jones, who had in the meantime become a multimillionaire financier with Citigroup, was *on* the Cornell board.

Yale may have been an "intellectual space" under the old constitution. Under the new one, how could it be? Once Yale changed its rules to recruit minority students through affirmative action, as the law required it to, upholding purely meritocratic standards (as Kimball urged) would have been a contradiction in terms. Following rules of decorum (in which the Christakises placed so much faith) was only a roundabout route to the same disappointment. An institution could *claim* to be upholding its old standards—Yale did—but it could not actually uphold them. It had taken on political responsibilities that overrode its educational ones. The protesters were wise to this. Their incredulity at the Christakises' failure to "understand" the real terms of their service at Yale was surely unfeigned.

It would have been sadistic to blame those students simply for not fitting in. But you had only to look at them screaming on those cell phone videos to see that many did not feel they fit in, and that this was a problem for which someone other than they would have to be blamed. It was an often repeated paradox of civil rights: The faster racism and privilege are dismantled, the greater the psychological need to point to racism and privilege.

The events at Yale were another sign that the great constitutional innovation of the civil rights era—the proxy exercise by private institutions of governmental power—had turned into a formidable instrument of discipline. On American and British campuses, so-called no-platforming—the move to "deny fascists, organized racists and other haters the freedom to spread their poison"—was on the rise.

Only an eighth of Americans over the age of 70 believed that "government should be able to prevent statements that are offensive to minority groups." But a quarter of Americans aged 35 to 70 believed it, and fully 40 percent of adults under 35 did.

For just under half of younger adults, the only workable basis for ethnic co-existence was a tabula rasa. There was something fittingly American about this. To say they believed in "new beginnings" and "dreaming big" was the usual way Americans liked to think of themselves. Another way to put it, though, was to say that Americans were given to razing and fleeing rather than to repairing and nurturing. So grand and noble were Americans' "dreams" in their own sight that carrying them out became a special dispensation, an emergency in the face of which others had better get out of the way. As they moved inland in the seventeenth, eighteenth, and nineteenth centuries, Americans had obliterated whole cultures with a clean conscience, as if the continent were unpeopled. In the half-century after the mid-1960s, America's leaders, still dreaming their big dreams, obliterated their own cultural institutions in a similar spirit.

"Who we are as Americans"

What Americans had to show at the end of that half-century was a version of what they had had at the beginning: a mix of energy and conformism, pride and disappointment. These things were hard to disentangle. Americans were certainly content with the achievements of civil rights. What it promised and delivered—a rough kind of racial equality in the states that had lacked it—was an extraordinary achievement. There were unexpected collateral blessings, too, beyond a freer life for many blacks: the lifting of a burden of guilt from certain whites, scope for working women, a less anguished life for gays. What the reforms aspired and failed to do—produce "harmony" between the races or peace between the sexes—may have been beyond the power of any government reform to achieve.

But the costs of civil rights were high. New inequalities arose. Fewer things were decided democratically. Free speech was suppressed. By the election year of 2016, Americans would be so scared to speak their mind on matters even tangential to civil rights that their political mood was essentially unreadable. Americans' grievances against diversity were now bottled up, in a way that was reminiscent of French people's late-nineteenth-century obsession with reconquering Alsace and Lorraine. ("Think of it always," the nineteenth-century French statesman Léon Gambetta had said. "Speak of it never.") Polls and elections surely underestimated opposition to the broad changes of the last fifty years, but even so there were signs of how many Americans felt they had been made worse off. According to a 2011 Pew Research Center survey, 23 percent of those born in the Baby Boom generation and before believed America's new diversity was a "change for the better"; 42 percent called it a "change for the worse."

American politics had re-sorted itself around that question— which came down to the question of whether one had benefited from or lost by the transfers of rights, goods, and privileges carried out under the new constitutional dispensation that began in 1964. The Democrats were the party of those who benefited: not just racial minorities but sexual minorities, immigrants, women, government employees, lawyers—and all people sophisticated enough to be in a position to design, run, or analyze new systems. This collection of minorities could, with discipline, be bundled into an electoral majority, but that was not, strictly speaking, necessary. The hierarchies of government, the judiciary, and the corporate world were Democratic in their orientations. Sympathetic regulators, judges, and attorneys took up the task of transferring as many prerogatives as possible from the majority to various minorities.

Republicans were the party, as we have noted, of yesteryear's entire political spectrum, of New Deal supporters and New Deal foes, of the people who would have voted for Richard Nixon in 1960 and the people who would have voted for John F. Kennedy. The lost world of that period seemed an idyll to many Americans. The parties represented two different constitutions, two different eras of history, even two different technological platforms. And increasingly, two different racial groups.

Once the heavily Democratic universities, and the nonprofit sector more broadly, began to drive the economy and the culture and to command the only remaining large pool of secure, high-paying jobs, the drift toward the new, minoritarian constitution gathered momentum, even when the Democrats were out of power. Isolated from the innovative, well-connected, and savvy populations of the top universities, Republicans, even when they were in an electoral majority, lost their ability to influence the system. It was only a matter of time before they lost their ability even to understand the logic of it.

Those who lost most from the new rights-based politics were white men. The laws of the 1960s may not have been designed explicitly to harm them, but they were gradually altered to help everyone *but* them, which is the same thing. Whites suffered because they occupied this uniquely disadvantaged status under the civil rights laws, because their strongest asset in the constitutional system—their overwhelming preponderance in the electorate—was slowly shrinking, because their electoral victories could be overruled in courtrooms and by regulatory boards where necessary, and because the moral narrative of civil rights required that they be cast as the villains of their country's history. They fell asleep thinking of themselves as the people who had built this country and woke up to find themselves occupying the bottom rung of an official hierarchy of races.

"Built this country"? Not so fast. An idea of Americans as something other than a people had begun to take hold of the political class: Ours was a "creedal" nation, a country united not by race or by history but by belief in certain ideas. This sounds like open-mindedness, but if not managed carefully, it can turn into the opposite. A country you can join by simply changing your mind is a country you can fall out of by doing the same. On literally dozens of occasions as president, Barack Obama described highly specific political opinions, always those of his own party, as expressing "who we are" as Americans. Not since the McCarthy era had Americans been told that to disagree with the authorities was to forfeit one's membership in the American nation. Obama always seemed to enjoy playing with fire that way.

Every signal sent from the commanding heights of American culture for half a century would have led him to believe he held an unbeatable hand. The powers of American democracy had been fortified with strains of theocracy, and Obama was the inheritor of a massive accumulated power to shame. There are, however, great problems with shame as a means of governing. For one thing, opposition does not disappear but only becomes unspeakable, making the public even less knowable to its rulers. For another, shame as a government weapon works only on people capable of *feeling* shame. It thus purges high-minded people from the opposition and ensures that, when the now-mysterious public does throw up an opposition, it will be led by shameless people and take a shameless form.

Civil rights never became self-regenerating as the Americans of 1964 had hoped it would. The legitimacy of civil rights legislation rested on the belief that it would be a transitional measure, leading to a stable, racially mixed society. Professing to oppose racial distinctions in the South, while introducing them on a nationwide basis via affirmative action and other programs, would have been illogical, hypocritical, and unjust if done on a permanent basis. The extra rights of protection and redress that minorities enjoyed were admissible as stopgaps—not as permanent parts of the Constitution.

Permanent, though, is what they became. In a world in which no one was able to say what he really thought, American politics turned into a bizarre tacit bargain, like an embarrassing family secret kept among 300 million people. White people were supposed to console themselves that their superior economic standing somehow "compensated" them for their inferior status as citizens. As their economic standing eroded, though, the consolation rang hollow and the compromise grew unstable.

The Civil Rights Act of 1964 was, as we have noted, a legislative repeal of the First Amendment's implied right to freedom of association. Over decades it polarized the political parties and turned them into something like secret societies, each of them loyal to a different constitutional understanding. Democrats, loyal to the post-1964 constitution, could not acknowledge (or even see) that they owed their ascendancy to a rollback of the basic constitutional freedoms Americans cherished most. Republicans, loyal to the pre-1964 constitution, could not acknowledge (or even see) that the only way back to the free country of their ideals was through the repeal of the civil rights laws. The combination was a terrible one—rising tensions along with a society-wide inability to talk or think straight about anything.

The stifling of public discussion could calm things for only so long. The system required more than the majority's silence; it required the majority's resources. In this respect the post–Civil Rights Act constitution resembled New York's subway. That New York should have underground trains might seem the most "natural" thing in the world. But, every day, seven hundred pumps work around the clock to remove tens of millions of gallons of water from the city's underground. Left alone for even a brief period, the subway would be reclaimed by a mighty network of rivers, springs, and inlets surging underground.

The work of integrating Americans by race and sex, as it is now understood, has come to require a similarly unstinting maximum vigilance. What would the country's social structure look like after six months without affirmative action? Five years? The tiniest dissents at the margins of civil rights thus came to seem like existential threats, and the most routine alternations of power as assaults on the American way.

Civil rights has always been what William James called a "moral equivalent of war," to return to a phrase we used earlier. At its outset in the 1960s, middle-class Americans were prosperous, exuberant, enraged at the death of their president, and certain they had the resources to wage such a war. They were wrong about that.

Ronald Reagan, for all the prosperity Americans enjoyed under his presidency, never found anything like the resources to carry out the projects Lyndon Johnson devised in the 1960s. He merely averted the social confrontation to which events had been building in the 1970s by devising a new system for financing those projects. That is what today's national debt is. The financial collapse of 2008 was a sign that the government had exhausted the resources of the not-yet-born and would now need to tap the resources of the living. Whether it could manage this was impossible to say. Meanwhile, the country's economic and political leaders were more isolated from ordinary citizens than they had been for more than a century. The American people were a closed book to them.

In June 2015, with the presidential election heating up, the talk-show host Bill Maher invited a handful of journalists to discuss the future of American politics. A dozen Republicans well respected within the party were seeking the nomination. Maher asked one of his guests, the conservative journalist Ann Coulter, which candidate had the best chance of winning the general election.

Her reply was surprising: She didn't think any of them would get the nomination. A self-promoting New York real estate developer, however, had announced his candidacy three days before, appearing in a Manhattan office building he pretended to own, making a few off-the-cuff-sounding remarks about Mexican immigration and how great America could be, and eliciting the unanimous ridicule of the press corps. Coulter stonily spoke his name. Her fellow panelists seemed to think she was cracking a joke. They twisted their faces into histrionic expressions of puzzlement to play along. The studio audience roared with laughter.

Notes

2. RACE

7 **new edition of the *Narrative***: Frederick Douglass, *Narrative of the Life of Frederick Douglass, an American Slave, Written by Himself*, edited by Benjamin Quarles (Cambridge, Massachusetts: Belknap Press, 1960). Reviewed by W. R. Brock in *Race & Class* 2 (January 1960): 76–77.

7 **almost unmentioned in print**: Robert S. Levine, *The Lives of Frederick Douglass* (Cambridge, Massachusetts: Harvard University Press, 2016), 11–13.

10 **"the greatest racial consciousness-raising"**: Derrick A. Bell, Jr., "*Brown v. Board of Education* and the Interest Convergence Dilemma," in *Critical Race Theory: The Key Writings That Formed the Movement*, edited by Kimberlé Crenshaw, Neil T. Gotanda, Gary Peller, and Kendall Thomas (New York: New Press, 1995), 21.

10 **"Naturally the *Narrative*"**: Douglass, *Narrative*, xxi.

11 **had turned against Reconstruction**: See Charles Beard, *Contemporary American History, 1877–1913* (New York: Macmillan, 1914), 3. Over the past five decades, the history of Reconstruction has itself been reconstructed to accord with contemporary politics. See Ta-Nehisi Coates, "Hillary Clinton Goes Back to the Dunning School," *The Atlantic* (online), January 25, 2016; Gregory P. Downs, Eric Foner, and Kate Masur, "Why We Need a National Monument to Reconstruction," *New York Times*, December 14, 2016.

11 **"Second Reconstruction"**: C. Vann Woodward, *The Strange Career of Jim Crow* (New York: Oxford University Press, 2002 [1955]), 3–10.

12 **30-item questionnaire**: Civil Rights Movement Veterans, crmvet.org.

14 **"an opinion which is often read"**: Herbert Wechsler, "Toward Neutral Principles of Constitutional Law," *Harvard Law Review* 73, no. 1 (November 1959): 32.

14 **"If the freedom of association"**: Ibid., 34.

15 **"A liberal society stands or falls"**: Leo Strauss, "Why We Remain Jews," lecture at Hillel House, University of Chicago, February 4, 1962, in Strauss, *Jewish Philosophy and the Crisis of Modernity: Essays and Lectures in Modern*

Jewish Thought (Albany: State University of New York Press, 1997), 314–15.

15 **"One of the most distinctive features"**: Harry J. Kalven, Jr., *The Negro and the First Amendment* (Columbus: Ohio State University Press, 1965), 66.

16 **barratry**: According to the *Oxford English Dictionary*, 2nd ed., barratry is "the offence of habitually exciting quarrels, or moving or maintaining law-suits." It is mentioned in Blackstone's *Commentaries*, vol. 4 (1768): 133.

16 **"private attorney general"**: Kalven, *The Negro and the First Amendment*, 80.

17 **"Mrs. Murphy"**: Discussions of Mrs. Murphy began while Kennedy was still alive, continued till the bill's final passage, and can be found *passim* in *Congressional Record—Senate*, including April 13, 1964, 7785, 7792, 7795.

17 **"real freedom will require"**: WGBH (89.7 FM) Boston, Transcript: "March on Washington for Jobs and Freedom." Educational Radio Network coverage, August 28, 1963, hour 6. Also read into the *Congressional Record—Senate*, September 3, 1963, 16228.

18 **"We would all agree"**: *Congressional Record—Senate*, April 13, 1964, 7751.

19 **"would give all persons"**: Gallup poll, June 21–26, 1963.

19 **"No memorial oration or eulogy"**: Lyndon B. Johnson, "Address Before a Joint Session of the Congress, November 27, 1963," lbjlibrary.net.

19 **The Gallup polling organization routinely asked**: Too fast: 50%; not fast enough: 10%: Gallup poll, August 15–20, 1963. Too fast: 30%; not fast enough: 15%: Gallup poll, January 30–February 5, 1964. Too fast: 57%; not fast enough: 18%: Gallup poll, October 1964.

20 **"Some people say"**: Gallup poll, October 8–13, 1964.

20 **got almost identical results**: Opinion Research Corporation poll, November 4–8, 1964.

21 **In 1961, they thought**: Gallup poll, May 28–June 2, 1961.

21 **In 1964, on the eve**: Gallup poll, May 22–27, 1964.

21 **Sixty percent even disapproved**: Gallup poll, August 15–20, 1963.

21 **"I can recall distinctly"**: Alan David Freeman, "Legitimizing Racial Discrimination Through Antidiscrimination Law," *Minnesota Law Review* 62, no. 1049 (1977–78): 1055n.

21 **"the same opportunities"**: Gallup poll, August 23–28, 1962.

21 **70 percent told pollsters**: Gallup poll, May 2–7, 1968. Gallup had gotten almost exactly the same results polling the year before.

22 **"What we find most amazing"**: Crenshaw et al., eds., *Critical Race Theory*, xvi.

22 **"Does the Senator not agree"**: *Congressional Record—Senate*, April 13, 1964, 7787.

23 **"was certainly the objective"**: Nathan Glazer, "Individual Rights Against Group Rights" (1978), in Glazer, *Ethnic Dilemmas, 1964–1982* (Cambridge: Harvard University Press, 1983), 269.

23 **"For one of the major groups":** Nathan Glazer, "The Peoples of America" (1965), in Glazer, *Ethnic Dilemmas*, 27.

24 **"The force of present-day Negro demands":** Nathan Glazer, "Negroes and Jews" (1964), in Glazer, *Ethnic Dilemmas*, 41. (Italics Glazer's.)

25 **Sixty percent of blacks believed:** Gallup poll for *Newsweek* Negro Survey, May 1969.

25 **By 69 to 9 percent:** Ibid.

25 **And when riots eventually came:** Ibid.

26 **"The time has arrived":** Hubert Humphrey, Speech to the Democratic National Convention, Philadelphia, July 14, 1948.

26 **"Revolution is never based":** Malcolm X, "The Black Revolution," in *Malcolm X Speaks*, edited by George Breitman (New York: Pathfinder, 1989 [1965]), 50.

27 **"opens the door":** Ibid., 53.

27 **"We were taking":** Martin Luther King, Jr., "Beyond Vietnam," Address to Clergy and Laymen Concerned About Vietnam, Riverside Church, April 4, 1967. Transcript online under "Beyond Vietnam" at kinginstitute.stanford.edu.

28 **"The civil rights movement itself":** David Halberstam, *The Best and the Brightest* (New York: Ballantine Books, 1992 [1972]), 428.

28 **"banditry":** E. J. Hobsbawm, *Primitive Rebels: Studies in Archaic Forms of Social Movement in the 19th and 20th Centuries* (Manchester: Manchester University Press, 1959).

29 **looting episodes in Memphis:** Ben A. Franklin, "Wiretaps Reveal Dr. King Feared Rebuff on Nonviolence," *New York Times*, September 15, 1985.

29 **toward the end of Barack Obama's first term:** Federal Bureau of Investigation, "Arrests by Race, 2011," Table 43a, Crime in the United States 2011. Online at ucr.fbi.gov.

29 **B'nai B'rith commissioned a poll:** B'nai B'rith/Opinion Research Center (University of Chicago)/Survey Research Center (University of California, Berkeley) poll, October 1964. The category of unsympathetic is a composite of two poll responses: much less sympathetic (13%) and somewhat less sympathetic (24%). So is the category of sympathetic: somewhat more sympathetic (11%) and much more sympathetic (4%).

30 **"Whatever the cause may be":** Beard, *Contemporary American History*, 24.

30 **"indigestible":** Allan Bloom, *The Closing of the American Mind: How Higher Education Has Failed Democracy and Impoverished the Souls of Today's Students* (New York: Simon & Schuster, 1987), 91.

30 **"Cornell," he wrote:** Ibid., 94.

31 **"You do not take":** Lyndon B. Johnson, "To Fulfill These Rights," commencement address at Howard University, June 4, 1965, in *Public Papers of the*

Presidents of the United States: Lyndon B. Johnson, 1965 (Washington, D.C.: U.S. Government Printing Office, 1966), vol. 2, entry 301, 636.

32 **"the next and the more profound stage":** Ibid.

32 **government-approved affirmative action program:** The classic account of how legislation, executive orders, bureaucratic rulemaking, and judicial interpretation combined to produce affirmative action is Nathan Glazer, "Affirmative Discrimination" (1979), in Glazer, *Ethnic Dilemmas*, 159–81.

32 **The American anti-racist regime developed:** Ibid., 164–67.

32 **"Good intent or absence":** Freeman, "Legitimizing Racial Discrimination Through Antidiscrimination Law," 1093–97.

33 **"I do not intend here":** James Q. Wilson, "A Guide to Reagan Country: The Political Culture of Southern California," *Commentary*, May 1967.

33 **"Members of white ethnic groups":** Nathan Glazer, "Blacks and Ethnic Groups" (1971), in Glazer, *Ethnic Dilemmas*, 71.

34 **"Affirmative action requires":** Crenshaw et al., eds., *Critical Race Theory*, xv.

35 **"Bleak though the system is":** Orlando Patterson, "Towards a Future That Has No Past—Reflections on the Fate of Blacks in the Americas," *The Public Interest* 27 (Spring 1972): 60–61.

3. SEX

36 **"a five-thousand-year-buried anger":** Robin Morgan, ed., *Sisterhood Is Powerful* (New York: Random House, 1970), xv.

37 **produced 60 percent:** William H. Branson, Herbert Giersch, and Peter G. Peterson, "Trends in United States International Trade and Investment since World War II," in *The American Economy in Transition*, edited by Martin Feldstein (Chicago: University of Chicago Press, 1980), 183.

37 **By the mid-1950s:** Michael Kazin, *The Populist Persuasion: An American History* (Ithaca, New York: Cornell University Press, 1995), 188.

37 **peaking in 1971:** Gillian Tett, "Trump, the Generals and the Political Front Line," *Financial Times*, October 27, 2017.

37 **"The intimate interaction":** Robert G. Kaiser, "The Great Days of Joe Alsop" (review of Gregg Herken, *The Georgetown Set: Friends and Rivals in Cold War Washington*), *New York Review of Books*, March 5, 2015.

37 **Advertisements from the color magazines:** Jim Heimann, ed., *All-American Ads of the 40s* (New York: Taschen, 2001), and *All-American Ads of the 50s* (New York: Taschen, 2001). Cited in Christopher Caldwell, "Selling Patriotism (and Tang) in Midcentury America," *Wall Street Journal*, February 22, 2002.

38 **they were the first players:** Fred Bierman and Benjamin Hoffman, "A History with Hair as Old as Baseball Itself," *New York Times*, August 9, 2008.

38   **President Kennedy himself smoked:** "Salinger's JFK-Cuban Cigar Stories," YouTube.

38   **his wife menthol cigarettes:** William Manchester, *The Death of a President* (New York: Harper & Row, 1967), 6.

38   **Mary, the most popular:** U.S. Social Security Administration. Available under "Top 5 Names in Each of the Last 100 Years," ssa.gov. Mary had lagged Linda in the years 1947 to 1951.

38   **Weeknight television:** Programming information from Tim Brooks and Earle Marsh, *The Complete Directory to Prime Time Network TV Shows, 1946–Present* (New York: Ballantine, 1979), 738–39.

38   **A *TV Guide* from early:** *TV Guide*, January 25–31, 1964, 14, 16.

39   **Most mothers owned sewing machines:** Thomas R. Tibbetts, "Expanding Ownership of Household Equipment," *Monthly Labor Review*, 87, no. 10 (October 1964). In 1961, 60 percent of urban households had sewing machines.

39   **were cabineted in wood:** See, e.g., the ads for Motorola and RCA TVs in Jim Heimann, ed., *All-American Ads of the 60s* (Cologne, Germany: Taschen, 2002), 385.

39   **"has been carried largely":** Peter F. Drucker, *The Age of Discontinuity: Guidelines to Our Changing Society* (New York: Harper & Row, 1968), 3–9.

40   **"post-industrial" problems:** Theodore Roszak, *Where the Wasteland Ends: Politics and Transcendence in Post-Industrial Society* (Garden City, New York: Doubleday, 1972), xxvii.

40   **City Hall Plaza:** Stephen Carr, Mark Francis, Leanne G. Rivlin, and Andrew M. Stone, *Public Space* (Cambridge, England: Cambridge University Press, 1992), 88–90.

40   **"Go right to it":** Chalmers M. Roberts, "President Approves D.C. Redevelopment," *Washington Post,* March 6, 1952. Cited in Christian James, "Southwest Renewal," at christianjames.us.

41   **"It resembled nothing so much":** John W. Aldridge, *In the Country of the Young* (New York: Harper & Row, 1970), 4.

41   **"the same passions and disciplines":** Tom Brokaw, *The Greatest Generation* (New York: Random House, 1998), xxviii. Quoted in George M. Marsden, *The Twilight of the American Enlightenment: The 1950s and the Crisis of Liberal Belief* (New York: Basic Books, 2014), xxi.

41   **"had been thrown into":** Marsden, *The Twilight of the American Enlightenment*, xii.

42   **"the human race is getting better":** Gallup poll, January 6–11, 1960.

42   **Between 1920 and 1958:** Betty Friedan, *The Feminine Mystique* (New York: Norton, 2001 [1963]), 58.

42 **"problem that has no name"**: Ibid., 20.

42 **a "sexual" one**: Ibid., 117, 142.

43 **"being a woman has prevented me"**: Louis Harris & Associates poll for Virginia Slims, October 1971.

43 **65 percent had never heard of her**: Ibid.

43 **Sixty-three percent had never heard**: Ibid.

43 **64 percent had never heard**: Ibid.

43 **"women's intuition"**: Gallup poll for the *Saturday Evening Post*, June 1962.

43 **Sixteen percent of married women**: Ibid.

44 **It was coined in 1968**: *Oxford English Dictionary*, 2nd ed., XV:112 (Oxford: Clarendon Press, 1989), credited to *Vital Speeches*, November 15, 1968, 90.

44 **"Because only one of them"**: David Halberstam, *The Best and the Brightest* (New York: Ballantine, 1992 [1972]), 206.

44 **If you asked women to name**: Roper poll for Virginia Slims, April 1974.

45 **"Presenting the Losers"**: Mike Mashon, "If This Isn't the Most Sexist TV Commercial Ever, It's Close," Library of Congress, February 24, 2015. Available at loc.gov.

45 **"Maybe the real you"**: Heimann, *All-American Ads of the 60s*, 657.

45 **"Everything to make it happen"**: Ibid., 80.

46 **"Men and Women Copopulating"**: John K. Setear, "Pro House Offers Copopular T-shirts to Commemorate Women's Presence," *Williams Record*, May 1, 1979.

46 **"Once I believed"**: Barry Mann and Cynthia Weil, "It's Getting Better," 1969.

47 **James Q. Wilson offered**: James Q. Wilson, *The Marriage Problem: How Our Culture Has Weakened Families* (New York: Harper, 2003), 55.

47 **The 1960s were as wildly skewed**: Ibid., 48.

48 **"a place where one could work"**: Christopher Turner, "If You Don't Swing, Don't Ring," *London Review of Books*, April 21, 2016.

48 **"The headboard of his bed"**: Ibid.

48 **When the journalist Tom Wolfe**: Ibid.

49 **"most of the efforts"**: Roper poll for Virginia Slims, April 1974.

49 **The Joy of Sex**: New York: Simon & Schuster, 1972.

49 **That did not stop the book**: Douglas Martin, "Alex Comfort, 80, Dies; a Multifaceted Man Best Known for Writing 'The Joy of Sex,'" *New York Times*, March 29, 2000.

49 **"They got an apartment"**: Billy Joel, "Scenes from an Italian Restaurant," 1977.

50 **Trojan Kling-Tite Naturalamb condoms**: Jim Heimann, ed., *All-American Ads of the 80s* (Cologne: Taschen, 2005), 236.

50 **Playboy Club "bunny"**: Gloria Steinem, "A Bunny's Tale," parts I and II, *Show*, May 1963 and June 1963.

50 **"Sex and race"**: Gloria Steinem, "After Black Power, Women's Liberation," *New York*, April 7, 1969.

51 **"the house-bound matriarchs"**: Ibid.

52 **"Would you like to see"**: Gallup poll for the *Saturday Evening Post*, June 1962.

52 **"legitimation"**: Nancy Fraser, "Feminism, Capitalism and the Cunning of History," *New Left Review* 56 (March–April 2009): 97–117.

53 **Between 1973 and the turn of the century**: Susan Watkins, "Which Feminisms?," *New Left Review* 109 (January–February 2018): 5–76, which cites Bureau of Labor Statistics data cited in Michael Kimmel, "Boys and School: A Background Paper on the 'Boy Crisis,'" Swedish Government Official Reports, SOU 2010:53, Stockholm, 2010, 15. Online at government.se.

54 **the repeal was vetoed**: Richard Perez-Pena, " '70 Abortion Law: New York Said Yes, Stunning the Nation," *New York Times*, April 9, 2000.

54 **By the time of *Roe***: Pew Charitable Trusts, "States Probe Limits of Abortion Policy," *Stateline*, June 22, 2006. Online at pewtrusts.org. According to Pew, the "trendsetting" states of Mississippi, Alabama, Colorado, New Mexico, and Massachusetts were followed by Alaska, Arkansas, California, Delaware, Florida, Georgia, Hawaii, Kansas, Maryland, New York, North Carolina, Oregon, South Carolina, Virginia, and Washington.

55 **We can tell because**: Gallup poll, December 8–11, 1972.

55 **Polls taken in the days after *Roe v. Wade***: National Opinion Research Center, University of Chicago poll, February 1973.

56 **"Christians should accustom themselves"**: Quoted in Andrew Hartman, *A War for the Soul of America: A History of the Culture Wars* (Chicago: University of Chicago Press, 2015), 94.

58 **"alienated from their own bodies"**: Wilma Diskin and Wendy Coppedge Sanford, "Preface," and Joan Sheingold Ditzion, "Our Changing Sense of Self," in Boston Women's Health Book Collective, *Our Bodies, Ourselves* (New York: Simon & Schuster, 1973 [1971]), 1–10.

58 **"Our culture," the authors wrote**: Ibid., 99.

58 **"the 'short arm' inspection"**: Ibid.

59 **When it came to abortion**: Ibid., 143–49.

59 **"When legal resources fail her"**: Ibid., 148.

59 **"If you're grabbed"**: Ibid., 97.

60 **"if this should occur"**: Bertrand Russell, *Marriage and Morals* (New York: Horace Liveright, 1929), 187–88.

61 **"My belief is"**: Ibid., 203.

61 **In the late spring of 1962**: Gallup poll for the *Saturday Evening Post*, June 1962.

62 **"I got so many women"**: Ray Davies, "The Good Life," unreleased, 1970, YouTube.

62 **In the winter of 1976:** Rick Perlstein, *The Invisible Bridge: The Fall of Nixon and the Rise of Reagan* (New York: Simon & Schuster, 2014), 614.

62 **X-rated videocassettes sold:** Jim Heimann, ed., *All-American Ads of the 70s* (Cologne: Taschen, 2004), 209.

62 **"He knew that the distance":** Martin Amis, *Yellow Dog* (New York: Vintage, 2005 [2003]), 74.

63 **By 2015, 45 percent:** Elizabeth S. Auritt et al., "The Class of 2015 by the Numbers," *Harvard Crimson*, June 2015. Online at thecrimson.com/2015/senior-survey/.

63 **"For those nights":** Heimann, *All-American Ads of the 70s*, 210.

63 **"Jackpot!":** Ibid., 436.

63 **"own at least one pair":** Ibid., 526.

63 **Steinem had heard it mentioned:** Margalit Fox, "Sheila Michaels, Who Brought 'Ms.' to Prominence, Dies at 78," *New York Times*, July 7, 2017.

63 **There was never much affirmative enthusiasm:** Roper Organization polls for Virginia Slims, April 1974 and October 6–20, 1979.

64 **"equal rights for women":** Roper Organization poll, June 14–21, 1975.

64 **"separate public toilets":** Harris poll for National Federation of Business and Professional Women. November 30–December 2, 1979.

65 **Anita Bryant led:** Roper Organization poll, January 7–21, 1978.

65 **What she was doing then:** Dade County Ordinance 77-4.

65 **giving them more rights:** George Fine Research poll for the *Washington Post*, January 1978.

65 **"women getting welfare money":** Opinion Research Corporation poll for Richard Nixon, May 7–25, 1971.

65 **"advocates of the Equal Rights Amendment":** Louis Harris & Associates poll, March 26–April 2, 1977.

4. WAR

66 **temporary home of 2.7 million:** Christopher Caldwell, "Letting Bygones Be Bygones," *Claremont Review of Books* 15, no. 2 (Spring 2015): 42–46.

68 **"Management is, in the end":** Phil Rosenzweig, "Robert McNamara and the Evolution of Modern Management," *Harvard Business Review*, December 2010.

68 **They claimed the percentage:** Samuel P. Huntington, "The Bases of Accommodation," *Foreign Affairs*, July 1968.

68 **"mad rationality":** Theodore Roszak, *The Making of a Counter Culture* (Berkeley: University of California Press, 1995 [1968]), 78. Roszak attributes the phrase to Lewis Mumford.

68 **"lunatic realism":** Theodore Roszak, *Where the Wasteland Ends: Politics and*

Transcendence in Post-Industrial Society (Garden City, New York: Doubleday, 1972), xxix.

68 **"We are what went wrong":** Loren Baritz, *Backfire: A History of How American Culture Led Us into Vietnam and Made Us Fight the Way We Did* (Baltimore: Johns Hopkins University Press, 1998 [1983]), 349.

68 **"I want to leave":** Lloyd C. Gardner, *Pay Any Price: Lyndon Johnson and the Wars for Vietnam* (Chicago: Ivan R. Dee, 1995), 197.

69 **White House counsel Clark Clifford:** Walter A. McDougall, *The Tragedy of U.S. Foreign Policy: How America's Civil Religion Betrayed the National Interest* (New Haven: Yale University Press, 2016), 288–89.

69 **The sociologist and Johnson advisor Daniel Patrick Moynihan:** Daniel Patrick Moynihan, "Who Gets in the Military?," *New Republic*, November 5, 1966. Cited in Christian G. Appy, *American Reckoning: The Vietnam War and Our National Identity* (New York: Viking, 2016), 132.

69 **"Do you really think":** David Halberstam, *The Best and the Brightest* (New York: Ballantine, 1992 [1972]), 610.

69 **"A strong rear":** Vo Nguyen Giap, *The Military Art of People's War* (New York: Monthly Review Press, 1970 [Hanoi: Foreign Languages Publishing House, 1961]), 160.

69 **Two twentieth-century wars had been:** Baritz, *Backfire*, 181.

69 **Not until the final years:** A Harris poll in October 1971 showed that 62 percent of Americans would favor leaving Vietnam even if it meant that the Communists might take over.

71 **"holding the line":** Harris poll for the *Washington Post*, March 1965.

71 **In August 1967, the *Post* asked again:** Harris poll for the *Washington Post*, August 1967.

71 **"having the UN try":** Gallup poll, February 10–15, 1966.

71 **The following month, voters:** Gallup poll, March 3–8, 1966.

71 **When reports emerged:** Gallup poll, December 12–15, 1969.

71 **The mining of Vietnam's harbors:** Harris poll, May 9–10, 1972.

72 **A slim majority approved:** Gallup poll, January 12–15, 1973.

72 **When Chicago police battered:** Gallup poll, September 1–6, 1968.

72 **"if there is any kind":** Opinion Research Corporation poll, October 7–10, 1968.

72 **The number of people:** A Harris poll done in October 1969 found that 6 percent thought Americans were withdrawing "too fast." A Roper poll two years later (October 18–27, 1971) found 3 percent said "too fast" versus 48 percent who said "too slow"—a ratio of 1 to 16. That is roughly equivalent to Nixon's own internal polling from April 5–6 the same year: 5 percent too fast, 46 percent too slow.

73   **At least 60 percent:** 61 percent. CBS News poll, October 14–16, 1969.

73   **A majority was convinced that:** Will hold its own: 38 percent; will not: 51 percent. CBS News poll, November 23–25, 1969.

73   **By contrast, Americans seemed:** Opinion Research Corporation poll for Richard Nixon, December 4–5, 1972.

74   **"fraggings":** Appy, *American Reckoning*, 214.

74   **"I never once heard":** Barry Romo in *Vietnam: Lost Films*, The History Channel, November 2011.

74   **The top-selling single:** *Billboard* Top 100, 1966. Available at billboard top100of.com.

74   **It was Barry Sadler's:** Appy, *American Reckoning*, 124.

74   **"our deeply felt apology":** Dan O'Connor, "McNamara Surrounded, Angered by Protestors," *The Heights* (Boston College), November 18, 1966.

75   **A petition of apology:** Steven Kelman, *Push Comes to Shove: The Escalation of Student Protest* (Boston: Houghton Mifflin, 1970), 61. Undergraduate population estimate of 4,780 based on four times the targeted class size in Efrem Sigel, "College Admits 1,362, Fewest Since 1930's," *Harvard Crimson*, April 15, 1963.

75   **In late 1968:** Baritz, *Backfire*, 181.

75   **"a bit of careless expediency":** "The Axe Falls" (editorial), *Harvard Crimson*, February 17, 1968.

75   **"I'm against the war":** Kelman, *Push Comes to Shove*, 82.

76   **"boys from Chelsea":** James Fallows, "What Did You Do in the Class War, Daddy?," *Washington Monthly*, October 1975.

76   **"spoiled brats":** Roger Rosenblatt, *Coming Apart: A Memoir of the Harvard Wars of 1969* (New York: Little, Brown, 1997), 48.

76   **"Part of the brutality":** Todd Gitlin, *The Sixties: Years of Hope, Days of Rage* (New York: Bantam, 1989 [1987]), 308.

77   **Whites made up 60 percent:** Arthur Flemming et al., *School Desegregation in Boston*, Staff Report Prepared for U.S. Commission on Civil Rights, June 1975 (typescript), 20 [in University of Maryland Law School library]. The figure for 1971–72 is 61 percent.

77   **"distinguished experts":** William M. Bulger, *While the Music Lasts: My Life in Politics* (Boston: Houghton Mifflin, 1996), 165.

78   **"afraid to ask the men":** James Webb, "The Draft: Why the Army Needs It," *The Atlantic*, April 1980, 44. Quoted in Baritz, 341.

78   **"I am convinced":** Irving Kristol, "The Disaffection from Capitalism," in *Capitalism and Socialism: A Theological Inquiry*, edited by Michael Novak (Washington, D.C.: American Enterprise Institute, 1979), 28. Quoted in Matthew Continetti, "The Theological Politics of Irving Kristol," *National Affairs* 20 (Summer 2014): 145–62.

78 **"On the one hand":** Kelman, *Push Comes to Shove*, 138–39.

79 **The Harvard theologian Harvey Cox argued:** Harvey Cox, *The Secular City: Secularization and Urbanization in Theological Perspective* (New York: Macmillan, 1965).

79 **"great awakenings":** Robert D. Putnam, David E. Campbell, and Shaylyn Romney Garrett, *American Grace: How Religion Divides and Unites Us* (New York: Simon & Schuster, 2010).

80 **"disordering all the senses":** Arthur Rimbaud, letter to Georges Izambard, May 13, 1871. In *Œuvres complètes* (Paris: Gallimard, 1972), 249. (Author's translation.)

80 **"These roads are truly different":** Robert Pirsig, *Zen and the Art of Motorcycle Maintenance* (New York: Harper, 2005 [1974]), 13.

81 **"a passport back to America":** In Bob Smeaton, dir., *Classic Albums: The Band* (London: Eagle Rock Entertainment, 1997).

82 **The mountain climber Guy Waterman:** Douglas Martin, "Guy Waterman Dies at 67; Wrote Books About Hiking," *New York Times*, February 20, 2000.

82 **Illinois-born John McClaughry:** Dirk Van Susteren, "In This State: A Thing or Two You Might Not Know About John McClaughry," *VTDigger*, November 24, 2013. Online at vtdigger.org.

83 **The United States had a population:** U.S. Bureau of the Census, *Current Population Reports*, ser. P-25, nos. 311, 917, 1095.

83 **70 million babies before 1964:** Sandra L. Colby and Jennifer M. Ortman, *The Baby Boom Cohort in the United States: 2012 to 2060*, Current Population Reports, May 2014, (Figure 3).

83 **Birth rates had been rising steadily:** Ibid., (Figure 1).

83 **In the first years of the twenty-first century:** Ibid., (Figure 3).

83 **For a generation, they made up:** "The Generation Gap and the 2012 Election," Pew Research Center, November 3, 2011.

83 **In 1970, the Bendix Corporation:** Jim Heimann, ed., *All-American Ads of the 70s* (Cologne: Taschen, 2004), 173.

84 **"And we don't see":** Ibid., 180.

86 **"the number of students tripled":** Eric Hobsbawm, *The Age of Extremes: A History of the World, 1914–1991* (New York: Pantheon, 1994), 296.

86 **its college enrollment more than quadrupled:** Bureau of the Census, *Statistical Abstract of the United States, 1972* (Washington, D.C.: U.S. Department of Commerce, 1972), tables 128, 200. (The exact figure in 1970 was 7,484,000.)

86 **By 2010, there would be:** Elizabeth M. Grieco et al., "The Size, Place of Birth, and Geographic Distribution of the Foreign-Born Population in the United States: 1960 to 2010" (Population Division Working Paper No. 96) (Washington, D.C.: U.S. Census Bureau, October 2012), 33.

87   **New Hampshire did not get one:** Online at www.littlemexicorestaurant.com.

88   **"In one of the fanzines":** Paul Cook, "Nothing Sacrilegious About This British Library Punk Show, Says Paul Cook of the Sex Pistols," *The Spectator* (London), May 28, 2016.

88   **"To the new generation":** Heimann, *All-American Ads of the 70s*, 129.

88   **Starting in 1978, General Motors began:** Jim Brennan, "Hooniverse Wagon Wednesday—The Worst Wagons Ever Produced," Hooniverse, May 18, 2011. Online at hooniverse.com.

88   **Magazine ads for Ford and Cadillac:** Heimann, *All-American Ads of the 70s*: Pinto 114, Cadillac 125.

5. DEBT

93   **"The cultural and Reagan revolutions":** Mark Lilla, "A Tale of Two Reactions." In *Left Hooks, Right Crosses: A Decade of Political Writing*, edited by Christopher Hitchens and Christopher Caldwell (New York: Nation Books, 2002), 267.

93   **" 'Do your own thing' ":** Kurt Andersen, "The Downside of Liberty," *New York Times*, July 4, 2012.

94   **The Ashland University historian:** Steven F. Hayward, *The Age of Reagan: The Conservative Counterrevolution* (Roseville, California: Forum, 2001).

94   **"For I doubt":** Spiro T. Agnew, Speech to the First Annual Vince Lombardi Award Dinner, Houston, Texas, January 21, 1971. Quoted in John R. Coyne, Jr., *The Impudent Snobs: Agnew vs. the Intellectual Establishment* (New Rochelle, New York: Arlington House, 1972), 445.

95   **The Princeton historian Sean Wilentz:** Sean Wilentz, *The Age of Reagan: A History, 1974–2008* (New York: Harper, 2008).

95   **"ruthlessly to cut the past away":** Philip Slater, *The Pursuit of Loneliness: American Culture at the Breaking Point* (Boston: Beacon Press, 1970), 143.

95   **"The truth is":** Ronald Reagan, "Address to the Nation on the Program for Economic Recovery," September 24, 1981. Transcript online at reagan library.gov.

96   **"In the United States":** Lionel Trilling, *The Liberal Imagination: Essays on Literature and Society* (New York: NYRB Books, 2008 [1950]), xv.

96   **"mystifying pleasantry":** Irving Howe, "This Age of Conformity" (1950), in Howe, *Selected Writings, 1950–1990* (San Diego: Harcourt Brace Jovanovich, 1990), 34–35.

97   **J. W. "River Rat" Edwards:** David Harris, "The Truckers Go to Washington: Democracy in Action on the Interstate," *Rolling Stone*, April 25, 1974.

97   **"When, wall-to-wall":** Cledus Maggard [Jay Huguely], "The White Knight," 1975.

98　**That was the year:** 94th Congress, Public Law 94-168 [H.R. 8674], December 23, 1975.

98　**"Drop a dime":** Kirsten A. Conover, "Drop-A-Dime Project Pays Off," *Christian Science Monitor*, August 18, 1989.

98　**It secured for another generation:** The phrase "exorbitant privilege" was used by French finance minister Valéry Giscard d'Estaing in the 1960s to describe America's relationship to its reserve currency.

99　**"I like to think of fire":** Ayn Rand, *Atlas Shrugged* (New York: Dutton, 1992 [1957]), 684.

99　**"his hand moving over":** Ibid., 107.

100　**"absolutely bewitched":** Buckley on *Charlie Rose*, PBS, June 17, 2003.

100　**"I give out *Atlas Shrugged*":** Katherine Mangu-Ward, "Young, Wonky, and Proud of It," *Weekly Standard*, March 17, 2003.

100　**"admirer":** Ronald Reagan, *Reagan: A Life in Letters*, edited by Kiron K. Skinner, Annelise Anderson, and Martin Anderson (New York: Free Press, 2003), 282.

100　**"The appalling disgrace":** Ayn Rand, "The Sanction of the Victims," speech to the National Committee for Monetary Reform, New Orleans, November 23, 1981, in Ayn Rand, *The Voice of Reason: Essays in Objectivist Thought* (New York: Meridian, 1990), 156.

100　**as governor of California:** Rick Perlstein, *The Invisible Bridge: The Fall of Nixon and the Rise of Reagan* (New York: Simon & Schuster, 2014), 103.

101　**being used twice as frequently:** Google Ngram Viewer.

101　**The expression "American Dream":** Christopher Caldwell, "Fantasy Politics," *New York Times Magazine*, November 5, 2010.

101　**its usage went up:** Google Ngram Viewer.

102　**the Obama administration would pay her:** Jason Furman and Jim Stock, "New Report: The All-of-the-Above Energy Strategy as a Path to Sustainable Economic Growth," White House press release, May 29, 2014.

102　**"an implicit deal":** William Strauss and Neil Howe, *Generations: The History of America's Future, 1584 to 2069* (New York: Quill, 1991), 14.

103　**"The national debt tripled under Reagan":** John Patrick Diggins, *Ronald Reagan: Fate, Freedom, and the Making of History* (New York: Norton, 2007), 178.

104　**"The answer to a government":** Ronald Reagan, "Address Before a Joint Session of the Congress on the Program for Economic Recovery," April 28, 1981. Online at reaganlibrary.gov.

105　**Its origins in a restaurant:** "Laffer Curve Napkin," National Museum of American History. Online at americanhistory.si.edu.

105　**"embrace the role of Scrooge":** Quoted in Bruce Bartlett, "Taxes and a

Two-Santa Theory," *National Observer*, March 6, 1976. Online at wallstreet pit.com.

105 **His article was widely read:** Ibid.

105 **fall of Rome:** Jude Wanniski, *The Way the World Works* (Washington, D.C.: Regnery Gateway, 1998 [1978]), 31.

105 **"Return to Normalcy":** Ibid., 130.

105 **Japan's post-war boom:** Ibid., 204–06.

106 **"permit the workers to keep":** Ibid., 105–06.

106 **Faced with the prospect:** Robert D. Novak, "Introduction" in Wanniski, *The Way the World Works*, ix.

106 **In an autumn 1981 economic address:** Reagan, "Address to the Nation on the Program for Economic Recovery."

106 **"We cut the government's":** Ibid.

106 **Government would continue to grow:** William A. Niskanen, "Reaganomics," *The Concise Encyclopedia of Economics*, Library of Economics and Liberty. Online at econlib.org.

107 **"Even if Congress manages":** George Gilder, *Wealth and Poverty* (New York: Basic Books, 1981), 225.

107 **"more trade barriers":** Niskanen, "Reaganomics."

107 **"from discretionary domestic spending":** Ibid.

108 **Although the size of the total credit market:** Richard Duncan, *The New Depression: The Breakdown of the Paper Money Economy* (Singapore: John Wiley & Sons, 2012), 59.

109 **They would swell:** "Figure 20 B: Total Pell Grant Expenditures and Number of Recipients, 1977–78 to 2017–2018." In Sandy Baum, Jennifer Ma, Matea Pender, and C. J. Libassi (New York: CollegeBoard, 2018), 27.

110 **According to one sympathetic account:** Christopher Jencks, "Did We Lose the War on Poverty?—II," *New York Review of Books*, April 23, 2015. Jencks cites a chapter by Bridget Terry Long in *Legacies of the War on Poverty*, edited by Martha J. Bailey and Sheldon Danziger (New York: Russell Sage Foundation, 2013).

110 **the largest collector of Pell Grant tuition:** Tamar Lewin, "Report Finds Low Graduation Rates at For-Profit Colleges," *New York Times*, November 24, 2010.

111 **the government's unfunded liabilities:** Roy H. Webb, "The Stealth Budget: Unfunded Liabilities of the Federal Government," *FRB Richmond Economic Review* 77, no. 3 (May–June 1991): 23–33.

111 **By the time of the 2016 election:** Antony Davies and James R. Harrigan, "Debt Myths, Debunked," *U.S. News & World Report*, December 1, 2016.

112 **electric typewriters:** See Jim Heimann, ed., *All-American Ads of the 60s* (Cologne, Germany: Taschen, 2002), 286.

112 **The biggest** *New York Times* **ever:** James Meek, "The Club and the Mob," *London Review of Books*, December 6, 2018, 13.

112 **especially true of illegal immigrants:** Christopher Caldwell, *Reflections on the Revolution in Europe: Immigration, Islam, and the West* (New York: Doubleday, 2009), 37–44.

113 **Even in the mid-1960s:** U.S. Bureau of the Census, *Statistical Abstract of the United States, 1965* (Washington, D.C.: U.S. Government Printing Office, 1965), table 116. Figures are from 1964.

113 **"Quota immigration under the bill":** Emanuel Celler, "Many Misinformed on Pending Immigration Revision Proposal" (remarks), 89th Congress, First Session, April 28, 1965.

114 **"This bill that we will sign":** *Public Papers of the Presidents of the United States: Lyndon B. Johnson, 1965* (Washington, D.C.: U.S. Government Printing Office, 1966), vol. 2, entry 546, 1038.

114 **"The American Nation":** Ibid., 1039.

114 **"Without injury or cost":** Nicholas deBelleville. Katzenbach, Statement before the Immigration and Nationality Subcommittee of the House Judiciary Committee, March 3, 1965.

114 **"The ethnic mix":** Edward Kennedy, Hearing of the Subcommittee on Immigration and Naturalization of the Committee on the Judiciary, U.S. Senate, February 10, 1965.

114 **Of these, only China:** Migration Policy Institute, "Largest U.S. Immigrant Groups over Time, 1960–Present," pie chart at its online "Migration Data Hub."

114 **"The bill will not aggravate":** Kennedy, Hearing of the Subcommittee on Immigration and Naturalization of the Committee on the Judiciary.

115 **In the three-and-a-half centuries:** American Committee on Immigration Policies, "Our Immigration Laws Protect You, Your Job and Your Freedom" (pamphlet), Washington, D.C., 1965.

115 **including a quarter-million slaves:** "Voyages," Trans-Atlantic Slave Trade Database, online at slavevoyages.org/assessment/estimates.

115 **In the half-century that followed:** Pew Research Center, "Modern Immigration Wave Brings 59 Million to U.S., Driving Population Growth and Change Through 2065," September 28, 2015, 6.

116 **Kennedy proposed:** Edward M. Kennedy, *Selected Readings on U.S. Immigration Policy and Law: A Compendium*, 96th Congress, 2nd Session (Washington, D.C.: U.S. Government Printing Office, October 1980).

116 **A Special Agricultural Worker (SAW) program:** Betsy Cooper and Kevin O'Neil, "Lessons from the Immigration Reform and Control Act of 1986," *MPI Policy Brief* 3 (August 2005): 4.

116 **Simpson-Mazzoli brought with it:** Ibid. Cooper and O'Neil called it "the

largest expansion of federal regulatory authority since the enactment of the Occupational Safety and Health Act in 1980"—but their date is a typo.

117 **In June 1986:** Gallup poll, June 19–23, 1986.

117 **"Everyone assumed":** Brad Plumer, "Congress Tried to Fix Immigration Back in 1986. Why Did It Fail?," *Washington Post*, January 30, 2013.

117 **That year, 47 percent:** Rodney Benson, "Fraying Asylum Policies, Great Migrations," *Le Monde Diplomatique* (English), May 1, 2015.

118 **"If it takes a man":** Gregory Korte, "Mexican Slur Has Long History in Politics," *USA Today*, March 29, 2013.

118 **"to explain the new immigration law's":** Marvine Howe, "Employers Warned on Alien Hiring," *New York Times*, August 9, 1987.

118 **Jack Kemp sought a waiver:** Carla Rivera, "Kemp May Ask Congress to Ease Immigration Act," *Los Angeles Times*, June 13, 1990.

118 **In policy terms:** See, e.g., Cooper and O'Neil, "Lessons from the Immigration Reform and Control Act of 1986."

119 **In 1983, four years after:** Wendell Rawls, Jr., "Mexican Food Trips Asian Refugee in Spelling Bee," *New York Times*, April 30, 1983.

119 **"unspoken (and sometimes spoken) criticism":** Nathan Glazer, "The Peoples of America" (1965), in Glazer, *Ethnic Dilemmas*, 27.

120 **"Consciously and unconsciously":** Martin Luther King, Jr., "Letter from a Birmingham Jail" (typescript of letter to Bishop C. C. J. Carpenter et al., April 16, 1963), 12. Collection of the Martin Luther King, Jr. Research and Education Institute, Stanford University. Online at kinginstitute.stanford.edu. (The typographical error "promise land" is in the original.)

121 **"The unity which will come":** Jean-Paul Sartre, "L'Orphée noir," in *Anthologie de la nouvelle poésie nègre et malgache de langue française*, edited by Léopold Sédar Senghor (Paris: Presses Universitaires de France, 1948), xiii–xiv. In English, "Black Orpheus," in Sartre, *"What Is Literature?" and Other Essays* (Cambridge, Massachusetts: Harvard University Press, 1988), 296. Quoted (and translated) in Michael Hardt and Antonio Negri, *Empire* (Cambridge, Massachusetts: Harvard University Press, 2000), 130.

121 **"Unlike our parents":** Christophe Guilluy, "L'antifascisme cache des intérêts de classe" (interview with Daoud Boughezala, Élisabeth Lévy, and Gil Mihaely), *Causeur*, February 2016. Quoted in Christopher Caldwell, "The French, Coming Apart," *City Journal*, Spring 2017: 46–55. (Author's translation.)

122 **"To be called African-Americans":** "Jackson and Others Say 'Blacks' Is Passé," *New York Times*, December 21, 1988.

122 **a writer in *Ebony* magazine:** Ibid. See also David Bradley, "The Omni-American Blues," *First Things*, March 2017, 45–50.

123 **Bork had had misgivings:** Robert Bork, "Civil Rights: A Challenge," *New Republic*, August 31, 1963, 21–24.

123 **"Robert Bork's America":** *Congressional Record—Senate*, July 1, 1987, 18518–19.

123 **"This is the most historic moment":** Ibid., 18519.

124 **This $50 billion "surplus" disguises:** George J. Borjas, "The Economic Benefits of Immigration," *Journal of Economic Perspectives* 9:2 (Spring 1995): 3–22. Cited in Borjas, *We Wanted Workers: Unraveling the Immigration Narrative* (New York: Norton, 2016), 157–58.

126 **"Observe Reagan's futile attempts":** Rand, "The Sanction of the Victims," in Rand, *The Voice of Reason*, 156.

127 **By 2010, it had:** The median household income in 1969 (this was what was measured in the 1970 census) was $9,590; see U.S. Bureau of the Census, *Statistical Abstract of the United States, 1972* (Washington, D.C.: U.S. Government Printing Office, 1972), table 532. The median home price in the fourth quarter of 1969 was $24,900; see U.S. Bureau of the Census and U.S. Department of Housing and Urban Development, "Median Sales Price of Houses Sold for the United States." Online at fred.stlouisfed.org. The ratio of median home price to median income was 2.5965 or 2 years, 217 days. The median household income in 2010 was $51,144; see Amanda Noss, "Household Income for States: 2010 and 2011. American Community Survey Briefs," U.S. Bureau of the Census, September 2012, table 1. The median home price in the fourth quarter of 2010 was $224,300 (U.S. Bureau of the Census and U.S. Department of Housing and Urban Development, "Median Sales Price of Houses Sold for the United States"). The ratio of the median home price to median income was 4.3857, or 4 years, 140 days.

128 **"All it takes is success":** Jim Heimann, ed., *All-American Ads of the 80s* (Cologne, Germany: Taschen, 2005), 218.

129 **claimed to be the inventor:** Lewis B. Cullman, "Stop the Misuse of Philanthropy!" *New York Review of Books*, September 25, 2014.

129 **"The newest member":** Heimann, *All-American Ads of the 80s*, 173.

129 **"Barbie: The Doll Dreams Are Made of":** Ibid., 263.

129 **"Starting April 23":** "Northwest Airlines 'No Smoking' Commercial—1988," YouTube.

6. DIVERSITY

132 **Until well into the Reagan era:** "Fonts in Use," fontsinuse.com.

132 **"we have used our wealth":** Daniel Boorstin, *The Image: A Guide to Pseudo-events in America* (New York: Vintage, 1992 [1962]), 3.

133   **"Some of you will fly"**: John F. Kennedy, "Remarks at U.S. Air Force Academy, Colorado Springs, Colorado, 5 June 1963," Papers of John F. Kennedy, President's Office Files, Speech Files.

133   **A year later, Lockheed:** Jim Heimann, ed., *All-American Ads of the 60s* (Cologne, Germany: Taschen, 2002), 350.

134   **By the 2016 presidential election:** 2016 times are from airport timetables. Nixon administration times are from a 1969 Boeing ad announcing that its new 747, traveling at 625 mph, could make it from New York to London in 6 hours, 3 minutes. See Heimann, *All-American Ads of the 60s*, 910.

134   **The train trip from New York:** Michael Tomasky, "The Next Amtrak Catastrophe," *Daily Beast*, May 13, 2015.

134   **"would narrow to a trickle":** Edmund Phelps, "Europe Is a Continent That Has Run Out of Ideas," *Financial Times*, March 3, 2015.

134   **"automatic highways":** Heimann, *All-American Ads of the 60s*, 362.

134   **The Presto Meat Toaster:** Jim Heimann, ed., *All-American Ads of the 70s* (Cologne, Germany: Taschen, 2004), 236, 239, 249.

135   **"crossing a telephone":** Heimann, *All-American Ads of the 60s*, 513.

135   **The first harvest of innovation:** Jim Heimann, ed., *All-American Ads of the 80s* (Cologne, Germany: Taschen, 2005), 178, 317.

135   **"the logical approach to computers":** Ibid., 178.

137   **"The gross national product":** Philip Slater, *The Pursuit of Loneliness: American Culture at the Breaking Point* (Boston: Beacon Press, 1970), 93.

137   **"post-materialist" economy:** Ronald Inglehart, *Culture Shift in Advanced Industrial Society* (Princeton: Princeton University Press, 1990), passim.

137   **"language really spoken by men":** William Wordsworth, preface to *Lyrical Ballads*, 1802 edition.

137   **"Data," said Lawrence Summers:** Andrew McAfee and Erik Brynjolfsson, "Human Work in the Robotic Future," *Foreign Affairs*, July–August 2016, 139–50.

138   **"The personal computer":** Eric Zemmour, *Le suicide français* (Paris: Albin Michel, 2014), 218–19. (Author's translation.)

138   **"evil . . . computerization enables":** Kevin Kelly, "Interview with the Luddite" (interview with Kirkpatrick Sale), *Wired*, June 1, 1995.

139   **"technology that's decentralized":** Ibid.

139   **"the specter of technology":** Robert Pirsig, *Zen and the Art of Motorcycle Maintenance* (New York: Harper, 2005 [1974]), 246.

140   **the adjective "compelling":** Google Ngram Viewer.

141   **"Authentic bush garments":** Banana Republic, Winter 1979 catalog (San Francisco, 1978). Quoted in Robyn Adams, "A Rare Look," *Abandoned Republic*, June 2, 2011. Online at secretfanbase.com/banana.

141 **"Israeli paratroopers messenger bags"**: Robert Klara, "Before Banana Republic Was Mainstream Fashion, It Was a Weirdly Wonderful Safari Brand," *Adweek*, March 16, 2016.

142 **In 1980, the Häagen-Dazs ice cream company:** *Häagen-Dazs, Inc., v. Frusen Glädjé Ltd.*, United States District Court, S.D., New York, June 9, 1980. [493 F.Supp. 73 (1980)].

142 **which had been named:** Calvin Trillin, "Competitors," *New Yorker*, July 8, 1985, 36.

143 **two friends in Odessa, Texas:** Teresa Tribolet, "A Brief History of Self-Storage," SpareFoot blog, January 18, 2013. Online at sparefoot.com /self-storage/blog.

143 **By 2015, there were:** Suzy Strutner, "America Has More Self-Storage Facilities than McDonald's, Because Apparently We're All Hoarders," *Huffington Post*, April 21, 2015. Online at huffpost.com.

143 **"can easily be transformed":** Leo Strauss, "Why We Remain Jews," lecture at Hillel House, University of Chicago, February 4, 1962, in Strauss, *Jewish Philosophy and the Crisis of Modernity: Essays and Lectures in Modern Jewish Thought* (Albany: State University of New York Press, 1997), 311.

144 **Bakke's scores:** *Regents of the University of California v. Bakke*, U.S. Supreme Court, 438 U.S. 265 (1978), no. 7811, June 28, 1978, 277n. (footnote 7).

144 **The averages for minorities admitted:** Ibid., 438: "Although disadvantaged whites applied to the special program in large numbers, *see* n 5, *supra*, none received an offer of admission through that process."

145 **"The handicap":** "The Bakke Decision: Did It Decide Anything?," *New York Review of Books*, August 17, 1978.

146 **"Free institutions are":** John Stuart Mill, *Considerations on Representative Government* (London: Parker, Son and Bourn, 1861), 296.

146 **"cloned":** The word comes from R. Shep Melnick, "The Odd Evolution of the Civil Rights State," Remarks at 2013 Federalist Society Annual Student Symposium, Austin, Texas, March 2, 2013. Printed in *Harvard Journal of Law & Public Policy* 37, no. 1 (2014): 118.

146 **the safeguards that had been in place:** *Alexander v. Sandoval*, 532 U.S. 275, 306–07 (2001). Cited in Melnick, "The Odd Evolution of the Civil Rights State," 131.

147 **"the conduct of nearly":** Melnick, "The Odd Evolution of the Civil Rights State," 113, 120–21.

147 **"The fundamental challenge":** Nathan Glazer, "Who's Available?," in Glazer, *Ethnic Dilemmas, 1964–1982* (Cambridge, Massachusetts: Harvard University Press, 1983), 183, 187.

148 **The city council in San Diego:** Paul F. Eckstein, "Instant Replay," *Los Angeles Times*, November 25, 1990.

148 **The more confrontational strategies:** Robert Anthony Watts, "Young Blacks Looking Up to Malcolm X," *Los Angeles Times*, January 17, 1993.

149 **"black holiday":** Ralph Jimenez, "N.H. Plan Eyes Swap of Holiday for King," *Boston Globe*, March 3, 1991.

149 **In May 1986:** Michael Rezendes, "Arizona Has Its King Day," *Boston Globe*, January 18, 1993.

149 **"It has the effect":** Ibid.

150 **its official federal name:** John Christian Hoyle, "Long-Standing Misnomer," *Christian Science Monitor*, February 13, 1998.

150 **The NFL made good:** Eckstein, "Instant Replay."

150 **The No campaign raised:** Rezendes, "Arizona Has Its King Day."

151 **"messages emphasizing American values":** Ibid.

151 **"battle for Arizona's soul":** Ibid.

151 **The adjective "iconic":** Google Ngram Viewer.

151 **U2 agreed to a deal:** Robert Hilburn, "U2 Shows Grace Under Pressure at Tour Opener," *Los Angeles Times*, April 4, 1987.

151 **"brought an end":** Eckstein, "Instant Replay."

151 **"I think it arouses":** Kenneth B. Clark, ed., *The Negro Protest* (Boston: Beacon Press, 1963), 41.

152 **"honor the too-often-neglected":** "Black History Month Is Supported by Ford," *New York Times*, February 11, 1976.

153 **Three standbys of Black History Month:** Kathleen O'Brien, "Part of the Mainstream?," *Star-Ledger* (Newark), February 26, 2009.

153 **At the start of the 1987 baseball season:** "Al Campanis Racist Remarks on Nightline (April 6, 1987)." Online at YouTube.

153 **"Why are black men":** William Weinbaum, "The Legacy of Al Campanis," ESPN, March 29, 2012. Online at ESPN.com.

154 **She demanded that the Dodgers cut:** Grahame L. Jones, "Dodgers Fire Campanis over Racial Remarks," *Los Angeles Times*, April 9, 1987.

154 **blacks and whites rooming together:** Jim Bouton, in *Ball Four* (New York: Dell, 1970), 346, 350, described outfielder Tommy Davis's reluctance to room with the white liberal knuckleballer Bouton, although the two were friends who had both recently been traded from the Seattle Pilots to the Houston Astros.

154 **"That's why you'd usually see":** Jack McCallum, "For Better or for Worse," *Sports Illustrated*, May 2, 1983, 70–84.

154 **"Al Campanis must have been":** Don Carleton, "Interview with Ted Koppel," Television Academy Interviews, June 14, 2005. Online at interview.television academy.com.

155 **"If they take over coaching":** "Jimmy the Greek Comments That Got Him Fired," YouTube.

155 **"reprehensible"**: Jay Sharbutt, "Jimmy 'The Greek' Is Fired by CBS," *Los Angeles Times*, January 17, 1988.

155 **Retired first baseman Bill White**: Richard Goldstein, "Al Campanis Is Dead at 81; Ignited Baseball over Race," *New York Times*, June 22, 1998.

155 **"slightly tinged by guilt"**: Richard L. Harris, "For Campanis, a Night That Lived in Infamy," *Los Angeles Times*, August 5, 2008.

157 **establishing the on-campus position**: Jason Vest, "The School That's Put Sex to the Test," *Washington Post*, December 3, 1993.

157 **"The Muse of Masturbation"**: Eve Kosofsky Sedgwick, "Jane Austen and the Masturbating Girl," *Critical Inquiry* 17 (Summer 1991): 818–37.

157 **"ice people"**: All quotes are from Leonard Jeffries, "Our Sacred Mission," speech at the Empire State Black Arts and Cultural Festival, Albany, New York, July 20, 1991.

158 **"this is a very diverse community"**: Charles Krauthammer, "On Campus, Flying the Flag Is a Provocation," *Washington Post*, February 8, 1991.

158 **"inappropriately directed laughter"**: Jerry Adler, Peter Prescott, and Patrick Houston, "Taking Offense," *Newsweek*, December 24, 1990.

158 **Stanford, Wisconsin, and Michigan**: John Taylor, "Are You Politically Correct?," *New York*, January 21, 1991.

158 **"Free speech, free press"**: *Beauharnais v. Illinois* (343 U.S. 250), U.S. Supreme Court, April 28, 1952. Quoted in Harry Kalven, Jr., *The Negro and the First Amendment* (Columbus: Ohio State University Press, 1965), 36–37.

158 **"Today a white man"**: Ibid., 37–38.

159 **Wu had put a sign**: Adler et al., "Taking Offense."

160 **"The objective of converting"**: " 'The Storm over the University': An Exchange," *New York Review of Books*, February 14, 1991.

160 **"more frightening"**: Taylor, "Are You Politically Correct?"

160 **"bad thing"**: CBS/*New York Times* poll, November 1993.

160 **The Peopling of America**: Taylor, "Are You Politically Correct?"

160 **"Resistance to this sort"**: Ibid.

160 **"silliness rather than catastrophe"**: "The Storm over the University."

161 **"Trendy Movement"**: Jeff Colpitts, "Trendy Movement Is on Its Last Legs," *Ottawa Citizen*, July 16, 1993.

161 **"two-step evolution"**: Paul Berman, *A Tale of Two Utopias: The Political Journey of the Generation of 1968* (New York: Norton, 1996), 221.

161 **"rights talk"**: The expression comes from a Harvard Law professor's book of that name; see Mary Ann Glendon, *Rights Talk* (New York: Free Press, 1991).

162 **"the managed destruction"**: Samuel Francis, "From Household to Nation," *Chronicles*, March 1996.

162 **"If Buchanan loses"**: Ibid.

163   **"Hey, hey! Ho, ho!":** "Jesse Jackson and students protest Western Culture program on Palm Drive, photo, 1987," Stanford Library exhibit. Online at exhibits.stanford.edu.

163   **"international" rather than "foreign":** William Safire, "A Foreign Affair," *New York Times*, April 7, 1991.

164   **Max Weber called "successors":** Max Weber, "The Social Psychology of the World Religions," in Weber, *From Max Weber: Essays in Sociology*, translated and edited by Hans Gerth and C. Wright Mills (New York: Oxford University Press, 1946), 297.

164   **only about a quarter of professors:** William G. Bowen and Julie Ann Sosa, *Prospects for Faculty in the Arts and Sciences* (Princeton: Princeton University Press, 2012 [1989]), 16. They cite the 1987 Survey of Doctoral Recipients, carried out biennially by the National Research Council, which showed that 22 percent of faculty that year were under age 40, i.e., born after 1947, the second year of the Baby Boom.

164   **A 1991 poll found:** Troy Duster, "They're Taking Over and Other Myths About Race on Campus," *Mother Jones*, September–October 1991, 30, 63. Cited in Nadine Strossen, "Thoughts on the Controversy over Politically Correct Speech," *SMU Law Review* 46 (1992): 119–44. The poll was carried out by the Higher Education Research Institute at UCLA. It showed: 4.9% far left, 36.8% liberal, 40.2% moderate, 17.8% conservative.

164   **In 1983, no Harvard undergraduate:** Author's recollection.

165   **That was also the year:** John Markoff, "Innovators of Intelligence Look to Past," *New York Times*, December 16, 2014.

165   **In fact, the percentage of people:** Samuel A. Stouffer, *Communism, Conformity and Civil Liberties: A Cross-Section of the Nation Speaks Its Mind* (New Brunswick, New Jersey: Transaction Publishers, 2009 [New York: Doubleday, 1955]). Cited in "Polls on Political Correctness," *AEI Political Report* 13, no. 6 (June 2017): 5–7.

166   **"What I am requiring":** William Bunch et al., "Beginning of the Rainbow," *Newsday*, December 17, 1992.

167   **Fernandez suspended:** Steven Lee Myers, "How a 'Rainbow Curriculum' Turned into Fighting Words," *New York Times*, December 13, 1992.

167   **"I don't know what":** Ibid.

167   **A journalist predicted:** William Tucker, "Revolt in Queens," *American Spectator*, February 1993, 26–31.

168   **"A curriculum that was designed":** Bunch et al., "Beginning of the Rainbow."

168   **"You have had, clearly":** John Diamond, "Gingrich: 'Active Homosexuals Shouldn't Teach Sex in School,'" Associated Press, March 7, 1995.

169   **The Appalachian Mountain Club's Galehead Hut:** Carey Goldberg, "For These Trailblazers, Wheelchairs Matter," *New York Times*, August 17, 2000.

170 **"human resources":** Google Ngram Viewer.

170 **"The commitment to multicultural education":** Bunch et al., "Beginning of the Rainbow."

171 **as New York mayor Michael Bloomberg discovered:** James Crawford, *Educating English Learners,* 5th ed. (Los Angeles: Bilingual Education Services, 2004). See also Melnick, "The Odd Evolution of the Civil Rights State."

7. WINNERS

174 **"the only way international competition":** Richard Baldwin, *The Great Convergence: Information Technology and the New Globalization* (Cambridge, Massachusetts: Belknap Press, 2016), 167.

175 **"virtual meetings":** Thomas L. Friedman, "It's a Flat World, After All," *New York Times Magazine,* April 3, 2005.

177 **By the end of the 1970s:** This section draws on the following sources: Christopher Caldwell, "Easy Credit, Hard Landing" [review of/essay on Raghuram Rajan, *Fault Lines: How Hidden Fractures Still Threaten the World Economy* (Princeton: Princeton University Press, 2010)], *Weekly Standard,* July 26, 2010. Christopher Caldwell, "Fannie and Freddie: A Fool's Errand" [review of Viral Acharya, Matthew Richardson, Stijn van Nieuwerburgh, and Lawrence J. White, *Guaranteed to Fail: Fannie Mae, Freddie Mac, and the Debacle of Mortgage Finance* (Princeton: Princeton University Press, 2014)], *Financial Times,* March 21, 2011. Christopher Caldwell, "Another Shock in the Making" [review of/essay on Charles W. Calomiris and Stephen H. Haber, *Fragile by Design: The Political Origins of Banking Crises and Scarce Credit* (Princeton: Princeton University Press, 2014)], *Longitude* 45 (January 2015): 104–05.

177 **the national debt stood:** It was $19,976,827,000,000.00, to be exact. See U.S. Department of the Treasury, "Fiscal Service, Federal Debt: Total Public Debt," Federal Reserve Bank of St. Louis. Online at fred.stlouisfed.org.

177 **the government's unfunded liabilities:** Antony Davies and James R. Harrigan, "Debt Myths, Debunked," *U.S. News & World Report,* December 1, 2016.

178 **The GSEs would now have:** Viral Acharya, Matthew Richardson, Stijn van Nieuwerburgh, and Lawrence J. White, *Guaranteed to Fail: How Hidden Fractures Still Threaten the World Economy* (Princeton University Press, 2011), 31.

179 **That meant lowering:** Housing and Community Development Act of 1992, Title XIII, "Government Sponsored Enterprises," sec. 1354, "Review of Underwriting Guidelines." Cited in ibid., 35.

179 **Clinton's allegation rested on a study:** Peter Passell, "Redlining Under Attack," *New York Times,* August 30, 1994.

180   **In the quarter-century after 1992:** Charles W. Calomiris and Stephen H. Haber, *Fragile by Design: The Political Origins of Banking Crises and Scarce Credit* (Princeton: Princeton University Press, 2014), 19, 208.

180   **ACORN:** Ibid., 223.

180   **"a new civil rights agenda":** Vice presidential debate, St. Petersburg, Florida, October 10, 1996.

181   **By 2007, high-risk mortgages:** Acharya et al., *Guaranteed to Fail*, 81.

181   **"income and mortgage credit growth":** Atif Mian and Amir Sufi, "The Consequences of Mortgage Credit Expansion: Evidence from the U.S. Mortgage Default Crisis," *Quarterly Journal of Economics* 124, no. 4 (November 1, 2009): 1449–96.

181   **By 2006, 46 percent:** Rajan, *Fault Lines*, 38, quoted Fannie Mae's former chief credit officer Edward Pinto, who noted that, by 2008, "the FHA, and various other government programs were exposed to about $2.7 trillion in subprime and Alt-A loans, approximately 59 percent of total loans to these categories. It is very difficult to reach any other conclusion than that this was a market driven largely by government, or government-influenced, money."

181   **Simon Johnson, an English-born:** Simon Johnson, "The Quiet Coup," *The Atlantic*, May 2009, 46–56.

182   **"the United States is singularly unprepared":** Rajan, *Fault Lines*, 14.

182   **"Easy credit has":** Ibid., 31.

182   **"The judgment calls historically made":** Ibid., 129.

185   **his poignant and gracefully written:** Barack Obama, *Dreams from My Father: A Story of Race and Inheritance* (New York: Times Books, 1995).

185   **David Remnick's sensitive study *The Bridge*:** David Remnick, *The Bridge: The Life and Rise of Barack Obama* (New York: Alfred A. Knopf, 2010).

185   **The mere rumor:** Richard L. Berke, "New Hampshire Poll Finds Powell with an Edge," *New York Times*, October 19, 1995.

185   **"looked kind of Hispanic":** "911 Transcript on Harvard Scholar Arrest," *Billings* (Montana) *Gazette*, July 27, 2009.

186   **But according to the police report:** Cambridge Police Department, Incident Report no. 9005127, July 16, 2009.

186   **"I don't know":** "Obama: Police Acted 'Stupidly' in Scholar Arrest," YouTube. Uploaded July 22, 2009.

186   **"The president used the right adjective":** Michael A. Fletcher and Michael D. Shear, "Obama Voices Regret to Policeman," *Washington Post*, July 25, 2009.

187   **Within 48 hours:** "Obama Apologizes for Criticism of Police During Henry Gates 'Alleged' Break-in," YouTube. Uploaded November 26, 2011.

187   **"110 percent":** Jonathan Saltzman, "Sergeant at Eye of Storm Says He Won't Apologize," *Boston Globe*, July 23, 2009.

187   **He donated those handcuffs:** Nicholas Jofre, "Gates Donates His Handcuffs to the Smithsonian," *Harvard Crimson*, February 17, 2010.

188   **Running for re-election in 2012:** "Trust in Government by Race and Ethnicity" (table), Pew Research Center, "Public Trust in Government: 1958–2017," December 14, 2017. Online at people-press.org.

188   **"would like nothing better":** *Grutter v. Bollinger*, U.S. Supreme Court, 539 U.S. 306 (2003), June 23, 2003, 5. Court's paraphrase.

188   **"We expect that":** *Grutter v. Bollinger*, 31.

189   **"Our diversity":** *Meet the Press*, NBC, November 8, 2009. Quoted in Peter Baehr and Daniel Gordon, "Paradoxes of Diversity," in *SAGE Handbook of Political Sociology*, edited by William Outhwaite and Stephen Turner (London: SAGE Publications, 2018), 977.

189   **"Perhaps foremost," Bolden said:** Toby Harnden, "NASA's New Mission: Reach Out to Mars and Muslims," *Daily Telegraph*, July 7, 2010. Original interview at "new NASA goal = Muslim outreach—Bolden," YouTube, July 6, 2010.

190   **"Either we must allow":** Bertrand Russell, *The Impact of Science on Society* (London: George Allen & Unwin, 1952), 95.

190   **In hundreds of cities:** Jeffrey Weiss, "Lunch Rush," *Dallas Morning News*, October 12, 1993.

191   **Walmart discovered:** Viktor Mayer-Schönberger and Kenneth Cukier, *Big Data: A Revolution That Will Transform How We Live, Work, and Think* (New York: Houghton Mifflin Harcourt, 2013), 54.

191   **Target could identify:** Ibid., 58.

192   **"Society will need":** Mayer-Schönberger and Cukier, *Big Data*, 7.

192   **Google claimed to predict:** Ibid., 15.

192   **SWIFT:** Ibid.

192   **When pundits sought new ways:** Fareed Zakaria, "Sanctions Russia Will Respect," *Washington Post*, February 13, 2015.

193   **In their communication with investors:** John Cassidy, "How Eliot Spitzer Humbled Wall Street," *New Yorker*, April 7, 2003, 54–73.

193   **He fought crisis pregnancy centers:** Nancy H. Tilghman, "Dillon and Spitzer Clash over Abortion," *New York Times*, February 24, 2002.

193   **The New York attorney general's office:** Cassidy, "How Eliot Spitzer Humbled Wall Street."

194   **In 2002, he issued:** Ibid.

194   **Two years later:** David Johnston and Stephen Labaton, "The Reports That Drew Federal Eyes to Spitzer," *New York Times*, March 12, 2008.

194   **he had nonetheless supported:** Christopher Caldwell, "Snowden's Stand for a Globalised Generation," *Financial Times*, October 11, 2013.

195   **The NSA used a technique:** Chandra Steele, "The 10 Most Disturbing
       Snowden Revelations," *PC Magazine*, February 11, 2014. Online at pcmag.com.

195   **It spied on:** James Bamford, "The Most Wanted Man in the World," *Wired*,
       August 2014.

195   **"bricked":** Ibid.

195   **Verizon, for example, was ordered:** FISA court order, Docket BR 13-80,
       April 25, 2013. Cited in Lorenzo Franceschi-Bicchierai, "The 10 Biggest
       Revelations from Edward Snowden's Leaks," Mashable, June 5, 2014. Online at
       mashable.com.

195   **Mark Zuckerberg taped over:** Katie Rogers, "Mark Zuckerberg Covers His
       Laptop Camera. You Should Consider It, Too," *New York Times*, June 22, 2016.

196   **high-tech companies were lobbying:** Robin Blackburn, "The Corbyn Project,"
       New Left Review 111 (May–June 2018): 5–32.

196   **A 1992 Supreme Court decision:** Christopher Caldwell, "Amazon's Tax-Free
       Landscape Needs Bulldozing," *Financial Times*, July 16–17, 2011. The Supreme
       Court decision discussed there, *Quill Corp. v. North Dakota*, would be over-
       turned in 2017.

196   **half-trillion-dollar company:** $550 billion as of December 2017.

197   **Half a decade later:** Wolf Richter, "A Key Advantage Amazon Has over
       Walmart Is Doomed," *Business Insider*, October 10, 2017.

197   **Taking in more than half:** Samuel Earle, "Vatican 2.0," *Times Literary Supple-
       ment*, November 17, 2017.

197   **"earn a virtual reward":** Jodi Kantor and David Streitfeld, "Inside Amazon:
       Wrestling Big Ideas in a Bruising Workplace," *New York Times*, August 16, 2015.

197   **"We noticed recently":** Christopher Caldwell, "OkCupid's Venal Experiment
       Was a Poisoned Arrow," *Financial Times*, August 2–3, 2014.

198   **more than a third of Americans:** James Bridle, "The Science of Seduction," *The
       Observer*, February 9, 2014.

198   **Now they would be set:** Lawrence Lessig, *Code and Other Laws of Cyberspace*
       (New York: Basic Books, 1999).

199   **"As the network power":** David Singh Grewal, *Network Power: The Social
       Dynamics of Globalization* (New Haven: Yale University Press, 2008), 34.
       Quoted in Christopher Caldwell, "Network Power That Works Too Well,"
       Financial Times, May 23, 2008.

199   **Google soon commanded 88 percent:** Christopher Caldwell, "Is Google Now
       a Monopoly?," *Financial Times*, February 26, 2010.

199   **Facebook, if you include:** Earle, "Vatican 2.0."

200   **By 2016, about a third:** Harold Meyerson, "The First Post-Middle-Class Elec-
       tion," *American Prospect*, June 29, 2016.

200   **A chubby French-Canadian adolescent:** Daniel Solove, *The Future*

of Reputation: Gossip, Rumor, and Privacy on the Internet (New Haven, Connecticut: Yale University Press, 2007), 44–48.

200 **viewed 900 million times:** "Star Wars Kid Is Top Viral Video," BBC News, November 27, 2006.

200 **"The college campus":** Peter F. Drucker, *The Age of Discontinuity: Guidelines to Our Changing Society* (New York: Harper & Row, 1968), 35.

200 **Arrest-related ads popped up:** Claire Cain Miller, "When Algorithms Discriminate," *New York Times*, July 13, 2015.

201 **The COMPAS algorithm:** Jesse Emspak, "How a Machine Learns Prejudice," *Scientific American*, December 29, 2016.

201 **A *Guardian* report described:** Stephen Buranyi, "Rise of the Racist Robots— How AI Is Learning All Our Worst Impulses," *The Guardian*, August 8, 2017.

202 **The computer did, however:** Julia Angwin, Jeff Larson, Surya Mattu, and Lauren Kirchner, "Machine Bias," ProPublica, May 23, 2016. Online at propublica.org.

202 **"diversifying the range of inputs":** Navneet Alang, "Turns Out Algorithms Are Racist," *New Republic*, August 31, 2017. Online at newrepublic.com.

202 **By 2016, in all but a handful:** "State-by-State Overview: Changing Gender Markers on Birth Certificates," Transgender Law Center, December 2016. Online at transgenderlawcenter.org.

202 **"With data inevitably drawn":** Earle, "Vatican 2.0."

202 **"even strangers were shocked":** Jodi Kantor, "Dave Goldberg Was Lifelong Women's Advocate," *New York Times*, May 4, 2015.

203 **In 2016, the masters voted:** Jalin P. Cunningham, Melissa C. Rodman, and Ignacio Sabate, "Harvard House Masters Now Called 'Faculty Deans,'" *Harvard Crimson*, February 25, 2016.

203 **had reduced its intake:** Ron Unz, "The Myth of American Meritocracy," *American Conservative*, December 2012, 14–51. The article did not rely on Harvard's tallies, which are not made available to the public, but made estimates of ethnic composition through the use of surnames.

203 **ran a story and video explaining:** "Luxury Fashion Line Empowers Women" was the banner to a video accompanying "OITNB Inspired Alysia Reiner to Empower Women," *Cheddar*, December 11, 2017. Online at cheddar.com.

203 **"Jackie Robinson, Business Pioneer":** April Joyner, "Jackie Robinson, Business Pioneer," *Ozy*, April 19, 2016. Online at ozy.com.

204 **The share of wealth held:** Emmanuel Saez and Gabriel Zucman, "Wealth Inequality in the United States Since 1913: Evidence from Capitalized Income Tax Data," *Quarterly Journal of Economics* 131, no. 2 (May 2016): 519–78.

204 **The so-called Buffett rule:** Arthur Laffer, "Class Warfare and the Buffett Rule," *Wall Street Journal*, January 11, 2012.

205 **"There must be great scope":** Andrew Carnegie, "The Gospel of Wealth," in Carnegie, *The Gospel of Wealth and Other Timely Essays* (New York: Century, 1901), 4.

205 **"If the American people":** Rosalind S. Helderman, "For Clintons, Speech Income Shows How Their Wealth Is Intertwined with Charity," *Washington Post*, April 22, 2015.

205 **A dedicated political agitator:** Marguerite Griffin and Tim Bresnahan, "Income Tax Charitable Deduction Summary," *Insights on Wealth Planning*, Northern Trust, November 2013.

205 **"a capitalist venture":** Olivier Zunz, *Philanthropy in America: A History* (Princeton: Princeton University Press, 2011), 3.

206 **Eliot Spitzer's father used part:** Fred Siegel and Michael Goodwin, "Troopergate, New York–Style," *Weekly Standard*, August 20–27, 2007.

206 **Mark Zuckerberg's $100 million gift:** Alex Kotlowitz, "Getting Schooled," *New York Times Book Review*, August 23, 2015.

206 **Until a court intervened:** Valerie Strauss, "The Secret E-mails About Mark Zuckerberg's $100 Million Donation to Newark Schools," *Washington Post*, January 6, 2013.

206 **"We all pay":** Rob Reich, "What Are Foundations For?," *Boston Review*, March 1, 2013. Online at bostonreview.net. Quoted in Gara LaMarche, "Democracy and the Donor Class," *Democracy: A Journal of Ideas*, 34 (Fall 2014).

206 **"entitled to peculiar favor":** *Edmund Jackson v. Wendell Phillips and others*, 14 Allen 539, 96 Mass. 539, Suffolk County, Massachusetts, January 1867.

207 **Harry Hopkins:** Zunz, *Philanthropy in America*, 129.

207 **"In effect":** Martin Shefter, "New York City and American National Politics," in *Capital of the American Century: The National and International History of New York City*, edited by Martin Shefter (New York: Russell Sage Foundation, 1993), 103. Quoted in Zunz, *Philanthropy in America*, 211.

207 **"patriotic billionaire":** Matt Miller, "How Billionaires Could Save the Country," *Washington Post*, August 31, 2011.

208 **"the Good Club":** Paul Harris, "They're Called the Good Club—and They Want to Save the World," *The Observer*, May 31, 2009.

208 **the word "governance":** Google Ngram Viewer.

209 **Bill Gates had used his foundation:** "Foundation Fact Sheet," Bill & Melinda Gates Foundation. Online at gatesfoundation.org.

209 **The educator Diane Ravitch complained:** Diane Ravitch, "When Public Goes Private, as Trump Wants: What Happens?," *New York Review of Books*, December 8, 2016.

209 **They were abetted:** Ibid.

209 **"First, break all the rules"**: Marcus Buckingham and Curt Coffman, *First, Break All the Rules: What the World's Greatest Managers Do Differently* (New York: Simon & Schuster, 1999).

210 **President Obama sought to scale:** Eden Stiffman, "Grants Roundup: Funds Pour into My Brother's Keeper Alliance," *Chronicle of Philanthropy*, May 6, 2015.

210 **"President Obama is taking action":** "Fact Sheet: Opportunity for All: President Obama Launches My Brother's Keeper Initiative to Build Ladders of Opportunity for Boys and Young Men of Color," White House, February 27, 2014, https://obamawhitehouse.archives.gov/the-press-office/2014/02/27 /fact-sheet-opportunity-all-president-obama-launches-my-brother-s-keeper-.

210 **"The My Brother's Keeper Initiative logo":** "Logo and Usage," White House, https://obamawhitehouse.archives.gov/my-brothers-keeper#section-logo.

210 **Between 2012 and 2014:** Luigi Zingales, "Does Finance Benefit Society?," Address to the American Finance Association, January 2015. Cited in Martin Wolf, "Why Finance Is Too Much of a Good Thing," *Financial Times*, May 27, 2015.

210 **U.S. financial enforcement agencies collected:** *Historical Tables: Budget of the United States Government, Fiscal Year 1994* (Washington, D.C.: Office of Management and Budget, 1993), table 1.1.

211 **a move for which his defenders claimed:** Bruce Ackerman, "Like the Emancipation Proclamation, Obama's Order Forces Democracy," *Los Angeles Times*, November 21, 2014.

211 *New York Times* **columnist Joe Nocera:** Joe Nocera, "Tea Party's War on America," *New York Times*, August 2, 2011.

212 **1 × 2 × 3 × 4:** Amos Tversky and Daniel Kahneman, "Judgment Under Uncertainty: Heuristics and Biases," in *Judgment Under Uncertainty: Heuristics and Biases*, edited by Daniel Kahneman, Paul Slovic, and Amos Tversky (Cambridge, England: Cambridge University Press, 1982), 15.

213 *Nudge:* The discussion of *Nudge* draws on the following sources: Christopher Caldwell, "The Perils of Shaping Choice," *Financial Times*, April 4, 2008. Christopher Caldwell, "Coaxers and Coercers on Common Ground," *Financial Times*, March 1, 2013.

213 **"largely an empirical question":** Cass Sunstein, "It's for Your Own Good!," review of Sarah Conly, *Against Autonomy: Justifying Coercive Paternalism, New York Review of Books*, March 7, 2013.

214 **"So I left him":** Plato, *The Apology* 21, in *The Dialogues of Plato,* Jowett translation (New York: Macmillan, 1892), 113–14.

216 **"We agree that":** Richard Thaler and Cass Sunstein, *Nudge: Improving Decisions About Health, Wealth, and Happiness* (New Haven, Connecticut: Yale University Press, 2008), 238.

216   **When *New Republic* editor Andrew Sullivan:** Andrew Sullivan, "Here Comes the Groom," *New Republic*, August 28, 1989: 20–22.

216   **The first male strippers started performing:** Henry Weinstein, "Chippendale Club Owner Kills Himself," *Los Angeles Times*, October 25, 1994.

216   **men sued to be admitted:** "Men Sue Chippendales," *Los Angeles Times*, July 1, 1988.

216   **To promote its new line:** "Calvin Klein Underwear Advertisement on Billboard," Bettmann Archive object number U2092058-34, Getty Images, October 4, 1982. Online at gettyimages.com.

217   **By the middle of the decade:** Jim Heimann, ed., *All-American Ads of the 80s* (Cologne, Germany: Taschen, 2005), 241.

217   **left them with a lifelong stigma:** Randy Shilts, *Conduct Unbecoming: Gays and Lesbians in the U.S. Military* (New York: St. Martin's Press, 1993), 34, 135.

218   **There was a small-scale riot:** Lillian Faderman, *The Gay Revolution: The Story of the Struggle* (New York: Simon & Schuster, 2015), 115–17.

218   **In 1973:** Michael J. Klarman, *From the Closet to the Altar: Courts, Backlash, and the Struggle for Same-Sex Marriage* (New York: Oxford University Press, 2012), 22. Cited in Christopher Caldwell, "Gay Rites," *Claremont Review*, Winter 2012–2013, 22–26.

218   **In 1983:** Ibid., 22.

218   **In 1991:** Ibid.

219   **"Being queer isn't setting up house":** Paula Ettelbrick, "Since When Is Marriage the Path to Liberation?," *Out/Look*, Fall 1989. Quoted in Faderman, *The Gay Revolution*, 584.

219   **As the AIDS virus spread:** This section draws on Christopher Caldwell, "How Aids Gave Gays Marriage," *Financial Times*, May 22–23, 2004.

219   **In 1985, a majority:** "Poll Indicates Majority Favor Quarantine for AIDS Victims," *New York Times*, December 20, 1985. Cited in Caldwell, "How Aids Gave Gays Marriage."

219   **When gays began to sue:** The chronology that follows is drawn from Klarman, *From the Closet to the Altar*, 3–77.

221   **"cornucopia of substantial benefits":** *Hillary Goodridge & Others v. Department of Public Health*, 440 Mass. 309, Suffolk County, March 4, 2003–November 18, 2003, 336.

221   **"discrimination on the basis":** David Cole, "Gay Marriage: Unthinkable or Inevitable?," *New York Review of Books*, April 29, 2015.

221   **the challenge first posed:** Faderman, *The Gay Revolution*, 587.

222   **public displays of affection:** Klarman, *From the Closet to the Altar*, 175.

222   **talking about sex:** Roberta Kaplan with Lisa Dickey, *Then Comes Marriage: How Two Women Fought for and Won Equal Dignity for All* (New York: Norton, 2015), 122.

222 **"tactical brilliance"**: Ibid., jacket copy.

222 **"an almost military assault"**: Harry Kalven, Jr., *The Negro and the First Amendment* (Columbus: Ohio State University Press, 1965), 66.

223 **saddling the 79-year-old Windsor**: Kaplan, *Then Comes Marriage*, 111.

223 **"If Thea had been 'Theo,'"**: Ibid., 115.

223 **Only estates in the richest micro-fraction**: Urban Institute and Brookings Institution Tax Policy Center, *The Tax Policy Center Briefing Book: A Citizens' Guide to the Tax System and Tax Policy* (Washington, D.C.: Urban-Brookings Tax Policy Center, 2018), 322–23. Online at taxpolicycenter.org/briefing-book.

223 **In addition to their liquid assets**: Kaplan, *Then Comes Marriage*, 95.

223 **was bankrolled by**: From the "HRC Story" page of the Human Rights Campaign, https://www.hrc.org/hrc-story/corporate-partners. Accessed January 4, 2019.

224 **Google's employees gave**: Nate Silver, "How Rare Are Anti-Gay-Marriage Donations in Silicon Valley?," FiveThirtyEight, April 4, 2014. Online at five thirtyeight.com.

224 **Reuters discovered in 2014**: Darel E. Paul, "Culture War as Class War," *First Things* 285 (August–September 2018): 42.

224 **it permitted Windsor to tap**: Kaplan, *Then Comes Marriage*, 56.

225 **pro–gay marriage activists pressured**: Ibid., 148–49.

225 **Kaplan wrote**: Ibid., 243–44.

225 **"felt like old home week"**: Ibid., 318.

225 **"Edie did not live differently"**: Ibid., 125.

225 **"The real dialectic of revolution"**: Rosa Luxemburg, *Die russische Revolution: Eine kritische Würdigung*, in Luxemburg, *Gesammelte Werke*, vol. 4 (August 1915 bis Januar 1919) (Berlin: Dietz Verlag, 1974 [1922]), 341. (Author's translation.)

226 **"Do you think marriages"**: Justin McCarthy, "U.S. Support for Gay Marriage Stable After High Court Ruling," Gallup, July 17, 2015.

226 **"If you look back"**: Maureen Dowd, "Not Feeling Groovy," *New York Times*, July 4, 2004.

226 **In the 2008 presidential election**: Christopher Caldwell, "American Oligarchy," *Weekly Standard*, May 10, 2010.

227 **David Koch barely scraped**: Kenneth P. Vogel, "Big Money Breaks Out," *Politico*, December 29, 2014.

227 **"The Sioux Falls *Argus Leader*"**: Jack Shafer and Tucker Doherty, "The Media Bubble Is Real—and Worse than You Think," *Politico*, April 25, 2017.

227 **"odious law"**: Kaplan, *Then Comes Marriage*, 39.

228 **"A Supreme Court ruling"**: Klarman, *From the Closet to the Altar*, 207.

228 **"this proffered change"**: *Hillary Goodridge and Others v. Department of Public Health*, 362.

228 in *Obergefell* he had imposed: Supreme Court of the United States, Opinion of the Court, *Obergefell v. Hodges*, Nos. 14-556, 14-562, 14-571, and 14-574. Scalia's dissent, 3.

228 "A system of government": *Obergefell v. Hodges*, Scalia's dissent, 5.

228 "The strikingly unrepresentative character": *Obergefell v. Hodges*, Scalia's dissent, 6. (Italics in original.)

229 "It is of no moment": *Obergefell v. Hodges*, Kennedy's decision, 24.

230 "WENNER: You got up there": Jann S. Wenner, "The Day After: Obama on His Legacy, Trump's Win and the Path Forward," *Rolling Stone*, December 15–29, 2016.

230 "How could *I* be against": Faderman, *The Gay Revolution*, 610.

231 "dumb bitch": " 'God Was Testing My Faith,' Says Miss California After Perez Hilton Calls Her a 'Dumb Bitch' in Gay Marriage Row," *Daily Mail*, April 21, 2009.

232 Corporations and celebrities rallied: Alan Blinder, "North Carolina Lawmakers Met with Protests over Bias Law," *New York Times*, April 25, 2016.

232 "the story of the extension": Richard B. Morris, *The Forging of the Union, 1781–1789* (New York: Harper & Row, 1987), 193. Quoted in Opinion of the Court (Ruth Bader Ginsberg), *United States v. Virginia*, 518 U.S. 515, 557 (1996). Quoted in turn in *Goodridge*, 339.

8. LOSERS

234 A sparsely watched Thursday-morning tirade: CNBC, February 19, 2009. Online at YouTube: "CNBC's Rick Santelli's Chicago Tea Party."

234 "I don't want government-run health care": Sarah Arnquist, "Obama on Health Care for Seniors," *New York Times*, July 29, 2009. Online at newoldage .blogs.nytimes.com.

234 "The tea party image": Jeff Cox, "5 Years Later, Rick Santelli 'Tea Party' Rant Revisited," CNBC, February 24, 2014. Online at cnbc.com.

234 "The Old Right": Samuel Francis, "Beautiful Losers," in Francis, *Beautiful Losers: Essays on the Future of American Conservatism* (Columbia: University of Missouri Press, 1993), 225. The first writer to claim that modern American conservatism mistook a historical fact for a future threat was Garet Garrett in his 1938 essay "The Revolution Was," in Garrett, *The People's Pottage: The Revolution Was, Ex-America, The Rise of Empire* (Caldwell, Idaho: Caxton Printers, 1953).

235 "The liberal organisation of society": Viktor Orbán, "Prime Minister Viktor Orbán's Speech at the 25th Bálványos Summer Free University and Student Camp," July 26, 2014, official government translation. Online at kormany.hu.

236 **"managed democracy"**: Ivan Krastev, in "Why Are American Liberals So Afraid of Russia?," *New York Times*, August 16, 2017, argues that Americans fear the United States is turning into a Russian-style democracy.

236 **"Does the owner"**: Susan Davis, "Rand Paul Taking Heat for Civil Rights Act Comments," *Wall Street Journal*, May 20, 2010.

237 **"Though this nation"**: Department of Justice, "Attorney General Eric Holder at the Department of Justice African-American History Month Program," Speech, Washington, D.C., February 18, 2009. Online at justice.gov.

237 **But by the end of Obama's term:** Quinnipiac University poll, November 2016. Cited in "Contemporary Attitudes about Political Correctness," *AEI Political Report* 13, no. 6 (June 2017): 2.

238 **Hannah Arendt had pointed out:** Hannah Arendt, *The Origins of Totalitarianism* (New York: Harcourt Brace Jovanovich, 1973 [1951]), 275–90.

238 **"forced outside the pale of the law"**: Ibid., 286.

239 **In 2010, the fifteen most common:** United States Census Bureau, "Frequently Occurring Surnames from the 2010 Census: Top 1,000 Surnames" (Excel table). Online at census.gov. Nguyen is 38, Baker 44, Turner 54, Cook 65, Cooper 70, Patel 95, Powell 101, Wong 274, Wang 282, Yang 290, Davidson 301, Pearson 308, Benson 365.

239 **"In fifteen of the largest"**: Arthur Meier Schlesinger, "The Significance of Immigration in American History," *American Journal of Sociology* 27, no. 1 (July 1921): 71–85.

240 **98 percent European descent:** U.S. Department of Commerce, *Historical Statistics of the United States, Colonial Times to 1970*, Part 1, "Series A 172–194. Population of Regions, by Sex, Race, Residence, Age and Nativity," September 1975, 22. Ninety-eight percent is a statistical measure, not a narrative hyperbole, for the European-descended population of both the Northeast and North Central regions, which received virtually all the immigrants. The census at the time classified all residents as "white," "Negro," or "other." In the census of 1880, which may be taken as the onset of the first wave of mass immigration, the Northeast had 14,507,000 people, of whom 14,274,000 (98.4 percent) were white; the North Central region had 17,364,000 people, of whom 16,691,000 (or 97.7 percent) were white. Those figures were essentially unchanged by the end of the migration. In the 1920 census, the Northeast had 29,662,000 people, of whom 28,958,000 (97.6 percent) were white. The North Central region had 34,020,000 people, of whom 33,164,000 (or 97.5 percent) were white.

240 **More than half (53 percent):** William H. Frey, *Diversity Explosion: How New Racial Demographics Are Remaking America* (Washington, D.C.: Brookings Institution Press, 2014), 15.

240 **It fell by 12 percent:** Ibid., 25.

241 **By the election of 2016:** Ibid., 137.

241 **"largely accounted for":** Anne Case and Angus Deaton, "Rising Morbidity
     and Mortality in Midlife Among White Non-Hispanic Americans in the 21st
     Century," *Proceedings of the National Academy of Sciences* 112, no. 49 (December
     8, 2015): 15078-83.

241 **In 2016, 63,600 people:** Holly Hedegaard, Margaret Warner, and Arialdi M.
     Miniño, "Drug Overdose Deaths in the United States, 1999–2016," NCHS
     Data Brief no. 294, December 2017.

242 **bringing the rate of overdose deaths:** Centers for Disease Control and Preven-
     tion, "Unintentional Drug Poisoning in the United States," Fact Sheet, ca. 2007.

242 **a death-by-overdose rate:** Ibid.

242 **By the time of the 2016 election:** Hedegaard et al., "Drug Overdose Deaths in
     the United States, 1999–2016."

242 **"limited comment":** Case and Deaton, "Rising Morbidity and Mortality in
     Midlife Among White Non-Hispanic Americans in the 21st Century."

243 **the incarceration rate peaked:** Adam Shatz, "Out of Sight, Out of Mind,"
     London Review of Books, May 4, 2017.

244 **"take an honest look":** Kevin D. Williamson, "Chaos in the Family, Chaos in the
     State: The White Working Class's Dysfunction," *National Review*, March 28, 2016.

244 **In his influential book:** Charles Murray, *Coming Apart: The State of White
     America, 1960–2010* (New York: Crown Forum, 2013).

244 **"For this, most of all":** Lyndon B. Johnson, "To Fulfill These Rights,"
     commencement address at Howard University, June 4, 1965, in *Public Papers of
     the Presidents of the United States: Lyndon B. Johnson, 1965* (Washington, D.C.:
     U.S. Government Printing Office, 1966), vol. 2, entry 301, 639.

244 **Lakshman Achuthan:** Lakshman Achuthan, "Only Retirement-Age Whites
     Gain Job Share: For Whom the Bell Tolls," Economic Cycle Research Institute,
     December 16, 2016. Online at businesscycle.com. Cited in Eduardo Porter,
     "Where Were Trump's Votes? Where the Jobs Weren't," *New York Times*,
     December 13, 2006.

244 **Whites lived disproportionately:** Porter, "Where Were Trump's Votes?"

245 **"Gradually another America":** Aleksandr Solzhenitsyn, *Between Two Mill-
     stones* (Notre Dame, Indiana: Notre Dame University Press, 2018), 291.

245 **"coalition of the ascendant":** See Ronald Brownstein, "Disenchanted with
     Obama for Different Reasons," *National Journal*, September 10, 2010.

245 **Whites were aging, hedonistic, and barren:** See Frey, *Diversity Explosion*, 133.

245 **"We often talk openly":** @*This Hour with Berman and Michaela*, CNN,
     October 31, 2014.

246 **"With white people heading":** Gary Younge, "It's the Racism, Stupid," *The
     Nation*, February 11, 2016.

246 **"They were central"**: Fareed Zakaria, "America's Self-Destructive Whites," *Washington Post*, December 31, 2015.

246 **"These are guys"**: Katharine Q. Seelye, "Gov. Paul LePage of Maine Says Racial Remark Was a 'Slip-up,'" *New York Times*, January 8, 2016.

247 **"At Prudential"**: "Diversity and Inclusion: The Power of People," Prudential, 2018. Online at prudential.com.

247 **"emancipate yourselves"**: Bob Marley, "Redemption Song," 1980. The Garvey speech was reprinted in *Black Man* 3, no. 10 (July 1938) and is referenced in Elizabeth Patterson, "Iconic Song Had Basis in Whitney Pier," *Cape Breton Post*, February 16, 2017.

247 **A couple of weeks after:** Meg Robbins and Harry Rube, "Students Debate Articles of Impeachment at BSG Meeting," *Bowdoin Orient*, March 4, 2016.

248 **Uninvolved undergraduates interviewed:** Catherine Rampell, "Why Write About Tiny Sombreros?," *Washington Post*, March 4, 2016.

248 **The BBC announced:** Jonathan Jones, "BBC Looks Beyond the West to Retell the Story of Civilisation," *The Guardian*, February 24, 2018.

248 **"foremost public intellectual"**: Carlos Lozada, "The Radical Chic of Ta-Nehisi Coates," *Washington Post*, July 16, 2015.

249 **"If blacks would only try harder"**: P. J. Henry and David O. Sears, "The Symbolic Racism 2000 Scale," *Political Psychology* 23, no. 2 (June 2002): 253–83. Quoted in Andrew Hacker, "2014: Another Democratic Debacle?," *New York Review of Books*, January 9, 2014.

249 **"My grandmother died"**: Farai Chideya, "Because #BlackLivesMatter, Black Healthcare Must Matter," *The Guardian*, July 23, 2015.

249 **"any deviation from statistical parity"**: Nathan Glazer, "Liberty, Equality, Fraternity—and Ethnicity," in Glazer, *Ethnic Dilemmas, 1964–1982* (Cambridge, Massachusetts: Harvard University Press, 1983), 214.

250 **But the average American believed:** Joseph Carroll, "Public Overestimates U.S. Black and Hispanic Populations," Gallup News Service, June 4, 2001. Poll taken March 26–28, 2001.

250 **In the second decade of the century:** Frank Newport, "Americans Greatly Overestimate Percent Gay, Lesbian in US," Gallup News Service, May 21, 2015.

250 **"Freedom is inside of me"**: Patti Smith, televised interview with Lennart Wretlind, Stockholm Konserthuset, Stockholm, Sweden, October 3, 1976. See "Patti Smith—Interview, Stockholm October 1976," YouTube, January 29, 2017.

251 **Fox News and MSNBC bleeped it out:** Joanne Ostrow, "Media Outrage Misdirected in Case of Obama Comments on Racism," *Denver Post*, June 24, 2015.

252 **"While these terms"**: Nadine Strossen, "Thoughts on the Controversy over Politically Correct Speech," *SMU Law Review* 46, no. 1 (1993): 119–144.

252 **"attaching themselves to"**: Shelby Steele, *Shame: How America's Past Sins Have Polarized Our Country* (New York: Basic Books, 2015), 74.

252 **"These individuals are"**: Amanda Kemp, "Blacks Feel Unwanted," *Stanford Daily*, April 28, 1987.

253 **"an entire nigger presidency"**: Ta-Nehisi Coates, "The First White President," *The Atlantic*, October 2017.

253 **"You shoulda seen"**: YG [Keenon Daequan Ray Jackson], "Twist My Fingaz," 2016.

253 **"Players turn to friends"**: Future, "Real Sisters," 2015.

253 **"She used to niggas"**: Hit Boy, "Stay Up," 2015.

254 **The epithet "white supremacist"**: Google Ngram Viewer.

254 **"My job is to listen"**: Douglas Ernst, "DNC Chair Candidate Says Her Job Is to 'Shut Other White People Down,' " *Washington Times*, January 24, 2017.

254 **so-called doll study**: K. B. Clark, "Effect of Prejudice and Discrimination on Personality Development," Midcentury White House Conference on Children and Youth, 1950. Quoted in U.S. Supreme Court, *Brown et al. v. Board of Education of Topeka et al.*, 347 US 483, 494n, May 17, 1954.

255 **In 2008, an unusual literary scandal**: The following paragraphs draw on Christopher Caldwell, "Tall Tales of the Would-Be Victim," *Financial Times*, March 7, 2008, an essay about the scandal surrounding Margaret Jones, *Love and Consequences: A Memoir of Hope and Survival* (New York: Riverhead, 2008).

255 **The president of the Spokane chapter**: Jamelle Bouie, "Is Rachel Dolezal Black Just Because She Says She Is?," *Slate*, June 12, 2015.

255 **Dolezal's fault was to have said**: Leah Sottile, "Broad Questions About Race," *Washington Post*, June 16, 2015. Buzz Bissinger, "Caitlyn Jenner: The Full Story," *Vanity Fair*, July 2015. Hilary Weaver, "Rachel Dolezal Is Back, Refusing to Apologize for Lying About Being Black," *Vanity Fair*, February 28, 2017.

256 **"You know, race didn't create"**: Interview with Savannah Guthrie, *Today*, April 12, 2016.

256 **Dolezal had four black siblings**: Gabrielle Fonrouge, "Dolezal Tells of Her Journey," *New York Post*, March 24, 2017.

256 **"This," he wrote**: Charles M. Blow, "The Delusions of Rachel Dolezal," *New York Times*, June 18, 2015.

257 **She had claimed**: William Saletan, "Rachel Dolezal's Truth," *Slate*, June 16, 2015.

257 **"She's making these claims"**: Sandy Banks, "Getting a Clearer View of a White Woman's Black Deception," *Los Angeles Times*, June 16, 2015.

257 **"It's no different from"**: Ibid.

257 **"who, as a result"**: Martin Luther King, Jr., "Letter from a Birmingham Jail" (typescript of letter to Bishop C. C. J. Carpenter et al., April 16, 1963), 11-B.

Collection of the Martin Luther King, Jr. Research and Education Institute, Stanford University. Online at kinginstitute.stanford.edu.

257 **"bloody heirloom":** Ta-Nehisi Coates, "The First White President," *The Atlantic*, October 2017.

258 **"No racist word":** Mark Edmundson, *Why Football Matters: My Education in the Game* (New York: Penguin, 2014), 6.

258 **When the actor Ben Affleck discovered:** John Koblin, "A PBS Show, a Frustrated Ben Affleck, and a Loss of Face," *New York Times*, June 25, 2015.

259 **not one of the top ten shows:** Elizabeth Kolbert, "TV Viewing and Selling, by Race," *New York Times*, April 5, 1993.

260 **"I know it's our job":** Lawrence Schiller and James Willwerth, *American Tragedy: The Uncensored Story of the Simpson Defense* (New York: Random House, 1996). Quoted in Christopher Caldwell, "Johnnie Cochran's Secret," *Commentary*, March 1997, 39–43.

260 **"Ten years from now":** Christopher Caldwell, "Why the Simpson Case Endures," *Weekly Standard*, July 28, 1996.

260 **By the twenty-first century:** Carl Bialik, "Most Black People Now Think O.J. Was Guilty," FiveThirtyEight, June 9, 2016. Online at fivethirtyeight.com.

261 **A disproportionate number:** U.S. Census Bureau, *Statistical Abstract, 2012*, table 325, "Arrests by Race."

262 **high on THC:** U.S. Department of Justice, *Report Regarding the Criminal Investigation into the Shooting Death of Michael Brown*, March 4, 2015, 25. Toxicologists found 12 nanograms per milliliter of delta-9-THC in Brown's blood. Under Washington State's I-502 marijuana legalization law, 5 nanograms is the level above which motorists are booked for driving under the influence.

262 **Brown's DNA was found:** Ibid., 6, 21.

262 **"consistent with Brown's hand":** Ibid., 18.

263 **Johnson claimed:** Ibid., 44–46.

263 **There were no credible witnesses:** Ibid., 83n.

263 **Chants of "Kill the police":** Ibid., 8–9.

263 **"the killer of Mike Brown":** Ta-Nehisi Coates, *Between the World and Me* (New York: Random House, 2015), 130.

264 **drawn from Erykah Badu's song:** Amanda Hess, "Earning the 'Woke' Badge," *New York Times Magazine*, April 24, 2016.

264 **drawn from the dystopic:** Serge Kovaleski, Julie Turkewitz, Joseph Goldstein, and Dan Barry, "An Alt-Right Makeover Shrouds the Swastikas," *New York Times*, December 11, 2016.

265 **"Contrary to what":** Todd Gitlin, "What Will It Take for Black Lives to Matter?," *American Prospect* 28, no. 4 (Fall 2017): 23.

265 **all were forced to apologize:** See the discussion about the three—Hillary

Clinton, Vermont senator Bernie Sanders, and former Maryland governor
Martin O'Malley—in Wesley Lowery and David Weigel, "Democrats Struggling to Connect with Black Activists," *Washington Post*, July 23, 2015.

265 **One of them:** Chris Moody, "O'Malley Apologizes for Saying 'All Lives Matter'
at Liberal Conference," CNN, July 19, 2015. Online at cnn.com.

265 **Days later, Joseph Curtatone:** Katherine Q. Seelye, "Police Protest a City
Hall's 'Black Lives Matter' Sign," *New York Times*, July 29, 2016.

266 **video released a year later:** CBS News aired it on June 20, 2017, days after the
policeman, Jeronimo Yanez, was acquitted of manslaughter. (He was removed
from the police department and disqualified from government work.)

266 **"It's not a setback":** Michael Barbaro and Yamiche Alcindor, "Black Lives
Matter Was Gaining Ground. Then a Sniper Opened Fire," *New York Times*, July
10, 2016.

267 **Baltimore had a black mayor:** "State Seeks Delay in 3 Freddie Gray Trials,
Pending Appeals," *Chicago Tribune*, February 8, 2016.

267 **"Part of the reason":** Mark Landler, "Obama Offers New Standards on Police
Gear in Wake of Ferguson Protests," *New York Times*, December 2, 2014.

267 **"I spoke to them":** U.S. Department of Justice, "Attorney General Holder
Visits Ferguson, Missouri," August 22, 2014. Online at justice.gov.

267 **Democrats were three times as likely:** David Weigel, "Three Words Republicans Wrestle With: 'Black Lives Matter,' " *Washington Post*, July 13, 2016.

267 **"end to the war":** "End the War on Black People," Movement for Black Lives.
Online at policy.m4bl.org.

267 **"digital":** Jessica Guynn, "Meet the Woman Who Coined #BlackLivesMatter,"
USA Today, March 4, 2015.

268 **Ta-Nehisi Coates insisted:** Coates, *Between the World and Me*, 28, 71.

268 **"atheist or at least non-denominational":** Guynn, "Meet the Woman Who
Coined #BlackLivesMatter."

268 **"These framings," Theoharis wrote:** Jeanne Theoharis, "MLK Would Never
Shut Down a Freeway, and 6 Other Myths About the Civil Rights Movement
and Black Lives Matter," *The Root*, July 15, 2016.

268 **"Black Lives Matter":** Randall Kennedy, "Black Lives Matter, the Next Stage of
the Civil Rights Movement," *Philadelphia Inquirer*, December 4, 2016.

269 **"Henceforth," Kimball proposed:** Roger Kimball, "More Mush from the
Wimp," *RealClearPolitics*, December 7, 2015.

270 **"They acknowledged that":** George W. S. Trow, *Within the Context of No
Context* (New York: Atlantic Monthly Press, 1997 [1981]), 50.

271 **The Yale faculty had sent:** Eugene Volokh, "Administrator's defending student
free speech is apparently reason to remove the administrator, according
to some Yale students," The Volokh Conspiracy (blog), *Washington Post*,
November 7, 2015.

271 **"an occasion for adults"**: "Email from Erika Christakis," Foundation for Individual Rights in Education, October 30, 2015. Online at www.thefire.org.

271 **"Then why the fuck"**: Haley Hudler, "Yale Students Demand Resignations from Faculty Members over Halloween Email," Foundation for Individual Rights in Education, November 6, 2015. Online at thefire.org (Video 3).

271 **The Christakises announced:** Erika Christakis, "My Halloween Email Led to a Campus Firestorm," *Washington Post*, October 28, 2016.

272 **"I am sick"**: "Yale University—Full Version—New Videos of The Halloween Email Protest." YouTube.

272 **The Christakises canceled:** David Shimer and Victor Wang, "Months After Controversy, Christakises Resign Silliman Posts," *Yale Daily News*, May 25, 2016.

272 **"an alliance of Yale students"**: "Next Yale Demands for the Administration," Foundation for Individual Rights in Education, November 18, 2015. Online at thefire.org.

272 **"who would enrich diversity"**: Kate Sinclair, "Student Demands: Who's Resigned, What's Renamed," *New York Times*, February 3, 2016.

272 **"more just and inclusive campus"**: Jonathan Haidt and Lee Jussim, "Hard Truths About Race on Campus," *Wall Street Journal*, May 6, 2016.

272 **"A new scientific truth"**: Max Planck, *Scientific Autobiography and Other Papers* (New York: Philosophical Library, 1949), 33–34. Quoted in Thomas Kuhn, *The Structure of Scientific Revolutions*, 3rd ed. (Chicago: University of Chicago Press, 1996 [1962]), 151n.

273 **By the new century:** Emily Cohn, "Tom Jones Reflects on a 'Selfless Revolution,'" *Cornell Daily Sun*, April 16, 2009.

273 **"deny fascists, organized racists"**: From the group Hope Not Hate (UK). Quoted in William Voegeli, "Unsafe Spaces," *Claremont Review of Books*, Winter 2015–2016, 8–14.

274 **"government should be able"**: Jacob Poushter, "40% of Millennials OK with Limiting Speech Offensive to Minorities," Pew Research Center, November 20, 2015. Quoted in Voegeli, "Unsafe Spaces."

275 **"Think of it always"**: J. R. von Salis, *Weltgeschichte der neuesten Zeit*, vol. 1, (Zürich: Orell Füssli Verlag, 1955), 9–14. (Author's translation.)

275 **According to a 2011 Pew Research Center survey:** Frey, *Diversity Explosion*, 32.

277 **"who we are"**: David Rutz, "46 Times Obama Told Americans 'That's Not Who We Are,'" *Washington Free Beacon*, November 30, 2015.

279 **In June 2015:** *Real Time with Bill Maher*, HBO, June 19, 2015.

Bibliography

Where a later edition is used, the date of original publication is in square brackets.

Acharya, Viral, Matthew Richardson, Stijn van Nieuwerburgh, and Lawrence J. White. *Guaranteed to Fail: Fannie Mae, Freddie Mac, and the Debacle of Mortgage Finance.* Princeton: Princeton University Press, 2014.

Aldridge, John W. *In the Country of the Young.* New York: Harper & Row, 1970.

Amis, Martin. *Yellow Dog.* New York: Vintage, 2005 [2003].

Appy, Christian G. *American Reckoning: The Vietnam War and Our National Identity.* New York: Viking, 2016.

Arendt, Hannah. *The Origins of Totalitarianism.* New York: Harcourt Brace Jovanovich, 1973 [1951].

Baldwin, Richard. *The Great Convergence: Information Technology and the New Globalization.* Cambridge, Massachusetts: Belknap Press, 2016.

Baritz, Loren. *Backfire: A History of How American Culture Led Us into Vietnam and Made Us Fight the Way We Did.* Baltimore: Johns Hopkins University Press, 1998 [1983].

Beard, Charles. *Contemporary American History, 1877–1913.* New York: Macmillan, 1914.

Berman, Paul. *A Tale of Two Utopias: The Political Journey of the Generation of 1968.* New York: Norton, 1996.

Bloom, Allan. *The Closing of the American Mind: How Higher Education Has Failed Democracy and Impoverished the Souls of Today's Students.* New York: Simon & Schuster, 1987.

Boorstin, Daniel. *The Image: A Guide to Pseudo-events in America.* New York: Vintage, 1992 [1962].

Boston Women's Health Book Collective. *Our Bodies, Ourselves.* New York: Simon & Schuster, 1973 [1971].

Bouton, Jim. *Ball Four.* New York: Dell, 1970.

Brokaw, Tom. *The Greatest Generation.* New York: Random House, 1998.

Brooks, Tim, and Earle Marsh. *The Complete Directory to Prime Time Network TV Shows, 1946–Present.* New York: Ballantine, 1979.

Buckingham, Marcus, and Curt Coffman. *First, Break All the Rules: What the World's Greatest Managers Do Differently.* New York: Simon & Schuster, 1999.

Bulger, William M. *While the Music Lasts: My Life in Politics.* Boston: Houghton Mifflin, 1996.

Calomiris, Charles W., and Stephen H. Haber. *Fragile by Design: The Political Origins of Banking Crises and Scarce Credit.* Princeton: Princeton University Press, 2014.

Carr, Stephen, Mark Francis, Leanne G. Rivlin, and Andrew M. Stone. *Public Space.* Cambridge, England: Cambridge University Press, 1992.

Coates, Ta-Nehisi. *Between the World and Me.* New York: Random House, 2015.

Comfort, Alex. *The Joy of Sex: A Gourmet Guide to Lovemaking.* New York: Simon & Schuster, 1972.

Cox, Harvey. *The Secular City: Secularization and Urbanization in Theological Perspective.* New York: Macmillan, 1965.

Crenshaw, Kimberlé, Neil T. Gotanda, Gary Peller, and Kendall Thomas, eds. *Critical Race Theory: The Key Writings That Formed the Movement.* New York: New Press, 1995.

Diggins, John Patrick. *Ronald Reagan: Fate, Freedom, and the Making of History.* New York: W. W. Norton, 2007.

Douglass, Frederick. *Narrative of the Life of Frederick Douglass, an American Slave, Written by Himself.* Edited by Benjamin Quarles. Cambridge, Massachusetts: Belknap Press, 1960.

Drucker, Peter F. *The Age of Discontinuity: Guidelines to Our Changing Society.* New York: Harper & Row, 1968.

Duncan, Richard. *The New Depression: The Breakdown of the Paper Money Economy.* Singapore: John Wiley & Sons, 2012.

Edmundson, Mark. *Why Football Matters: My Education in the Game.* New York: Penguin Press, 2014.

Faderman, Lillian. *The Gay Revolution: The Story of the Struggle.* New York: Simon & Schuster, 2015.

Francis, Samuel. *Beautiful Losers: Essays on the Future of American Conservatism.* Columbia: University of Missouri Press, 1993.

Frey, William H. *Diversity Explosion: How New Racial Demographics Are Remaking America.* Washington, D.C.: Brookings Institution Press, 2014.

Friedan, Betty. *The Feminine Mystique.* New York: Norton, 2001 [1963].

Gardner, Lloyd C. *Pay Any Price: Lyndon Johnson and the Wars for Vietnam.* Chicago: Ivan R. Dee, 1995.

Giap, Vo Nguyen. *The Military Art of People's War.* New York: Monthly Review Press, 1970 [Hanoi: Foreign Languages Publishing House, 1961].

Gilder, George. *Wealth and Poverty.* New York: Basic Books, 1981.

Gitlin, Todd. *The Sixties: Years of Hope, Days of Rage.* New York: Bantam, 1989 [1987].

Glazer, Nathan. *Ethnic Dilemmas, 1964–1982.* Cambridge, Massachusetts: Harvard University Press, 1983.

Grewal, David Singh. *Network Power: The Social Dynamics of Globalization.* New Haven: Yale University Press, 2008.

Halberstam, David. *The Best and the Brightest.* New York: Ballantine, 1992 [1972].

Hardt, Michael, and Antonio Negri. *Empire.* Cambridge, Massachusetts: Harvard University Press, 2000.

Hartman, Andrew. *A War for the Soul of America: A History of the Culture Wars.* Chicago: University of Chicago Press, 2015.

Hayward, Steven F. *The Age of Reagan: The Conservative Counterrevolution.* Roseville, California: Forum, 2001.

Heimann, Jim, ed. *All-American Ads of the 40s.* New York: Taschen, 2001.

———. *All-American Ads of the 50s.* New York: Taschen, 2001.

———. *All-American Ads of the 60s.* Cologne, Germany: Taschen, 2002.

———. *All-American Ads of the 70s.* Cologne, Germany: Taschen, 2004.

———. *All-American Ads of the 80s.* Cologne, Germany: Taschen, 2005.

Hobsbawm, E. J. *The Age of Extremes: A History of the World, 1914–1991.* New York: Pantheon, 1994.

———. *Primitive Rebels.* Manchester: Manchester University Press, 1959.

Howe, Irving. *Selected Writings, 1950–1990.* San Diego: Harcourt Brace Jovanovich, 1990.

Inglehart, Ronald. *Culture Shift in Advanced Industrial Society.* Princeton: Princeton University Press, 1990.

Kahneman, Daniel, Paul Slovic, and Amos Tversky, eds. *Judgment Under Uncertainty: Heuristics and Biases.* Cambridge, England: Cambridge University Press, 1982.

Kalven, Harry, Jr. *The Negro and the First Amendment.* Columbus: Ohio State University Press, 1965.

Kaplan, Roberta, with Lisa Dickey. *Then Comes Marriage: How Two Women Fought for and Won Equal Dignity for All.* New York: Norton, 2015.

Kazin, Michael. *The Populist Persuasion: An American History.* Ithaca, New York: Cornell University Press, 1995.

Kelman, Steven. *Push Comes to Shove: The Escalation of Student Protest.* Boston: Houghton Mifflin, 1970.

Klarman, Michael J. *From the Closet to the Altar: Courts, Backlash, and the Struggle for Same-Sex Marriage.* New York: Oxford University Press, 2012.

Kuhn, Thomas. *The Structure of Scientific Revolutions,* 3rd ed. Chicago: University of Chicago Press, 1996 [1962].

Lessig, Lawrence. *Code and Other Laws of Cyberspace.* New York: Basic Books, 1999.

Levine, Robert S. *The Lives of Frederick Douglass.* Cambridge, Massachusetts: Harvard University Press, 2016.

Luxemburg, Rosa. *Gesammelte Werke.* Berlin: Dietz Verlag, 1974 [1922].

Malcolm X. *Malcolm X Speaks.* Edited by George Breitman. New York: Pathfinder, 1989 [1965].

Manchester, William. *The Death of a President.* New York: Harper & Row, 1967.

Marsden, George M. *The Twilight of the American Enlightenment: The 1950s and the Crisis of Liberal Belief.* New York: Basic Books, 2014.

Mayer-Schönberger, Viktor, and Kenneth Cukier. *Big Data: A Revolution That Will Transform How We Live, Work, and Think.* New York: Houghton Mifflin Harcourt, 2013.

McDougall, Walter A. *The Tragedy of U.S. Foreign Policy: How America's Civil Religion Betrayed the National Interest.* New Haven: Yale University Press, 2016.

Mill, John Stuart. *Considerations on Representative Government.* London: Parker, Son and Bourn, 1861.

Morgan, Robin, ed. *Sisterhood Is Powerful.* New York: Random House, 1970.

Novak, Michael, ed. *Capitalism and Socialism: A Theological Inquiry.* Washington, D.C.: American Enterprise Institute, 1979.

Obama, Barack. *Dreams from My Father: A Story of Race and Inheritance.* New York: Times Books, 1995.

Perlstein, Rick. *The Invisible Bridge: The Fall of Nixon and the Rise of Reagan.* New York: Simon & Schuster, 2014.

Pirsig, Robert. *Zen and the Art of Motorcycle Maintenance.* New York: Harper, 2005 [1974].

Putnam, Robert D., David E. Campbell, and Shaylyn Romney Garrett. *American Grace: How Religion Divides and Unites Us.* New York: Simon & Schuster, 2010.

Rajan, Raghuram. *Fault Lines: How Hidden Fractures Still Threaten the World Economy.* Princeton University Press, 2010.

Rand, Ayn. *Atlas Shrugged.* New York: Dutton, 1992 [1957].

———. *The Voice of Reason: Essays in Objectivist Thought.* New York: Meridian, 1990.

Reagan, Ronald. *Reagan: A Life in Letters.* Edited by Kiron K. Skinner, Annelise Anderson, and Martin Anderson. New York: Free Press, 2003.

Remnick, David. *The Bridge: The Life and Rise of Barack Obama.* New York: Alfred A. Knopf, 2010.

Rosenblatt, Roger. *Coming Apart: A Memoir of the Harvard Wars of 1969.* Boston: Little, Brown, 1997.

Roszak, Theodore. *The Making of a Counter Culture.* Berkeley: University of California Press, 1995 [1968].

———. *Where the Wasteland Ends: Politics and Transcendence in Post-Industrial Society.* Garden City, New York: Doubleday, 1972.

Russell, Bertrand. *The Impact of Science on Society.* London: George Allen & Unwin, 1952.

———. *Marriage and Morals*. New York: Horace Liveright, 1929.

Salis, J. R. von. *Weltgeschichte der neuesten Zeit*, vol. 1. Zürich: Orell Füssli Verlag, 1955.

Slater, Philip. *The Pursuit of Loneliness: American Culture at the Breaking Point*. Boston: Beacon Press, 1970.

Solove, Daniel. *The Future of Reputation: Gossip, Rumor, and Privacy on the Internet*. New Haven: Yale University Press, 2007.

Stouffer, Samuel A. *Communism, Conformity and Civil Liberties: A Cross-Section of the Nation Speaks Its Mind*. New Brunswick, New Jersey: Transaction Publishers, 2009 [1955].

Strauss, Leo. *Jewish Philosophy and the Crisis of Modernity: Essays and Lectures in Modern Jewish Thought*. Albany: State University of New York Press, 1997.

Strauss, William, and Neil Howe. *Generations: The History of America's Future, 1584 to 2069*. New York: Quill, 1991.

Thaler, Richard, and Cass Sunstein. *Nudge: Improving Decisions About Health, Wealth, and Happiness*. New Haven: Yale University Press, 2008.

Theoharis, Jeanne. *The Rebellious Life of Mrs. Rosa Parks*. Boston: Beacon Press, 2013.

Trilling, Lionel. *The Liberal Imagination: Essays on Literature and Society*. New York: NYRB Books, 2008 [1950].

Trow, George W. S. *Within the Context of No Context*. New York: Atlantic Monthly Press, 1997 [1981].

Wanniski, Jude. *The Way the World Works*. Washington: Regnery Gateway, 1998 [1978].

Wilentz, Sean. *The Age of Reagan: A History, 1974–2008*. New York: Harper, 2008.

Wilson, James Q. *The Marriage Problem: How Our Culture Has Weakened Families*. New York: Harper, 2003.

Woodward, C. Vann. *The Strange Career of Jim Crow*. New York: Oxford University Press, 2002 [1955].

Zemmour, Eric. *Le suicide français*. Paris: Albin Michel, 2014.

Zunz, Olivier. *Philanthropy in America: A History*. Princeton: Princeton University Press, 2011.

Index